52.00

HOSKING'S
PENSION SCHEMES
AND
RETIREMENT BENEFITS

AUSTRALIA
The Law Book Company Ltd.
Sydney : Brisbane : Melbourne : Perth

CANADA
The Carswell Company Ltd.
Agincourt, Ontario

INDIA
N.M. Tripathi Private Ltd.
Bombay
and
Eastern Law House Private Ltd.
Calcutta and Delhi

M.P.P. House
Bangalore
and
Universal Book Traders
New Delhi

ISRAEL
Steimatzky's Agency Ltd.
Jerusalem : Tel Aviv : Haifa

PAKISTAN
Pakistan Law House
Karachi

HOSKING'S
PENSION SCHEMES
AND
RETIREMENT BENEFITS

Sixth Edition

Bob Escolme, M.A., F.I.A., F.P.M.I.

David Hudson, F.P.M.I., Solicitor

Paul Greenwood, B.Sc., F.I.A.

Principals, William M. Mercer Fraser Limited

LONDON
SWEET & MAXWELL
1991

FIRST EDITION 1956
SECOND EDITION 1960
THIRD EDITION 1968
FOURTH EDITION 1977
FIFTH EDITION 1985
SIXTH EDITION 1991

Published by
Sweet & Maxwell Limited of
South Quay Plaza, 183 Marsh Wall, London, E14 9FT
Computerset by Promenade Graphics Ltd. Cheltenham
Printed by and bound in Great Britain by BPCC Hazell Books
Aylesbury, Bucks. Member of BPCC Ltd.

British Library Cataloguing in Publication Data
Escolme, R.
  Hosking's pension schemes and retirement benefits.—6th.
  ed.
  1. Great Britain.   Superannuation schemes
  I. Title II. Hudson, D. III. Greenwood P.
  IV. Hosking,   Gordon A. (Gordon Albert) *1907—*.
  Hosking's pension schemes and retirement schemes
  331.2520941

  ISBN 0–421–41350–6

ACKNOWLEDGMENTS

Some figures are quoted from the Annual Survey of Occupation Pension Schemes, published by the National Association of Pension Funds. We are grateful to the Association for permission to quote the Survey. Copies may be purchased from the National Association of Pension Funds, 12–18 Grosvenor Gardens, London SW1W 0DH.

The table at the end of Part 1 comes from the Government Actuary's 1989 survey of occupational pensions and we are grateful for permission to reproduce it. Copies of the survey can be bought from HMSO.

PREFACE

"We remarked, in our preface to the fourth edition in 1977, that the taxation and Social Security backgrounds, against which occupational pension schemes operate, have changed considerably since the publication of the third edition in 1968".

That was the opening paragraph of the fifth edition in 1985. With appropriate changes to the various years and edition numbers it would be apt now as the opening to the preface of the (1991) sixth edition—except in one important respect. The rate of change since 1985 has far outstripped that of earlier periods.

Scheme administrators, finance and personnel executives and pension advisers have had to assimilate and implement new practices on account of, among other things, the requirements of the following:

Data Protection Act (1984)

Social Security Act 1985	— Preserved pension indexation
	— Transfer/buy-out rights
	— New disclosure of information rights
Sex Discrimination Act 1986	— Equal retirement ages

Financial Services Act (1986)

Social Security Act 1986	— Personal pensions
	— Voluntary memebership
	— SERPS cutback and changes in contracting-out terms
	— Money purchase contracting-out
	— Contracting-out incentive for new schemes
Finance Act 1986	— Controls on over-funding
Finance Act 1987	— First restrictions on tax-free retirement cash
Finance Act 1989	— £60,000 cap for approved pension schemes
	— Unapproved funded and non-funded schemes
Social Security Act 1989	— More sex discrimination legislation
Social Security Act 1990	— Preserved pension indexation extended to all service

	— Future service pension accruals after Appointed Day to be indexed in retirement
	— First call on scheme surpluses to extend indexation to pensions accrued before Appointed Day (expected to be January 1, 1992 in both causes)
	— Any scheme deficit on wind-up to be a debt on the employer
Cases at the European Court about sex discrimination in pension schemes	— Following *Barber* v. *Guardian Royal Exchange* (G.R.E.), equality of pension ages early and late retirement pensions, etc.

In 1985 we also wrote that "The stability which has prevailed since 1975 begins to look fragile and pensions may well be plunged, yet again, into the party political turmoil which ruled from 1958 to 1975." Certainly, that political accord was broken by much of what was introduced by the Social Security Act 1986 and we have been promised substantial change following a return of a Labour government.

In every practical sense it is immaterial which of these changes have been socially or fiscally necessary, which have justification based on dubious reasoning, which could be put down to party political dogma and which spring from the genuine or bureaucratic requirements of European membership. The fact that we have, and must continue to have, politicians and bureaucrats (European as well as the indigenous), combined with the size to which pension funds have grown, will ensure that change will continue to be the order of the day even if changes in socio-economiic matters do not require some of it. The sixth edition of *Hosking's Pension Schemes and Retirement Benefits* is assuredly not the last.

Most of the chapter headings of the fifth edition (called Parts) and most of their sections have been retained. However, they have been rewritten where appropriate and some new ones have been added. Part 9 of the fifth edition (*The 1984 Government Enquiry—Early Leavers, Personal Pensions, Disclosure of Information*) is redundant. The 1984 Government Enquiry led to some of the legislation listed at the beginning of this preface and all that is incorporated in the appropriate places in Parts 1 to 10. Part 9 of the fifth edition has been replaced with the new Part 11—*Unapproved Pension Schemes*, following the 1989 Finance Act. Few people are affected as yet (1990) but the prices as opposed to earnings indexation of the cap will change that with time. Part 11 can therefore be expected to become more important and to change as practice and custom in dealing with the cap emerges. The preceding parts are concerned almost exclusively with Inland Revenue approved pension schemes.

Part 10 on Sex Discrimination is also completely new. This separate part reflects the importance of the subject, not least of all because of the significantly added expense that European Court judgments can imply for occupational schemes.

The introduction to *Hosking's* fifth edition consisted essentially of a brief history of U.K. occupational pension provision. We have retained most of it, and we have added to it to bring it up to date as at October 1990.

CONTENTS

TABLE OF CASES

TABLE OF EUROPEAN LEGISLATION

TABLE OF STATUTORY INSTRUMENTS

TABLE OF STATUTES

PART 1

INTRODUCTION

.

A BRIEF HISTORY OF UK OCCUPATIONAL PENSIONS

To October 1984, as written at the time

Until the middle of the nineteenth century the means of providing for old **1–01** age were, broadly speaking, the same the world over. Village and even town communities were relatively small. Most people knew most other people and would lend a helping hand, where needed. Family homes within those communities tended to comprise several generations and the support of the old family members by their children and grandchildren was largely taken for granted.

The development of large scale industrial enterprise changed all this, as much else, in Europe and North America. Country folk moved into ever growing cities. Family units became much smaller. The generations no longer lived together. It became more difficult and less congenial for the young to support their own parents and grandparents in old age.

A name which will be unexpected in the context may now appropriately **1–02** be mentioned. The earliest formal system of what we now call Social Security was inaugurated over a century ago in Prussia by Bismarck, the (otherwise) "Iron Chancellor". Other industrialised nations followed suit.

In Britain the first statutory provision for the payment of old age pen- **1–03** sions, (financed through taxation), to certain groups of employees was made in 1908.

A sprinkling of occupational pension "schemes" (but not funds) had been inaugurated in the nineteenth century. A notable example of these is the one applying to members of the Civil Service which continues to operate on a pay as you go basis. 1921 saw the passage of an Act of Parliament requiring local authorities to set up funded occupational pension schemes for their staff and empowering them, if they saw fit, to extend these to manual employees.

1921 was a vintage year for pension legislation because, also in that year, the Finance Act for the first time provided for the concept of an approved occupational pension scheme. Given Inland Revenue approval, employer's and employees' contributions to such a scheme were to rank as deductible expenses and the investment income of the growing pension fund was to be exempt from income tax provided, *inter alia*, that the only benefit of consequence was a taxable pension and that, if the scheme were contributory, this pension should not exceed £2,000 per annum.

Side by side with occupational schemes for national and local government employees, others were gradually coming into operation for those employed by the household names of British industry and commerce. Even by 1936 however, the membership of occupational pension schemes in the

1

United Kingdom was no more than 2.6 million and of these 1.0 million were public sector employees.

1–04   Somewhat remarkably, the stimulus to further growth in the United Kingdom of State provision for old age dates from June 1941 when German armies were at the gates of Egypt and starting their thrust into the vast plains of the Soviet Union. In that month the British Government invited Sir William Beveridge to make recommendations regarding the post war shape of Social Security.

Legislation, in great part based upon the Beveridge proposals, took effect in 1948. The state retirement pension for a single person was to be £1.30 per week. This represented, as does its 1984 counterpart of £34.05 per week, roughly one fifth of current national average earnings.

1–05   The United Kingdom growth in occupational pension schemes since the Second World War has taken place against a constantly changing legislative background, both as to Social Security and to taxation. In the former case, legislation has led to ever increasing complexity. Happily, in the latter case the opposite has been true. With the benefit of hindsight this view might now be open to question. On the Social Security side the 20 years 1958–1978 saw several different proposals for fundamental change put forward by Government and Opposition. The late and unlamented "Graduated Pension Scheme" came (in 1959) and went (in 1975), suffering at its departure from pernicious anaemia induced by inflation. Finally, in 1974–1975 a truce was called. Subject to endless discussion, negotiation and bargaining, it proved possible to find support within both major political parties for the Social Security Pensions Act 1975. This introduced the earnings related State Pension which came into operation on April 6, 1978. It also expanded upon a concept (inherent also in the 1959 scheme) which remains almost unique in the world, namely the "contracting-out facility."

On the tax side, the Finance Acts of 1970 and 1971 tidied up what had in the preceding half century become somewhat of a jungle. These have, thank goodness, left us since April 6, 1980 with one single "code of approval," compliance with which carries complete exemption from taxation on the "pension build up." Also, anomalously, it allows a part of the emerging retirement benefit to be taken as a tax-free lump sum. It is believed by some that this anomaly is, fortunately, with us indefinitely because a tax-free lump sum at retirement has formed part of the Civil Service occupational pension provision for well over a century.

1–06   Leaving aside the legislative background, one or two other features of the occupational pension scheme these past twenty years are worthy of mention. One is the notable extent to which the rigid distinction between the insured pension scheme and the privately invested pension scheme has been blurred. It must always be remembered that there is no sense in which the salary inflation risk to which pension schemes are subject can be insured although, since the Government introduced index linked stocks, some life offices have introduced contracts whose benefits move in line with the Retail Prices Index during the period of retirement. With increased competition, life office premiums for group life assurance policies have become much lower and the trustees of many medium and smaller schemes which are basically privately invested use the life companies to reinsure the risks involved in their liability under the scheme rules to pay lump sums (and/or widows' pensions) on members' death in service.

In the other direction, the increasing level of inflation has rendered the old "non profit group deferred annuity" method of insuring the trustees' pension liabilities more and more inappropriate, so that life offices have moved steadily toward the privately invested concept. Some indeed go as far as offering investment management services (only) for an individual employer's pension scheme while a few advertise that they are able to provide a privately invested scheme.

Inflation has played a large part in two other developments. Over 90 per **1–07** cent. (at 1984 figures) of occupational scheme members now look forward to a "final salary" pension, *i.e.* one based upon salary at retirement or the average salary over a very few years before retirement. At the same time, especially during the rampant inflation of 1974–1981, the benefits afforded to early leavers came under increasing scrutiny and criticism culminating in legislation.

From October 1984 to October 1990

The first page of the Preface, with its list of legislation, summarises the **1–08** amount and extent of the changes brought about by the Conservative Government over this period. That period has largely coincided with a substantial turn-around in the financial fortunes of most schemes, to the point that many of them have become substantially over-funded (as seen by employers), or in surplus (as seen by the Government, scheme members and their trade unions).

The emergence of substantial surpluses has resulted in or been a contributory factor to some of the legislation, in particular to the pension aspects of the Finance Act 1986 and the Social Security Act of 1990.

The requirements of the Social Security Act 1990, when added to those of the Social Security Act 1986, and the general and substantial increase in complexity brought about by all this legislation, can be expected to result in some growth in the number of money purchase schemes at the expense of final pay schemes. For this reason, *Hosking's* now contains a more thorough treatment of money purchase schemes than did the fifth and earlier editions.

Shortly before the draft for the sixth edition was completed the far- **1–09** reaching and confusing judgment was made by the European Court in *Barber* v. *G.R.E.* Basically, if it is necessary to know the sex of an occupational pension scheme member in order to determine that member's pension or death benefits then sex discrimination is involved. And, following *Barber* v. *G.R.E.* it is unlawful. What is confusing is that it is not known (October 1990) to what extent the judgment is retrospective since the judges, learned as they no doubt were concerning the Treaty of Rome, quite simply failed to make themselves clear on this point. For United Kingdom employers the difference in value between no retrospection and the retrospective effect it is possible to read into the judgment has been estimated to be of the order of £30 billion.

The NAPF obtained leading Counsel's Opinion on the matter, published in October 1990. Briefly, this was to the effect that the equality requirements of the judgment do not apply to pensions accrued for service up to May 17, 1990. In final pay schemes "accrued" here means in relation to final pensionable salary, which would of course be determined after May 17 if requirement was after that date.

1–10   The Government Actuary's surveys of occupational pension schemes provide a useful summary of community practice. They are, however, infrequently produced and not as up to date as the NAPF's, narrower based, annual surveys. The Government Actuary's latest survey was conducted in 1989 and the results are expected to be published at any time now. His previous survey was conducted in 1983 and the following membership figures, taken from that survey and from his 1979 survey, will be of some historical interest.

Employees in occupational pension schemes (millions)

Year	Private Sector	Public Sector	Total	Total membership as % of total employees
1936	1.6	1.0	2.6	25%
1953	3.1	3.1	6.2	28%
1956	4.3	3.7	8.0	35%
1963	7.2	3.9	11.1	48%
1967	8.1	4.1	12.2	53%
1971	6.8	4.3	11.1	49%
1975	6.0	5.4	11.4	49%
1979	6.1	5.5	11.6	50%
1983	5.8	5.3	11.1	52%

PART 2

SCHEME DESIGN

SCHEME DESIGN

Why do employers have pension schemes?

2–01 There are two types of problem which an appropriate pension scheme can solve for an employer. One is concerned with the employer's need to retire employees in due time, while continuing to motivate those who have not yet reached retirement age. We call this the retirement problem. The other concerns the employer's need to recruit staff in those categories which community practice treats as occupationally pensionable; if your competitor for the sort of staff you are trying to recruit offers pensions then you may well feel obliged to do the same.

An employer whose workforce consists entirely of temporary or seasonal workers does not have the first problem. As a result, such workers are not generally regarded as occupationally pensionable and so their employers do not have the second problem either. Part-time employees are perhaps different. EEC-inspired legislation outlawing indirect discrimination may be changing, or may force change in employer's general attitudes about the pensioning of part-time employees—see Chapter 43.

–02 Since employees of many small employers have no expectation of occupational pensions there has not been a community practice of providing occupational pensions for them. Such employers have not had the second problem and, perhaps as a result, do not have the first one either. This may change, as a result of the government's encouragement for non-pensioned employees to opt out of the State earnings related pension scheme (SERPS) by means of an appropriate personal pension scheme.

–03 Because of community practice, medium sized employers and the larger ones have been obliged to have a pension scheme at least for established white collar staff and, increasingly, for all full-time permanent employees. Such employers also have a pension scheme for such staff in order to solve the retirement problem.

What type of pension provision?

–04 The State flat rate and earnings related pension schemes are jointly financed on a pay-as-you-go-system by employers and employees (and by the self-employed). Outside the State system there are two types of pension scheme: defined benefit and defined contribution schemes. In the United Kingdom the overwhelming majority of defined benefit schemes provide pensions related to length of pensionable service with the employer and salary at, or averaged over a period near, retirement age if the employee has not left earlier. We call these final salary schemes. Defined contribution schemes, usually known as money purchase schemes, require a given rate of contribution (invariably related to pay) and the pen-

sion is what can be provided by the <u>accumulated result of investing the con-</u>
<u>tributions.</u>

Money purchase schemes can be adopted by individuals, in which case
they are known as personal pension schemes (see Chapter 29). Such
schemes are open both to self-employed individuals and to employees who
are not pensioned by the employer through an occupational scheme. In
addition a personal pension scheme may be used by the employees for contracting-out of the State earnings related scheme where their occupational
scheme is not itself contracted-out. An employer can contribute to an individual employee's personal pension scheme, within prescribed limits
(assuming the personal pension scheme to be one approved by the Inland
Revenue for tax relief purposes).

2–05   Thus, bearing in mind general community practice, the employer has the
following broad choices in relation to pensioning any group of employees.

(i) Not to pension the employee. The employee can take out a personal
pension scheme operated by one of the recognised institutions
(insurance company, unit trust, building society, bank). And the
employee can choose to be contracted-out of the State Earnings
Related Scheme. If he does, his personal pension scheme attracts a
contribution from the Department of Social Security. This DSS contribution comes out of the employer's and employee's National
Insurance contributions, and may include by way of incentive to
contract-out an additional payment during the period from April 6,
1987 to April 5, 1993.

(ii) With choice (i) the employer can add to the employee's contributions, over and above the National Insurance contribution content
in a contracted-out personal pension scheme. Assuming the personal pension scheme to be approved by the Inland Revenue for tax
purposes, and assuming that the total of the employer's and
employee's contributions are within certain prescribed limits, then
the employer's contributions to the employee's personal pension
scheme are not treated as pay for tax or National Insurance contribution purposes. Personal pension schemes are treated in detail in
Chapter 29.

(iii) Pensioning the employee in a company operated money purchase
scheme.

(iv) Pensioning the employee in a company operated final salary
scheme.

Short of premature death, everyone needs a retirement income. Given
that the employer is going to assist a given category of employees with their
pension provision, the first question one might ask is whether the provision
should be on a final pay or on a money purchase basis. The answer is likely
to depend on such things as the <u>employee category</u> being considered. (Pensioning senior executives and other highly paid individuals can present
special problems, which we cover in Chapter 30). It will also depend on
such factors as <u>staff turnover</u> and <u>community practice.</u> This is because

there are some general and important differences between the two types of pension scheme. We summarise them briefly in the rest of this section.

In Chapters 1 and 2 we describe the different types of money purchase scheme and the principle features of final pay schemes. Chapter 3 is devoted to "hybrids," schemes which derive their design from both money purchase and final pay schemes. The remaining chapters in this section are devoted to factors of scheme design which are common to them all.

Points for and against final pay schemes

One important difference between the two types of scheme is that with the 2–06 final pay scheme the employer's contributions are not allocated on an individual basis until, in effect, the promised benefit is paid.

As a result of that, and because of the nature of the pension promise, the employees are insured against fluctuations in stock market values, relative to prices and wages inflation. The scheme member who stays in service until he retires on pension has a pension promise related to the standard of living achieved near retirement. "What pension will I get, if I stay in service?" can be answered in a very meaningful way with a final pay scheme. It is extremely difficult to give any sort of adequate answer with a money purchase scheme.

It also follows from the non-individual allocation of the employer's contributions that the employer should have a far greater flexibility with a final pay scheme than with a money purchase scheme. Although redundancies and early retirements when required cannot be known in advance, a significant amount of rational pre-funding for such contingencies can be done by the employer with a final pay scheme. A well-run final pay scheme can be of great assistance with manpower planning, something which is not possible with a money purchase scheme.

Final pay schemes are eminently suitable for solving the retirement 2–07 problem mentioned at the beginning of this chapter. Employees being retired on pension will measure the adequacy of that pension against their then pay rates. Depending on how stock markets have performed relative to inflation, members of money purchase schemes could in some periods receive very adequate pensions (even excessive pensions) and at other times very poor ones. When emerging pensions are poor the employer will be under pressure to increase them. Money purchase pensions, inevitably measured and expressed as a proportion of pay at retirement, can be extremely volatile.

In some but not all respects final pay schemes are more difficult to communicate to members than are money purchase schemes. The disclosure regulations for final pay schemes are more onerous and extensive than for a money purchase scheme and so are the requirements for accounting for pension costs in company accounts.

Points for and against money purchase schemes

These are generally the converse of the previous points, but there are a 2–08 number of points which should be made explicit.

The money purchase scheme gives the employer a definiteness of cost unless the pensions turn out to be very poor and the employer feels it necessary to increase them. Furthermore, the money purchase scheme does not have the "blank cheque" aspect of the final pay scheme. If a final pay scheme is wound up in deficit then, following the Social Security Act 1990, the employer will be required to make it good.

For the same total company outlay, more of the total in absolute terms, and as a percentage of pay, goes to financing the pensions of the older members in a final pay scheme than to financing the pensions of the younger members. (The older one is the more expensive it is to provide a given pension.) With most money purchase schemes the same employer percentage of pay contribution is allocated to each member, regardless of age. Given that most leavers are at the younger ages, money purchase schemes are generally more attractive to leavers than to stayers, the converse being the case with final pay schemes.

2–09   The concepts involved with, and the funding and actuarial control of, a money purchase scheme are much simpler than for a final pay scheme (the administration/record keeping aspects are in some ways simpler but in other ways more onerous).

From the members' point of view, the greatest advantage of a final pay scheme is for those who stay in service until retirement. However, "What pension will I get if I stay in service?" is hardly of interest to all those who leave long before reaching retirement age. For all members, whether they leave or stay, the money purchase scheme does have the definiteness and attraction of the deferred pay concept, a subject discussed in Scheme Design, the introduction to Part 2.

In general

2–10   From the employer's point of view, the final pay scheme is generally the more attractive if a significant proportion of his occupationally pensionable employees stay in service until an age when retirement on pension becomes a possibility. The same is true for those employees who stay in service until such an age. The employer needs a final pay plan so as to be able to retire the employees concerned on adequate pensions (thereby not demotivating those still below retirement age) and to fund the requisite pensions appropriately.

One problem for the employer is that neither he nor the employees know in advance which employees are going to need to be retired on pension from the employer's service and which will have left at earlier ages. The answer for "stayers" is a final pay scheme while for early leavers it is a money purchase scheme. A hybrid, or mixed scheme, may be an expensive solution.

Chapter 1

FINAL PAY SCHEMES

Balance of cost schemes

Traditionally there have been two principle types of final pay scheme, **2–11** which we call "balance of cost schemes" and "deferred pay schemes." By far the greater majority of final pay schemes are balance of cost schemes. While such a scheme is in operation its rules require the employer to pay the (balance of the) cost of the scheme after taking into account the members' contributions, if any.

For the greater security of the members' pensions, it is usual to have the scheme set up under trust and for the employer to fund his promises—that is, contribute to the pension scheme trust, in addition to the employee members' contributions if any (Chapter 45 discusses non-funded schemes). The trust's funds are segregated from the business and cannot fall into the hands of a liquidator unless, possibly, on a wind-up all scheme promises and any additional statutory requirements have been fulfilled. The rate at which the pension promises are funded is decided after seeking actuarial advice—funding is the subject of Chapter 22.

In deciding on the employer's contribution rate, it is necessary to make assumptions about such things as future investment returns and rates at which salaries will increase in the future. Clearly, calculating recommended contribution rates is very much an estimating process and it should be no surprise that pension schemes can become under-funded or over-funded.

With a balance of cost scheme which becomes under-funded (and whose **2–12** rules require the benefits to be funded), it will sooner or later be necessary for the employer to increase his payments to the scheme. This will not happen if in the interim the investment experience, etc., improves sufficiently to correct the under-funding.

Conversely, a balance of cost scheme which has become over-funded is, by definition, one which has received too much money from the body which undertook to meet the balance of the cost—the employer. This over-funding can be corrected in a variety of ways, only one of which is to increase the benefits. The converse of increasing the employer's contributions when the scheme becomes under-funded is to reduce them when it becomes over-funded. (The subject is considered more fully in Part 5).

However, since the scheme is set up under trust, there is a widespread misconception that all the assets must necessarily belong to the employee members and pensioners and their dependants. The misconception appears to extend in the minds of many people to the point where there is complaint if, having paid too much in the past, the employer reduces his rate of future contribution. What is probably happening is that the balance

of cost scheme is being confused with the type of final pay scheme described next. Be that as it may, the Social Security Act which is referred to
below overrides scheme rules and dictates to a substantial extent how surplus is to be calculated and used.

Deferred pay

2–13 In the balance of cost scheme what is promised by the employer is a given
set of benefits, In a few final salary schemes not only do the scheme rules
set down given final pay benefits but also the employer's contribution rates
and, if any, those of the members. The rules of such schemes go on to say
what is to happen if the actuary to the scheme recommends that on any
given occasion the under-funding or over-funding which has occurred
should not be carried forward. With under-funding the benefits would have
to be reduced or (without saying whose) the contributions increased. And
with under-funding, the rules will require that the benefits be increased or
(without saying whose) the contributions reduced. However, see below for
how the Social Security Act 1990 has overridden the rules of these
schemes.

2–14   It has been possible to operate one of these schemes so that in a sense
both any over-funding and any under-funding belongs to the members.
Traditionally, over-funding which was not to be carried forward would produce benefit increases or reductions in the members' contributions (or a
mixture of both) and conversely with any under-funding that is not to be
carried forward. From a joint, or collective, point of view one could regard
these schemes as representing the members' deferred pay.

With balance of cost schemes under-funding and over-funding should
belong to the employer and they are not, in the sense we have been discuss-
ing here, deferred pay schemes but, rather, benefits, the cost of which (or
the balance of the cost of which) the employer has undertaken to pay.

2–15   In fact, most final pay schemes are operated as a mixture of balance of
cost and deferred pay schemes. This is the case in the sense that when a
substantial surplus or over-funding is being corrected in a balance of cost
scheme it is invariably done by a mixture of benefit improvements (such as
granting pension increases to pensioners, over and above those promised
in the rules) and employer contribution reductions. This serves to blur the
distinction between final pay schemes which are on a balance of cost basis
and those which are on a deferred pay basis. The distinction has been
further blurred by the Social Security Act 1990, with its requirements on
the treatment of surplus and any deficiencies on a scheme wind-up.

The Social Security Act 1990

2–16 Traditionally, the rules of balance of cost schemes required the employer
to meet the balance of the cost, while the scheme was in operation. However, nearly all balance of cost schemes have had what might be described
as a let out clause: a clause which said that, subject possibly to some notice,
the employer could stop his contributions at any time. The rules of such

schemes went on to say that when the scheme was wound up in deficit the benefits would be reduced (pensioners being priority creditors). In other words, balance of cost schemes which were wound up in deficit ceased to be balance of cost schemes at that time: they turned into deferred pay schemes as described above.

However, this has been overridden by the Social Security Act 1990. For the future, the employer will be required to make up the shortfall should the scheme be wound up in deficit. The deficit will be measured in relation to the scheme's promised benefits for service to and salary at the date of wind-up.

And if the scheme is wound up in surplus then a first call on it will be to extend post-retirement indexation to any accrued pensions and pensions already in payment which do not already have the required indexation attaching to them. The indexation rate requirement is five per cent. per annum or, if lower, in line with movements in the Retail Prices Index.

While the final salary scheme is in operation, any pensions accrued after **2–17** a date not as yet announced (October 1990) will be required to have this post-retirement indexation attaching to them. This post-retirement indexing on the pension accruals is required to form part of the scheme's promises, particularly as regards the calculation of any surplus or deficit, both during the currency of the scheme and in its eventual winding-up. At each valuation during the currency of the scheme (after a date to be announced), as well as on wind-up, a first call on any surplus will be, as described above, to extend the post-retirement indexation to any accrued pensions and pensions already in payment which do not already have the indexation attaching to them.

Once the post-retirement indexation attaches to all accrued pensions and pensions in payment, then any over-funding can be corrected by being used for other benefit improvements, by contribution reduction or, scheme rules permitting, by cash return to the employer (see Chapter 24).

Clearly, any new final salary scheme set up before then should have the **2–18** post-retirement indexation from the start, with the remaining benefit levels designed with the cost of the indexation taken into account.

The requirements of the Social Security Act 1990 may make final pay schemes less popular with employers because of the "blank cheque" element it introduces. Generally speaking, final pay schemes are favoured by large employers, money purchase schemes by small employers. Following this legislation we can expect the cross-over line to be further towards the larger size of employer.

Chapter 2

MONEY PURCHASE SCHEMES

Introduction

2–19 The cost of a final pay scheme for any given year cannot be known with any precision. Therefore the costs of final pay schemes which appear in company accounts (see Chapter 25) can only be estimates. This must be so, if for no other reason, because an employee's final pay cannot be known until he leaves, dies or retires.

2–20 The cost to the employer of a money purchase scheme for a given year is however known with precision. It is known in the sense that the employer knows his total payroll once it has been paid. Company money purchase schemes are, except in one regard, deferred pay schemes. The exception invariably arises if the employee declines to join the company money purchase scheme. Invariably, in such circumstances, the employee's pay is not increased by the amount his employer would otherwise have put into the scheme on the employee's behalf.

Of course, as discussed earlier, the employer may be faced with additional costs if the results of the money purchase scheme turn out to be poor. The employer may feel he must augment inadequate pensions, if he wishes to retire his employees and continue to motivate those who have not yet reached retirement age.

2–21 What sets money purchase schemes apart from all others is that each member has allocated to his or her account a given employer contribution each year the amount of which is universally prescribed in advance, by a given formula. The formula could be quite complicated, perhaps referring to company profits. Nearly all money purchase schemes, however, provide for a fixed percentage contribution rate to be applied to the member's pay, or one that increases with age.

The contributions are invested and at retirement the member's pension is determined by what has directly or indirectly built up in the member's account as a result of the investment of the contributions. It is how the results (of the investment of the contributions) are distributed among the members' accounts that serves to distinguish the two main classes of money purchase scheme.

Unitised schemes

2–22 In these schemes the member's contributions, and the contributions of the employer, are invested on a unitised basis. The contributions may be invested directly in a unit trust, or in an insurance company's pension funds which are operated on a unit trust basis. Alternatively the trustees, with the aid of an investment manager, may invest the contributions directly in stock exchange and other securities, crediting each member's account with a unitised or proportionate value of the total invested contributions.

Money purchase schemes are not final pay schemes. But their success 2–23 can only be judged by the member in the first place by how much pension is produced in relation to the member's standard of consumption at retirement (*i.e.* in relation to final pay). And since final pay rates are likely to have been affected in substantial part by past inflation, the investment of a substantial proportion of the contributions is likely to be in assets which afford some protection against inflation, *e.g.* equities.

Stock exchange values, of gilt edged securities as well as equities, and 2–24 the value of property investments, can go down as well as up. The results of a unitised money purchase scheme can therefore be volatile, over short periods of time as well as between one generation of retirements and another. This is particularly so with the results of the volatile investment being used to purchase insurance company immediate annuities. Immediate annuity rates themselves are volatile.

What these money purchase schemes need is investment against inflation for the majority of the period leading up to retirement (with its volatility risk) combined with a switch to a less volatile form of investment in the last few years before retirement (*e.g.* into cash or indexed government securities).

It should not be forgotten that there have been substantial periods in the 2–25 past where investment returns on all forms of investment have been poor relative to the rates of inflation and even more so in relation to rates of pay increase.

Money purchase schemes operated on a unit trust basis may be unpopular with members. Given annual account statements, one could see the value of one's account go down even after a whole year's contribution input—because stock market values have decreased. A possible answer is a scheme operated on reversionary bonus lines.

Reversionary bonus schemes

These schemes are usually invested in with-profits insurance policies, 2–26 either in the form of deposit administration contracts or reversionary bonus contracts. With the former the capital value of and interest added, with the latter the accrued basic benefits and bonuses to date, are not reduced once credited to individual accounts. The position is almost certain to be different if one of these insurance contracts is surrendered.

What the insurance company is doing is to hold a reserve which is used to even out the fluctuations in stock market values. This reserve, or estate as it is often called, has been built up over the generations since the insurance company started with-profits business. Each generation contributes to the estate and each generation benefits from it, although whether the shares are equitable is not an automatic affair; the first generation may certainly have something to complain about, if still extant.

A few money purchase schemes are run on this reversionary bonus basis with the trustees investing directly in stock exchange securities and, perhaps, property. Some of these schemes have worked very well, but probably because they happen to have been started at the right time in relation to a sustained increase in stock market values.

2–27   Scheme membership since April 1988 has been voluntary. And it must be assumed that employees will have drawn to their attention the sort of returns produced by an established and successful with-profits insurance company. So it could well be unwise to start now a directly invested reversionary bonus scheme. Who will be guaranteeing the capital values—the employer? How much should be held back from the first generation in order to build up adequate reserves? And what are adequate reserves? Is it wise to operate a money purchase scheme in which, on occasion, the sum of the individual account values is greater than the value of the assets? However, starting a directly invested reversionary bonus scheme may well be a viable proposition if it is as a result of a switch from a final pay scheme in surplus, with some or all of that surplus being used so as to enable a conservative valuation of the members' money purchase scheme accounts.

Chapter 3

HYBRID PENSION SCHEMES

The money purchase scheme with a final pay guarantee

In the introduction to Part 2—Scheme Design—we pointed out that final 2–28
pay schemes tend to favour stayers as opposed to leavers and that with
money purchase schemes the opposite is the case. This has given rise to two
types of hybrid scheme.

One type of hybrid is essentially a money purchase scheme which
includes a guarantee to augment the money purchase pension up to a final
pensionable pay basis (should the formula decided on for the latter produce a larger pension than the money purchase pension). Schemes which
start life as a money purchase scheme and then have a final salary formula
guarantee added in this way are relatively rare as yet.

Generally, the money purchase contribution input, and its relation to the
top up formula, is such that relatively few augmentations are expected to
be necessary. However, the addition of the final pay formula guarantee
(for the sake of a few people) brings with it the additional levels of administrative complexity imposed by legislation and additional potential cost,
some of which is also imposed by legislation. Accounting for pension costs
in the company's accounts is also simpler for a money purchase scheme
than for a final pay scheme; and a hybrid may need to be treated as a final
pay scheme for accounting purposes.

Where final salary top up guarantees are likely to appear is with money 2–29
purchase schemes which have come into existence as the result of a switch
from an existing final pay scheme. A final pay guarantee may be added for
older employees who would lose out heavily on a strict switch to a money
purchase accumulation for their future service.

In such cases, particularly if the predecessor scheme is overfunded at the
time of the switch, it might be preferable to grant one-off additional pension augmentations and operate the new scheme as a straight money purchase scheme, rather than as a hybrid.

The final pay scheme with a money purchase underpin

The object here is to improve the lot of the early leaver, while continuing
to solve the pension problem with stayers. (See Part 2, Scheme Design—
Why do employers have pension schemes?).

The mechanics of a money purchase underpin, inserted in a final pay 2–30
scheme, might operate on the lines of the following example. For each in-
service member an additional record is maintained for the notional
accumulation of the member's contributions. The accumulation might be
at a rate of interest determined annually having regard to the total rate of

return earned on the scheme's funds (including capital appreciation and depreciation). Then, when the member leaves or retires, twice this accumulated sum will be compared with the value of the final pay formula pension, the member receiving the benefit of the larger sum, within Inland Revenue Limits, whichever it is.

If this sort of money purchase underpin is to look reasonable to members then the sum to be accumulated will need to be something like one and a half or twice the member's contributions, in a contributory scheme. The twice multiple is by way of matching the employee's contributions with an equal employer contribution. The results could be expensive and an alternative to consider is a switch of the final pay scheme to a non-contributory basis.

2–31   There are some final pay schemes having an underpin where the multiple of member contributions which is being accumulated is one, with a generous accumulation rate. The object here is to assure members that they are getting good value for their contributions.

2–32   Hybrids of the type discussed above vary not only as to the contribution multiple which is accumulated but also on how the resulting sums are accumulated. Our suggestion above of having regard to the total rate of return earned by the scheme's funds is only an example. An alternative is a fixed rate of interest, or one that is changed only infrequently. Another alternative is to use the yield produced by a given stock or share or index.

2–33   Most employers with final pay schemes take the view that the preservation and indexation requirements result in sufficient provision for early leavers. From the members' point of view, however, the reasonable final pay scheme with a generous money purchase underpin provides the best of both worlds.

CHAPTER 4

ELIGIBILITY

Personal pension provision

Personal pension provision may be appropriate for senior executives (or **2–34** some of them). This is discussed in Chapter 30. Full-time established staff may well be eligible in medium to large companies for a company pension scheme, more correctly called an occupational pension scheme.

Some employers with substantial numbers of seasonal or temporary workers have encouraged them to join personal pension schemes, perhaps providing a modest lump sum death in service benefit for those who join the "group" personal pension scheme. A group personal pension scheme is in fact a given individual personal pension scheme, the terms of which may have been improved by the institution operating it, for employees joining from the given employer.

In the rest of this chapter we discuss eligibility for occupational schemes.

Full-time and permanent employment

The rules of the occupational scheme will record which groups of **2–35** employees are eligible to join the scheme. Most but by no means all occupational schemes exclude employees who are not employed for the full normal working week. If part-time employees in a given job category are to be excluded from eligibility, and if there are full-time employees in the same job category who are not, then that may constitute a case of indirect sex discrimination. Such discrimination would need to be justifiable on non-sex grounds if it is to be maintained (see Chapter 43). Where the part-time employees are an established feature of the company's workforce then they are more likely to be included in the eligibility of the relevant occupational scheme.

Employment categories

Separate schemes, with different levels of benefit, for different categories **2–36** of employee are commonly operated for companies in the construction and manufacturing industries, other than pharmaceutical companies. In such cases *salaried staff*, *factory staff*, *administrative staff* and suchlike may be found in scheme rules setting out who is eligible.

Some of these phrases may well have precise meanings in a given company but different meanings across companies. Care is needed when a common scheme is being introduced following the merger of two companies. However, the trend over the years has been towards making no distinction in the pension provision between blue and white collar staff.

Voluntary membership

2–37 Before April 1988 it was possible to make pension scheme membership a condition of employment. It is now illegal and an employee who does join an occupational scheme can opt out of it at any time.

It is permissible to have the scheme rules and employment terms written in such a way that the eligible employee is automatically a member of the scheme as soon as he or she becomes eligible, and will continue to be a member until he or she opts out (in writing is the invariable requirement). Alternatively of course the rules can be written so that the newly eligible employee does not become a member unless he or she completes an application form. As might be expected, schemes which require explicit opting out rather than explicit joining tend to have a substantially higher proportion of new eligible employees in the scheme. In a contributory scheme it is essential for the employer to have proper authority from the employee to deduct contributions from pay. This can be in the contract of employment, or in a separate application for membership if that route has been adopted.

2–38   Substantial, or significantly increased, death in service benefits usually go with pension scheme membership. It is important therefore to know exactly who is and, among eligibles, who is not a member of the scheme at any given time. This is a point in favour of automatic membership with explicit opting out being a requirement. The point needs special care when transfers arise between one scheme and another following a merger or takeover.

2–39   With voluntary membership it is important to have a policy, and a corresponding rule in the scheme documentation, on whether and on what conditions subsequent membership is allowed if an eligible employee does not join at his or her first opportunity. Certainly, if any of the death in service benefits are insured it is essential that the late entrant should be clear that cover will only be provided subject to any evidence of health requirements of the insurance company.

Minimum and maximum entry ages

2–40 Schemes with an entry age of as low as 16 exist. More commonly, entry before the age of 21, possibly 25, is not permitted and the scheme's rules are written accordingly. The reason for not allowing younger entry is usually one of cost, particularly administrative cost, employee turnover being high at the younger ages.

A number of employers in fact reduced their minimum entry ages following the introduction of voluntary membership and the availability from 1987 of personal pension schemes and contracting-out with a government incentive. The reasoning behind such a change was based on the wish to have eligible employees join the company scheme. It was feared that with a higher entry age a proportion would join personal pension schemes in the meantime and decline membership of the company scheme when they later became eligible.

A few employers moved their entry ages up significantly although it is rare to come across a scheme with a minimum entry age which is higher than 30. The reasoning here is based on the high turnover experience with younger ages and the greater interest generally shown in pensions the older the individual is.

Waiting periods

On the question of waiting periods, data taken from the National Associ- **2–41** ation of Pension Funds 1989 survey of occupational pension schemes has been used to construct the chart shown on page 20).

The NAPF's survey also gives the percentages for public sector schemes. The percentages differ significantly between the two sectors.

To summarise, the intention of having a waiting period is to exclude from the scheme the "floating employee" and this can most easily be done by a combination of minimum age and service conditions.

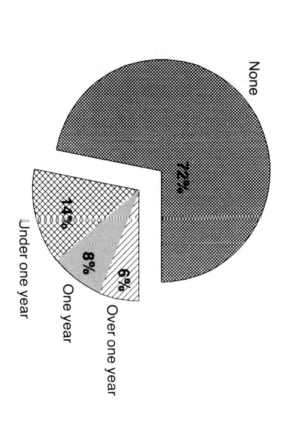

Figure 1

CHAPTER 5

CONTRIBUTORY SCALES

Scale contributions—Defined benefit schemes

Nearly 80 per cent. of approved final salary pension schemes require mem- **2–42**
bers to contribute towards part of the cost of the benefits. With such
schemes the members' contribution rates generally vary in the range of
three per cent. to six per cent. of pensionable salary. For the private sector,
the NAPF's 1989 survey gives 77 per cent. as the proportion of contributory schemes.

It has been argued that an employer with a non-contributory scheme will
tend to pay comparable employees less than an employer with a contributory scheme. Certainly, the Government takes account of the non-contributory nature of the Civil Service pension scheme in fixing the pay rates
of civil servants. And in the private sector, when seeking to hire an individual who is an occupational scheme member, the contributory/non-con-
tributory aspects of the two employers' schemes may be taken into account
in agreeing on the initial salary rate. Generally, however, in the private
sector, there is no discernable difference in the pay rates of employers with
contributory and employers with non-contributory pension schemes.

Certainly, when first considering a final pay scheme for a given category
of employees, the employer might first decide how much he can afford. He
might then go on to consider how much more attractive the scheme could
be made if members were to be required to contribute towards the cost.
Alternatively, the employer might consider the level of provision made by
others for the given employee category, the actuary's estimated cost of
that, and then whether he feels it necessary to ask members to contribute
towards that cost.

If scheme members are to be contracted-out of the State earnings related **2–43**
pension scheme they will enjoy a reduction in their National Insurance
contributions. Consequently, it is usual to find that contracted-out schemes
in the private sector are contributory unless, possibly, they were started
before 1978.

Some pension practitioners argue that requiring members to contribute
to part of the cost makes them more appreciative of the value of the pension scheme. There must be some truth in this if only because membership
of a scheme cannot be made a condition of employment. An employer with
a contributory scheme will have to persuade eligible employees of the
advantages of joining somewhat harder than an employer with a non-
contributory scheme.

Another factor in favour of contributory (approved) pension schemes is
that the employee contributors receive tax relief on their contributions.

(See Chapter 33 on how much a member can contribute to an approved pension scheme). For example, a five per cent. of salary contribution reduces the take-home pay of the standard rate taxpayer to only 3.75 per cent. of salary (to even less, if the employee is contracted-out), given a standard tax rate of 25 per cent.

2–44   There are several points in favour of non-contributory schemes. We are assuming the scheme is a balance of cost scheme, as explained in Chapter 1, at least for the first point in favour of a non-contributory scheme.

When a balance of cost scheme is in surplus the members and their representatives will claim that they should share in that surplus, and their claim may appear to be substantiated by the nature of the scheme if it is contributory. That the validity of the argument is questionable can be seen by considering the situation when the scheme is in deficit—but that does not prevent the argument from arising. Having the balance of cost scheme on a non-contributory basis does help a little to make the position clearer. Incidentally, "surplus" is used here on the assumption that all accrued pensions already have the post-retirement indexation required by the Social Security Act 1990.

2–45   A substantial argument in favour of non-contributory schemes is that they are simpler to administer—with a non-contributory scheme there is one less pay deduction to make and one less record to maintain for each member than with a contributory scheme. Further, if the member leaves or dies before going on pension from the scheme, the benefit represented by the member's contributions has normally to be dealt with and this does not of course arise with a non-contributory scheme. It should also be noted that employer contributions to a pension scheme do not attract the National Insurance contributions levy. So a non-contributory scheme, with correspondingly lower pay rates, saves on National Insurance contributions. Finally, there can be expected to be very few, if any, eligible employees and members opting out of a non-contributory scheme.

2–46   A few contributory final pay schemes have two scales of member contributions and two corresponding scales of benefit accrual (for example a pension of 1/60th of final pensionable pay for each year of contribution at a five per cent. rate and a pension of 1/80th of final pensionable salary for each year of contribution at a rate of $3\frac{1}{2}$ per cent. of pensionable salary). Such schemes would allow a certain amount of latitude, but not complete freedom, in moving from one scale to another.

A few schemes with a contribution rate of five per cent. or so introduced the option of a lower contribution (with a lower pension accrual) in 1988 when all schemes were required to be made voluntary.

Money Purchase Schemes

2–47 Detailed contribution records have to be kept for money purchase schemes so there is little, if anything, to be gained administratively by making a money purchase scheme non-contributory (except in the sense described next).

Since April 1988, when contracting-out of SERPS became possible with money purchase schemes, a number of minimum contracted-out money purchase schemes have been set up. Such schemes are minimum in the sense that the member's and company's contributions consist of the contracting-out rebate and any incentive payments (see Chapter 37). Such schemes are non-contributory in the sense that the employee's take-home pay is unaffected by joining the scheme (in fact, take-home pay goes up slightly on joining the scheme, by virtue of the tax relief gained on the minimum contribution; the minimum contribution being offset by the contracting-out reduction in National Insurance contributions).

Apart from such minimum money purchase schemes, it seems the common practice to have the member's and company's scale contribution rates the same, with there being the usual facility for additional voluntary contributions (AVCs) as described next.

With a money purchase scheme the member's contributions, and the company's, can be seen to be of direct benefit to the member. As a result, it is more common in money purchase schemes than in final pay schemes to have the contribution rate apply to total earnings. In a final pay scheme, it is administratively simpler, and more equitable, to have the member's contribution rate apply to a definition of pensionable pay which does not fluctuate as much as total earnings might fluctuate. **2–48**

Additional Voluntary Contributions

With certain minor exceptions all approved pension schemes, whether contributory or non-contributory, are required to allow members to contribute voluntarily over and above any scale contribution required of them by the scheme's rules. These contributions are called Additional Voluntary Contributions (AVCs) even where the scheme itself has no compulsory contributions for its members. **2–49**

There are relatively few final pay schemes where additional voluntary contributions secure additional pension on a final pay basis; the additional final pay pension in such cases is promised on a scale determined by the rate of additional voluntary contribution being paid and the age at which the additional contribution started to be paid at that rate. Most final pay schemes (and all money purchase schemes) have the AVCs securing additional pension on a money purchase basis. In final pay schemes the AVCs are commonly paid into a building society or insurance company contract even though the main scheme itself may be invested directly in stock exchange securities.

The greatest tax relief attraction of an approved pension scheme is the tax-free cash which it can pay out at retirement. The amount of retirement benefit which can be paid out in this form is restricted (see Chapter 34), and above a given level is related to the amount of pension provided by the scheme. Within the limits allowed, the more pension that the scheme provides for the individual, the larger the amount of pension which can be commuted for a tax-free cash sum. Although the additional pension provided by the AVCs which started to be paid after April 7, 1987 cannot itself be commuted for cash (except in the circumstances described below) it **2–50** does increase the total pension provided by the scheme and therefore the amount of main scheme pension which can be commuted.

2–51 The rules of the approved scheme can restrict the amount of the pension which can be commuted for cash to an amount below the maximum allowed by the Inland Revenue. Some do, on the questionable grounds that the member should not be allowed to decide these things for himself. The fear is that the cash will be spent and that the residual pension will be inadequate. This paternalistic approach denies the individual the opportunity to maximise his after tax income in retirement (for example, by taking the maximum tax-free cash and using it to buy an annuity which is taxed more favourably than the pension which produced the cash in the first place.)

2–52 The Civil Service Scheme and other central and local government schemes promise and provide pension and tax-free cash separately: a pension of 1/80th and retirement cash of 3/80ths of final pensionable salary for each year of pensionable service. The member has no choice here in how much of the total retirement benefits to take in lump sum form. With schemes of this nature, the pension provided by AVCs can, as far as Inland Revenue approval is concerned, be partly commuted for tax-free retirement cash. The various maxima and other approval restrictions are summarised in Chapter 34.

Free-Standing AVC Schemes

2–53 As mentioned above, approved pension schemes must provide an AVC facility for the scheme members. In addition, a member of an approved pension scheme is permitted to contribute to external Inland Revenue approved AVC schemes operated by banks, unit trusts, building societies and insurance companies. These external AVC schemes are known as free-standing AVC schemes.

The trustees in relation to the scheme AVC facility, and the operator of the free-standing AVC scheme, must check by prescribed means that the projected benefits provided by the AVCs are not expected to bring the member's total benefits above the limits allowed by the Inland Revenue for tax approval purposes. If in the event they do then the surplus AVC monies must be returned to the member, less a 35 per cent. tax deduction which is not capable of repayment or offset against other tax liabilities. Higher rate taxpayers are charged at the higher tax rate on the amount of the refund received, grossed up for basic rate income tax.

CHAPTER 6

BENEFITS ON RETIREMENT

Pre-scheme service

In setting up a new final salary scheme, for a category of previously non- **2–54** pensionable employees, the question arises over how much credit initial members should get for service before the new scheme starts. From the members' point of view, it might seem logical that service should count as fully pensionable back to the youngest entry age now applicable to new eligible employees. However much credit existing members actually get will be determined by how much the employer feels he can afford, relative to the additional goodwill engendered.

Given that some pension is to be provided in relation to pre-scheme ser- **2–55** vice, it will have to be expensed in the company's profit and loss account, whether or not the benefits are funded. And it can only be expensed over the remaining service lives of the members concerned (*i.e.* over the period after the start of the scheme) while the profit derived from the pre-scheme service cannot be altered however generous or otherwise the employer might seek to be in relation to that pre-scheme service.

A similar point can arise when one company takes over another, the two **2–56** companies' staff schemes, say, are to be merged and one scheme is more generous than the other.

Completely new final pay schemes are most likely to arise when a new company is being set up; for example, an overseas company setting up in the United Kingdom for the first time (as opposed to taking over an existing company). Pre-scheme service questions do not arise in these circumstances.

Where a money purchase scheme is to be introduced for a category of employees not previously pensionable, the common practice is to take no general action in relation to pre-scheme service—that is, service before the scheme starts attracts no extra or special contributions from the employer. An employer who wishes to set up a money purchase scheme, and give some recognition for pre-scheme service, should seek expert advice. There is no naturally deriving formula for giving pre-scheme benefits on an equitable basis in a money purchase scheme, other than based on records of past pay if they still exist.

Final pay formula

For historic reasons, connected with earlier public sector provision, the **2–57** most common pension promise in the private sector is 1/60th of final pensionable salary for each year of pensionable service. In fact, the Civil Service Scheme provides a pension of 1/80th of final pensionable pay, and 3/80ths of final pensionable pay in cash, for each year of pensionable service. Assuming that each £9 of cash is equivalent to £1 per annum of pension, this is equivalent to a pension accrual rate of 1/60th, one-quarter of which is commuted for cash. However, we return to this topic later in this chapter (Post-retirement increases in final salary schemes) and in chapter 42 (Achieving equality in new final salary schemes).

There is much to be said in a final pay scheme for expressing the formula in pension form, part of which can be commuted for cash (as opposed to explicitly promising a smaller non-commutable pension plus retirement cash). "After 40 years of service I only received a half-pay pension" one might hear a long serving civil servant say, ignoring the pension equivalent of the retirement cash.

For senior staff it is still common to find pension accruals which are more generous than 1/60th (commonly, a two-thirds pension or 40/60ths after 20 years of service rather than 40). Many such generous schemes had their inception in days of high marginal tax rates and before pension preservation on leaving service was a legal requirement (see Chapter 35), let alone before such preservation had operated for sufficiently long to have had a significant effect. Given the existence of such a scheme, it might be thought difficult for a company hiring experienced senior staff to discontinue its very generous provision for new senior people.

2–58   Another significant variation among schemes is in the definition of final pensionable pay. It is common to see final pensionable pay as being the best consecutive three year average of pensionable pay in the last ten years of service. Pensionable pay itself might relate to basic pay only, on administrative grounds, or may be based on total earnings. And there may be an adjustment to take account of the pension the employer and employee are providing through the State system (see "Taking account of the pension provided through the state system" later in this chapter).

Money purchase schemes

2–59 The variations that can arise with money purchase pension schemes will include the employer's and members' compulsory contribution rates, and the definition of pensionable pay to which those contribution rates are to be applied. Pensionable pay may be total earnings, or defined in some way so as to result in pensionable pay varying less than total pay from week to week or month to month.

It is difficult to make recommendations for total contribution rates, beyond possibly the minimum for contracting-out, on any logical basis. Eventually, the member will compare the actual pension he is to receive on retirement with his earnings at that time. Also, what the contribution rates should be in order to achieve such and such a total related to unknown future pay can only be calculated on the basis of assumptions which are certain to be wrong. A total contribution rate of ten per cent. to which AVCs can be added, would be considered generous (the more so the smaller is the proportion of it which the member is required to pay).

A fundamental variation in money purchase schemes relates to a guarantee to protect the capital, or the absence of such a guarantee.

Unitised and reversionary bonus schemes

As discussed in Chapter 2, a unitised money purchase scheme is one under **2–60** which the total value of a member's account varies with the underlying value of the scheme's investments. Such a scheme may be run like a unit trust, with the member's and company's contributions on behalf of the member buying an increasing total of units (the value of which varies). Or one could accumulate the contributions and add interest (which in some years might be negative, representing a fall in asset values). Of course, what matters is not so much the volatility in the capital values in the years substantially before retirement, but rather the volatility in the values shortly before retirement. As a result, unitised money purchase schemes will often have a facility for switching the individual's account into a cash or gilts fund, possibly restricted to or achieved uniformly over a period of five years before pension age.

A possibility here is for the scheme rules to require an even switch into a cash or gilts funds over, say, the five years to pension age, unless the member instructs the trustees in some way to the contrary. To leave the decision entirely to the members will result in no action being taken in many cases, with the recriminations that will inevitably follow the stock market fall. To give the member no choice in the matter will result in criticism when the member retires during a bull market. The suggestion is a compromise.

An alternative, designed to overcome the problems associated with the **2–61** volatility of capital values represented by investments, is for someone or somebody to guarantee the capital values. Banks and building society deposits provide a capital guarantee—the cost to the members will almost certainly be a substantial loss of total investment return compared with that produced by a more balanced portfolio. One answer is an appropriate with-profits contract with an insurance company.

A typical contract would also guarantee the capital values of the accounts. It would guarantee a lowish rate of interest addition to which would be added bonus interest from year to year and perhaps a further sum at maturity. The guaranteed and bonus rates of interest when added to the accounts would become part of the guaranteed capital.

If investments are not all to be in bank deposits (with their low total yield **2–62** over the years relative to inflation) then the capital guarantee must come from some reserve. Each generation of with-profit policyholders contributes to this reserve (called the estate of the insurance company) and each generation benefits from it. The reserve itself is invested of course and is used, in effect, to smooth out (via the with-profits bonus system) most if not all of the volatility in stock market values. How equitable the practice is as between policyholders in one generation, and between generations, it is not possible to say. It is certain though that reducing the volatility has a cost in a smaller total investment yield for the members' pension accounts taken as a whole.

Taking account of the pension provided through the State system

2–63 Employers and employees pay for the State pension on a pay-as-you-go
basis, through their National Insurance contributions. And since the object
of a pension scheme is to provide for consumption during retirement, what
matters to the individual is his total pension in retirement. In addition,
what matters to the individual and the employer is the total cost. Accordingly it is a common, though not universal, practice to take explicit account
of the State pension system when deciding on the pension formula of final
salary pension schemes.

It was at one time feared that the State pension system would provide
more and more in due course, in earnings terms (with employers and
employees meeting the cost). It was at this time felt by many advisers to be
particularly important to "integrate" the occupational promise with the
pensions provided through the State system. There grew up the practice of
promising such and such a total pension, inclusive of the State provision, or
of making up the State pension to a given total. Given that the State pension could be regarded as accruing throughout the working life of an individual, and given that an employee's working life could be divided between
different employers, it would be necessary to integrate on some sort of pro-
portional basis.

A direct method of doing this is for the occupational scheme to provide
say 1/60th of final pensionable salary for each year of pensionable service
less 1/40th of the rate of State pension payable at retirement. This formula
is open to criticism: consider for example two employees with one of them
retiring just before an increase in the State pension and one just after.

2–64   An almost equivalent formula which brings in the averaging used for
defining final pensionable pay is derived from regarding the State basic
pension as pensioning a first slice of salary, with the occupational scheme
pensioning the remainder. Thus pensionable salary in the occupational
scheme might be defined as salary less one and a half times the State basic
pension in force at any given time. Final pensionable salary might be the
best consecutive three year average of pensionable salary in the last ten
years of service. The one and a half times deduction is derived from the
fact that

$$40/60\text{ths of (final salary} - 1\tfrac{1}{2} \times \text{State basic pension)}$$
$$= 2/3\text{rds of final salary less the State basic pension}$$

This gives a total pension of two-thirds final pensionable salary when the
payment of the State pension is added in (assuming the member to have
the National Insurance contribution record required for a full State pension). For someone with less than 40 years of pensionable service with the
employer, proportionately less of the State pension is taken into account.

The one and half times State basic pension deduction from salary to
arrive at pensionable salary in a 1/60ths scheme is not readily understood
by members. Partly for such reasons, a deduction of once times the State

basic pension is commonly found in 1/60ths schemes. This appears superficially to be more reasonable, although it results over 40 years in only two-thirds of the State basic pension being taken into account.

Taking account of only two-thirds of the State basic pension as opposed **2–65** to 100 per cent. can be justified on the following grounds. When the full State basic pension is added to the member's occupational pension, and the total is expressed as a percentage of final pay, the resulting total percentage increases the smaller is the member's final pay. The lower an individual's pay the closer to a 100 per cent. of that pay his pension needs to be in order to purchase the ordinary necessities of life.

When the State basic pension is taken into account it is universally the single person's pension which is used. It would of course be inequitable to provide a married employee with a company pension of a smaller amount than that provided for the single colleague, solely on the grounds that he is married.

To put the discussion into perspective, the following figures are those **2–66** applicable at June 1989, where "national average earnings" (the average earnings of male manual worker on adult rates, taken from the Government's earnings survey) were £11,050 per annum and a State basic pension for a single person was £2,262 a year.

Final pay £ per annum	Total pension consisting of [2/3 (final pay − State pension) + State pension] as % of final pay
5,525 (half "national average earnings")	80%
11,050 ("national average earnings")	73%
22,100 (two times "national average earnings")	70%
44,200 (four times "national average earnings")	68%

At April 1989 just following an increase, the State basic pension for the single person was 20 per cent. of "national average earnings." At November 1980, just following an increase it was 23.7 per cent. of then national average earnings. For some years prior to 1980 there was a statutory requirement to increase the State basic pension in line with earnings, or price increases if that gave a higher figure. In earlier periods it was the practice to make such increases. Since 1980, however, the statutory commitment has been one of increases in line with prices, although some of the increases since then have been a little higher. This explains the drop from 23.7 per cent. to 20 per cent. when the State basic pension is expressed as a percentage of "national average earnings."

With an ageing population, and an increase in the proportion of the **2–67** number of pensioners to the number of people in the working population, one might expect to see this percentage continuing to be allowed to drift lower. Certainly, any need for an integrated occupational pension scheme on the basis that State pensions might increase significantly (as a percentage of earnings) would not seem to be too great.

The State earnings related pension scheme is very complicated, even more so since 1988 when the accrual rate was reduced, and in a complicated way, for employees retiring after the year 2000. The easiest way to integrate with the State earnings related scheme is to contract-out of it (something which is not permitted with the State basic scheme). Basically, there is no difficulty in the general level of final pay schemes meeting the conditions required for contracting-out; contracting-out results in the member's State earnings related pension being reduced in respect of the period during which he is contracted-out in exchange for which both employee and employer pay a reduced National Insurance contribution. The subject of the State earnings related pension scheme and contracting-out of it is discussed in greater detail in Chapters 37, 38 and 39.

Money purchase scheme integration

2–68 Since a money purchase scheme provides a pension from the accumulated investment of the member's contributions and those of the employer on his behalf, it is not possible to integrate with the State basic pension scheme in any explicit manner. Implicitly, one might make some adjustment by having a contribution rate for the employee and employer which, because of the State provision, is smaller than it might otherwise be. To calculate a contribution salary for a money purchase scheme in the same way as pensionable salary is calculated from salary in a final pay scheme makes some rough and ready sense. Thus, one might have a contribution from both employer and employee of, say, five per cent. of pay minus an amount equal to once times the State basic pension for the single person. This lowers the contribution burden for the lower paid employee in greater proportion than for the higher paid employee, although of course it also lowers the eventual pension.

Lump sum retirement benefit

2–69 As part of a total retirement benefit which is within Inland Revenue limits for an approved pension scheme, it is possible with no diminution of tax relief on contributions or investment returns, to provide a tax-free lump sum relating to both salary and length of service. The normal scale allowed by the Inland Revenue is 3/80ths of final salary for each year of service up to a maximum of 120/80ths of such salary after 40 years (*i.e.* one and half times salary). There is, moreover, provision for this maximum scale to be granted, in certain circumstances, after only 20 years' service.

The provision of a lump sum in this way can be made quite independently from the scale of the member's pension (which will then naturally be lower than it would otherwise have been). Alternatively, the whole of the retirement benefit can be expressed in the first place as a retirement pension, with the member having the option to commute a part of the pension for a lump sum up to the limits laid down by the Inland Revenue. The terms on which a member's pension is given up in return for a lump sum will be as laid down in the rules of the scheme and are commonly related to the age at retirement and the sex of the member. Such terms are once again subject to limits laid down by the Inland Revenue and relationships commonly found have been £9 of cash for a pension of £1 a year given up by men retiring at the age of 65 and £11 for women retiring at age 60. Following a decision in the *Barber* v. *Guardian Royal Exchange (G.R.E.)* case at the European Court (see chapter 42) there should no longer be any discrimination between the sexes in the pension to cash rate for men and women retiring at the same age.

Subject to the one and a half times final pay limit, members of new schemes after March 14, 1989, and members of then existing schemes who joined after May 30, 1989, can have a tax-free retirement lump sum of 2.25 × the pension provided (before any commutation). Where such tax-free retirement cash is provided the maximum approvable pension is appropriately reduced.

As explained in the next chapter, a widow's or widower's pension **2–70** becoming payable on the death of a member in retirement is commonly a fraction of the pension payable to the member (in about 80 per cent. of cases the fraction is one half). If a member reduces his or her own pension in return for a lump sum, then commonly this does not affect the amount of the pension payable to the widow or widower which is related to the full amount of the member's pension before any such commutation.

Retirement ages and pension ages

Legislation requires the normal retirement age for men and women in a **2–71** given job category to be the same (this requirement came into force in November 1987). Where no earlier normal retirement age common to both men and women can be established, the upper age limit for unfair dismissal is age 65 for both men and women. The State pension age, the earliest age at which State pensions become payable, is 65 for men and 60 for women.

Before November 1987 no distinction was made between normal retirement ages and normal pension ages (the age at which the pension normally started) in occupational schemes. The majority had normal retirement ages and normal pension ages coinciding with the State pension ages of 65 for men and 60 for women.

It is clear that an EEC Directive will require State schemes to have equal **2–72** pension ages for men and women one day. Effectively however equal pension ages have been required in occupational schemes since May 17, 1990 following The *Barber* v. *G.R.E.* case referred to above. Occupational schemes now have to have equal pension ages, even though State pension ages may remain unequal for some while yet.

Retirement at other than normal pension age

The circumstances we have described above essentially relate to the pro- **2–73** vision of a pension at the member's normal pension age, as defined in the rules. However, a number of members will, in a variety of circumstances, wish or be required to retire before reaching that age. There will also be a smaller number of members who will in fact stay in employment after normal pension age. The provisions of the scheme must allow for these alternative circumstances. The common practice is to use the same scale of retirement pension as for retirement at normal pension age, except that in the case of early retirement when the member is in good health, the scale amount of pension otherwise payable will be reduced appropriately so as to allow for the longer period of retirement. It is of course also reduced by virtue of the years of accrual missed on account of going early.

2–74   Early retirement due to ill health involves various ramifications which have prompted us, in Chapter 9, to give it separate consideration.

A possibly intractable problem arises when a member retires early in a final pay scheme integrated with the State basic pension. The same problem may arise with retirement at the normal pension age if that is below the individual's State pension age. The problem arises from the fact that the State pension cannot be drawn earlier than State pension age.

Some employees would say that they have a poor standard of living on full pay, let alone on a full pension which is less than full pay. Unless an ill-health pension, the early pension is certain to be less than the full pension as explained above. The member's total pension is cut back further, by virtue of the State part of the integrated total not starting till State pension age. A common approach among integrated final pay schemes has been for the scheme to pay an additional amount, related to the missing State pension, for the period from retirement up to the State pension age.

2–75   Care is needed in how this bridging payment is described in the members' explanatory literature and in the scheme rules. The point to be aware of is that (following the *Barber* v. *G.R.E.* case) it is easy in this context to be in contravention of the sex discrimination law. Given that the State pension ages are 65 for men and 60 for women it is likely that bridging payments if paid at all by a scheme, will be paid to men in circumstances where they are not normally paid to women. If this is not to be in breach of the sex discrimination law then the early retirement will need to be written in appropriate optional terms. Treating men and women differently in these circumstances is in contravention of the *Barber* v. *G.R.E.* judgment.

2–76   With funded final pay schemes the usual aim is to have each member's pension fully funded by the time pension age is attained. The pension will have a given value if it starts to be paid from that age. It will have a higher value if it starts later. It has a higher value because the funded or invested value will continue to be earning an investment return. Also, given that it starts later than planned, since the individual is older the pension will be payable for a shorter period. The pension or annuity payments could therefore be larger on this account as well.

2–77   It is usual with final pay schemes, but not universal, for pensions to be larger if they start after normal pension age than if they start at normal pension age. The increase factor itself increases the longer the start of the pension is delayed beyond normal pension age. Note however that with an Inland Revenue approved final pay scheme there are circumstances in which the amount of increase has to be restricted. For example, for members joining approved schemes after June 1, 1989, assuming the member is retiring between the ages of 50 and 75, the approved pension cannot be larger than the maximum Inland Revenue approvable pension calculated on the basis that the age at which the member is actually retiring is treated as normal pension age.

Early and late retirement with a money purchase scheme

2–78

The concept of a normal pension age has little meaning for a money purchase scheme. The earlier an individual retires on pension the less will have been accumulated up to the time of retirement and the more expensive will be the immediate annuity rate applied to the accumulated sum. Conversely, the later the individual retires the more will have been accumulated (stock market vagaries apart) and the cheaper the immediate annuity rate should be.

Post-retirement increases in final pay schemes

Even though the scale of pensions payable may be designed, after taking 2–79 into account the State pension arrangements, so as to provide the member with an adequate income after retirement, this will not be achieved if, during his period of retirement, the real purchasing power of the pension being paid is diminished owing to the effects of inflation. On the other hand, it is an unwise move for the typical pension scheme run by an employer in the private sector to guarantee that such pensions will be increased automatically year by year in line with the cost of living index. The compromise seen most often up till 1990 is that a scheme will contain no more than a comparatively modest "contractual" rate of pension escalation (if any) which will be combined with regular reviews by the trustees of the amounts of pension being paid. The effect of this approach has been for the typical pension scheme in the private sector to grant increases which have approximated to 60 per cent. of the rise in the cost of living in recent years. Having said that, there has been a wide divergence between schemes, ranging from those schemes which in practice have been able to match the whole of the rise in the cost of living to those schemes where the pensions in payment have remained unchanged.

However, from a date to be announced the Social Security Act 1990 2–80 requires all final salary and other defined benefit pension schemes to provide post-retirement increases on pensions accrued after that date, by reference to the Retail Prices Index (RPI), limited to 5 per cent. per annum. A similar indexation of pensions accrued before that date is required to be a first call on any surplus disclosed when the scheme is valued. The guaranteed minimum pension (GMP) in a contracted-out scheme (see Chapter 37) is subject to its own indexing requirements.

The cost of pension increases in excess of those contractually promised or required by the Act is met in various ways. In many cases advance provision is made on the advice of the actuary, and built into the financing pattern of the scheme. In other instances the costs of such increases are met by the company on a "pay-as-you-go" basis as and when these actually become payable.

Post retirement increases in money purchase schemes

2–81 In most money purchase schemes the member is given the option of converting his accumulated account at retirement into an annuity purchased from an insurance company of his choice. This "free market option" must be allowed in relation to that part of the account built up from the State contracting-out contributions, called "protected rights." The protected rights must be converted into an annuity which increases at a compound annual rate of three per cent. (or, possibly, in line with the Retail Prices Index if less).

In respect of the balance of the account it is usual for the member to be free to have a static annuity bought, or one increasing at three per cent. a year or at any other rate. For a given purchase price, the largest initial annuity is of course the static one and this is the choice usually made. For a given pot of money available to purchase pension benefits the initial size of the pension varies considerably with the level of increase purchased. The chart opposite illustrates the point.

2–82 There are a few directly invested money purchase schemes where the pensions are paid by the scheme and annuity purchases (at least for the non-protected rights part of the account) are not made. The pattern of pension increases in such schemes will typically follow the same pattern as for directly invested final pay schemes, except that they are not subject to the limited price indexation requirements of the Social Security Act 1990.

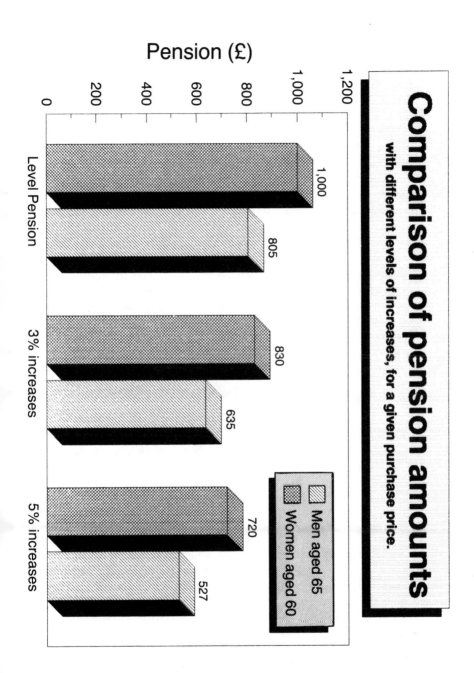

Figure 2

Chapter 7

BENEFITS ON DEATH

General

2–83 Pension schemes have always had associated with them death benefit schemes, whether directly or indirectly. Usually the pension trust provides for benefits to be paid in certain circumstances to the member's estate or dependants. Sometimes there is a separate death benefit trust with a common membership.

Although considerably less costly at the normal level of provision, death in service benefits are likely to be more valued by the young employee than is a prospective pension; the former can provide substantial security for the family should the employee not reach that far off retirement date.

2–84 Traditionally, there have been two schools of thought on the provision of death benefits for employees, at least in relation to death in service benefits. One school of thought has it that the principle purpose of the death benefit is the provision for need. This view would lead to substantially less provision for an employee who dies leaving no dependants than for the one who dies leaving one or more. This school of thought holds the view that it is a waste of money to provide death benefits where there is no need.

The other school of thought holds that the rate for a job, with the cost of any associated benefits included, should not vary with the fact that the individual may or may not have dependants at the time of death.

Overlaying both schools of thought has been the change in the role of women at work, changing attitudes to and legislation on sex discrimination. Notwithstanding that, there is still a substantial variation in the provision of death in service benefits.

Levels of provision and discrimination

2–85 There are numerous final pay schemes which provide death in service benefits of a multiple of salary (up to the Inland Revenue approval limit of four times) irrespective of whether the employee leaves a dependant, plus a return of the employee's contributions with perhaps a modest rate of interest, plus where applicable the relatively small widow's/widower's pension required for contracting-out of the State earnings related pension scheme.

More common among final pay schemes is the provision of a more modest lump sum, irrespective of dependency, plus a significant widow's pension. Typically, the widow's pension will be one half the member's retirement pension had he survived to pension age with no change in salary. A further total half pension might be provided for any surviving children for a limited period, with the children's total doubling if there is no surviving spouse.

The provision of widowers' pensions on death in service, apart from at the **2–86** level required for contracting-out, has been uncommon. Such continuing discrimination cannot be sustained following the *Barber* v. *G.R.E.* case.

On the death of a pensioner under a final salary scheme the usual provision is a widow's (or, now, widower's) half pension; that is, half of the pension to which the member was entitled before he/she may have reduced it by way of commuting a part for a retirement lump sum, increased in line with any additions provided since retirement on account of inflation.

The attitude towards the provision of death benefits, whether before or **2–87** after retirement, is increasingly being affected by the rise in the proportion of women at work. When both partners of the marriage are at work, or have accrued a pension, the death of either would clearly reduce the standard of living of the survivor. In this context, dependency no longer means dependant for the ordinary necessities of life, and non-discrimination is now an important factor.

Money purchase schemes

The usual death in service benefits associated with the money purchase **2–88** scheme are

(i) a return of the fund built up in the member's account;
(ii) a multiple of up to four times the member's annual pay, which may include or may be on top of the benefit of (i).

A part of the fund in (i) may be required to provide a widow's or widower's contracting-out pension.

Half a century or more ago, when money purchase schemes were first **2–89** popular, it was not uncommon to find associated with them (as with other types of scheme) separate widows' and orphans' pension funds, providing an income benefit related to the member's salary at death or the individual accumulated account. Such schemes may again emerge if money purchase schemes become popular at reasonable levels of benefit, as opposed to providing little more than the minimum for contracting-out plus an AVC facility.

If a money purchase scheme has been installed on a group basis at a level **2–90** of provision seriously intended to provide a reasonable life in retirement, then an additional associated widow's/widower's pension benefit should be provided on death of the pensioner. To rely on the member voluntarily to take a reduced pension so as to provide for a surviving spouse may well result in no such provision being made in a number of cases of need. To have compulsion in the matter of surrendering pension, given that the employee did not opt out of the scheme, would result in an inadequate pension unless the scheme is over-generous for single employees.

Death benefits for non-members

The member who opts out of the company pension scheme, and the eli- **2–91** gible employee who does not join in the first place, may well do so without consulting his/her spouse or any other person that might be dependent on the employee, or that such consultation was held may well be forgotten as and when the employee dies. When such an employee dies the spouse or dependants may look to the employer for some provision.

Where a pension and death benefit scheme provides a significant death in service benefit it is common to find a death in service benefit provided for employees who opt out, albeit at a reduced level. Any income benefit for a member's spouse or dependant, related to the employee's pension, would not be provided for the survivors of the employee who opts out, since that employee will have accrued no pension. Where a death in service benefit is provided for those who opt out it is invariably in the form of a lump sum, with the total death in service benefits increasing on joining the pension and death benefit scheme.

Insuring death benefits

2–92   If the pension scheme is directly invested (*i.e.* not insured) in relation to the members' pensions, then it is usual to find that any income benefits payable on death are also not insured. Such a result is usually the outcome of what is basically an investment decision. However, it is common to find that multiple salary lump sum death benefits are insured even though the scheme is directly invested in relation to the members' pensions, even in some very large schemes. This is because group life assurance premium rates in the United Kingdom are very competitive.

2–93   Where death benefits are insured it is important to be clear, and for the employee literature as well as the trust deed and rules to be clear, on the benefits payable when the insurance is unobtainable. The given group insurance contract taken out by the trustees will have a limit set, above which evidence of good health will be required by the insurers before going on risk for the individual concerned, at least in relation to any amounts above that limit. The insurance contract may also have conditions attaching to it related to whether the individual member was actively at work on the day he became a member. And the insurers are almost certain to require at least a simple medical questionnaire completed (with the possibility of it leading to a medical examination) if the eligible employee is joining at a date later than when he or she first became eligible, with cover being declined or subject to a reduction if the medical examination reveals poor health.

2–94   Pension schemes where the trustees insure the lump sum death benefits can be classified into two broad categories. One is the category of the large scheme which is quite capable of carrying its death benefit risks, and which promises death benefits whether or not insurance is obtained. The other category is the scheme where the given death benefits are promised only if the trustees are able to obtain insurance.

Where benefit does depend upon insurance it is important that all concerned are clear on the issue.

CHAPTER 8

BENEFITS ON LEAVING SERVICE ✓

Preservation

A member of an occupational pension scheme who leaves service with two **2–95** or more years of membership has a right under the law to a preserved pension. Given that two years' membership, the preserved pension cannot be surrendered in exchange for a return of contributions.

That part of the preserved pension from a final pay scheme which **2–96** accrued after January 1, 1985 must be increased up to the scheme's pension age in line with the retail prices index or, if over the whole period the result is less, by five per cent. per annum compound. Many schemes which were in force before 1985 did not provide the indexation in respect of the pension accrued before 1985 except to the extent required if contracted-out. For leavers on or after January 1, 1991 this indexation has been extended, by the Social Security Act 1990, to the pension accrued over pre- as well as post-1985 service. With money purchase schemes, the preserved benefits must be credited with bonuses or investment returns related to the yields on the underlying assets.

It is not a requirement of the law, and it is not generally done in practice, for death in service benefits to be preserved. Post-retirement death benefits must be preserved if the member's pension is subject to preservation.

Buy-outs

As an alternative, the member with a preserved pension who left service **2–97** after January 1, 1986 can have the trustees apply the value of the preserved pension in the purchase of an appropriate insurance company deferred annuity policy, or have that sum invested in an approved personal pension scheme. This option must be available until the member is one year short of the scheme pension age. Many schemes have extended the option to pre-1986 leavers.

Transfers

A further choice open to the leaver with a preserved pension is for the **2–98** value of the benefits to be transferred to his or her new employer's pension scheme. The trustees of the new employer's scheme are not obliged by law to take transfer values, but in practice schemes usually do accept the transfer if that is what the new employee wants.

The cash equivalent of the preserved pension, which is to be used for a buy-out or a transfer value, must be calculated having regard to principles laid down by the Institute and Faculty of Actuaries.

There are basically two ways of dealing with a transfer into an occupational scheme. One is to credit the member with extra benefit calculated on money purchase principles. For example, the transfer-in might be applied in the purchase of units in an exempt unit trust, with the proceeds applied at eventual retirement in the purchase of an annuity. An alternative is to credit the new employee with a period of additional pensionable service in exchange for the transfer value. Unfortunately, even if the employee's new scheme were identical in its pension promises with the one he has left, it is highly likely that the added years granted will appear to be poor value compared with the period of membership served in the old scheme.

This is because the transfer value will usually be calculated as the value of the preserved pension. And the preserved pension is not usually increased in line with pay increases, only to the lower extent explained above.

The transfer club

2–99 Within the public sector, among the civil service, local government and the remaining nationalised industries, the level of pension scheme benefits per year of service varies little. As a result it has been possible to allow employees to transfer from one public sector employment to another with, broadly speaking, each year of service which ranked for benefit under the old employment ranking for benefit under the new.

This system has been extended to provide for transfers between a public sector and a private sector scheme, on condition that the private sector scheme enters into an agreement with the so-called "transfer club" for regulating the method of effecting such transfers. Most pension schemes in the transfer club relate to employees in the public sector.

2–100 It should be noted that for years to rank equally between two identical or near identical schemes, transfer values must be significantly larger than if the accrued pension is to be increased subsequently solely in line with prices (subject to a maximum of five per cent. compound). The same principle applies where the two schemes are not identical. Consequently, the value of transfer club membership can be costly for the employer as it benefits the leaver greatly, but benefiting the leaving employee does not benefit the remaining employer. It is not surprising, perhaps, that there are relatively few private sector pension schemes in the transfer club.

The net result of all this is that, generally, a person in the private sector who moves from one final pay scheme to another, following changes in employment, ends up with less total pension than the individual who stays in one final pay pension scheme throughout his career.

This is considered unfair if not outrageous by most of the press and by all politicians, and certainly by any pensionable employee who, perhaps, is forced to change jobs. However, short of requiring all employers to operate final pay schemes, or all employers to operate money purchase schemes, compulsory transfer club membership is inoperable.

Discharge of liability

2–101 It is essential that the correct procedures are followed whenever a preserved pension is replaced by a transfer to another occupational or personal pension scheme or by an insurance buy-out policy. If the correct procedures are not followed the trustees may not obtain an adequate discharge for what was the scheme's preserved pension liability. Trustees should check with their advisers on the procedure at least on the first occasion of a transfer to another occupational scheme, a transfer to a personal pension scheme and on the first occasion of the use of an insurance company buy-out policy.

Dealing with leavers' buy-out and transfer requests can be a time consuming operation for medium sized and larger schemes with a significant staff turnover. Some schemes delegate the work of dealing with such requests to their pension consultants.

CHAPTER 9

ILL-HEALTH PENSIONS AND PERMANENT HEALTH INSURANCE

Types of premature retirement

2–102 As we have mentioned earlier, although the scale of the member's pension from a final pay scheme is defined in the first place as an amount applying from the normal pension age, there are facilities for the benefit to become payable in other circumstances, in particular when the member is retiring from the service of the company before reaching the normal pension age. There are two possibilities with such early retirements. The first is where the member can be regarded as being in normal health for his age. In the second case, the retirement is arising because the member is considered no longer fit enough to carry on work. It should be noted that in the case of the retirement in good-health, the Inland Revenue will not generally permit a pension from an approved scheme to start unless the member is aged 50 or over.

Notwithstanding the recent enactment of much anti sex-discrimination legislation, the Inland Revenue will still approve a pension scheme with a normal pension age down to the age of 55 for women and, in such cases, early good health retirement for women down to the age of 45. In the case of ill-health retirement, however, there is no restriction as to the age at which such a pension can start. For the future it will be essential to ensure that the earliest date from which a pension can be paid is the same for men and women.

The level of ill-health pension in defined benefit schemes

2–103 In the normal way, it can be anticipated that members retiring due to ill-health will have a lower expectation of life than members retiring at the same age but in good health. Accordingly, it is appropriate for the scale of pensions awarded to ill-health retirements to be more generous than those provided on early retirement in good health. This is commonly achieved by basing the ill-health retirement pension on the pensionable service completed by retirement and the pensionable salary applying at the time but without the actuarial reduction which is frequently applied in the case of retirement in good health. Moreover, it is quite often found that the service ranking for benefit in the case of ill-health retirement is not only the pensionable service actually completed but all or part of the further amount of service which would have been completed had the member been able to remain in service until normal pension age. In this way, those relatively few members who are required to retire because of ill-health are at least provided with an adequate pension.

Inter-relation with State pensions

As has been mentioned earlier, it is commonly found in the design of **2–104** defined benefit pension schemes that there is a deductive item in the amount of pension which is intended to allow for the State pension benefits which the member will also receive. This will comprise both the basic State pension and the earnings-related State pension unless the pension scheme is contracted-out, when only the first of these will be applicable. It will be realised that when a member is forced to retire before normal pension age, there will be a period of time, perhaps lengthy, before any income is received from the State pension system. Accordingly, during this interim period, it is appropriate to pay an ill-health pension calculated without the deductive item. This enhanced amount of pension is then reduced when the member reaches state pension age and the State pension benefit becomes payable. However, if the pension scheme is to treat men and woment equally, this issue will cause considerable difficulty until state pension ages are the same for men and women.

The need for controls

It will be appreciated from what has been said above that, especially for a **2–105** member retiring at a comparatively young age, there can be a substantial difference between the amount of pension payable if the member is considered to be in good health and the pension payable if the retirement is taken as being due to ill-health. Accordingly, it is important for pension scheme trustees to have a set procedure for examining cases submitted to them on the basis of breakdown in health. This can take the form of the trustees asking for evidence as to the state of health of the proposed pensioner from a doctor who has no connection with the particular employee being considered or, ideally, who is acting for the trustees themselves.

Actuarial implications

As to the liabilities which will arise in respect of retirements due to ill- **2–106** health, it is common practice for the actuary, in deciding upon the financial basis of the scheme, to build in an allowance for a certain proportion of members to retire due to ill-health. Provided the numbers actually occurring do not exceed those anticipated by the actuary, then the granting of ill-health retirement pensions, even on the generous basis outlined above, will not put liabilities onto the scheme additional to those which have been anticipated.

Continuing trustee scrutiny

One difficult point which, under the rules of most pension schemes, the **2–107** trustees have to decide upon is whether or not an ill-health retirement pension should continue once it has been granted, irrespective of any improvement taking place in the health of the member. Obviously, however strict the procedure for obtaining medical evidence at the time an application for ill-health retirement is received, there will be a certain proportion of cases where after retirement the health of the member improves substantially to the extent that he may be able to, and possibly does, take on a part-time or full-time job. In such cases, it can reasonably be argued that the continued payment of an income to the former member from the scheme is no longer justified and that the resources so being utilised should be used elsewhere in the general running of the scheme. It should be noted that such scrutiny of a pension in course of payment to an ill-health pensioner is only applicable while that member is below normal pension age.. Once that age has been passed, then the pension should continue automatically without any further scrutiny of the level of ill-health applying.

2–108   It is difficult to advise firmly as to the attitude which should be taken by the trustees. We would only say that any investigation which is carried out should be done systematically for all ill-health pensioners and not concentrated upon the much smaller number where there is clear evidence that the member's state of health has improved considerably. When it is decided an ill-health retirement pension should be suspended or reduced until normal pension age, then the trustees should always be willing to reconsider their decision if subsequent evidence indicates that the member's state of health has once again deteriorated.

Permanent health insurance

2–109   It is appropriate to mention one other form of income to which members of the scheme may be entitled and which needs to be taken into account, in particular in deciding on the appropriate level of pensions for ill-health pensioners. We have in mind here permanent health insurance schemes set up by many companies. Such schemes may well cover the same employee as those included in the company pension scheme.

2–110   It should be noted that the regulations laid down by the Inland Revenue do not permit this type of benefit to form an integral part of the company approved pension scheme. Accordingly, bearing in mind the nature of the risk (that is with only a limited number of beneficiaries being expected but with a long benefit payment period being possible), it may be inadvisable for this particular type of scheme to be provided on a privately invested basis even if the pension scheme itself is run in that way. The alternatives are to insure the scheme or merely to provide the benefit from general corporate resources. The latter (non-insurance) is probably viable where upwards of say 1,000 eligible employees are involved, and an appropriate external agency is used for policing claims.

2–111   Obviously, if in certain circumstances an employee can receive a substantial increase under the permanent health insurance (PHI) policy taken out by the company, this should be reflected in the scale and conditions of the ill-health retirement pension provided from the company pension scheme. However, before considering this point, it is useful to set out the salient features of PHI schemes, as encountered at the present time.

Under these schemes an income will start to be paid to an employee **2–112** when that employee is unable to follow his or her usual occupation and after his illness or disability has lasted for a certain period of time, commonly called the "waiting period". The length of this waiting period varies between schemes, but the period most commonly encountered is 26 weeks. The income continues to be paid whilst the disability remains until the member reaches a given age usually the same as the normal pension age applying under the company pension scheme, if that pension age is the same for both men and women.

The scale of the benefit payable may be defined in a variety of ways. **2–113** Normally, however, the benefit will be a percentage of the salary being received by the member prior to the onset of the disability. Since, in such circumstances the employee involved can expect also to receive a significant income from the State, it is appropriate for the amount thus arising to be allowed for in determining the amount payable under the PHI scheme.

The amount of the benefit so payable may be level throughout, or there may be provision for increases to be granted at yearly intervals at a rate of, say three or five per cent. per annum compound. As we have mentioned above, the state of inability to work is not by any means always clear-cut, so that there will be instances arising where the employee will be fit enough to take on either part-time employment or employment in a less onerous field than that which he was carrying out prior to the start of the disability. In such cases, the insurance company may be entitled under the provisions of its policy to reduce, either wholly or partially, the level of the income benefit which it is paying, with the added proviso that if the member thereafter has to cease work on health grounds the benefit will be restored to its initial level.

It should be appreciated that, in the circumstances where an income **2–114** becomes payable under the PHI scheme, the employee involved has not in fact retired. He can be taken as being on very long-term absence from his employment. Moreover (since benefits are being paid from the PHI scheme and probably by the State) it is appropriate to have the member remain in suspended employment rather than for him to be retired. Accordingly, the ill-health retirement pension under the scheme will not start to be paid. Instead, the pension will become payable only when the member reaches normal pension age when, as explained above, the income from the PHI scheme would in any event stop. In this way, there would be some alleviation in the cost of running the company pension scheme against the premiums which would be payable by the company in respect of the PHI scheme. For the purpose of calculating the amount of pension so payable it is necessary to decide upon the notional remuneration of the member during the period of his suspended employment. A suitable definition for this purpose would be the salary being received just prior to the onset of the disability, indexed thereafter according to either the cost of living or salary levels in general.

PART 3

LEGAL DOCUMENTATION

LEGAL DOCUMENTATION

The documentation required for a pension scheme will depend on the type **3–01** of arrangement. A simple contractual obligation to provide a pension for one employee can be contained in the contract of employment, and the arrangement may qualify for approval by the Inland Revenue.

However, where funds are to be set aside, a trust is required if advantage is to be taken of the full range of exemptions from tax available to exempt approved schemes. The documentation for a scheme involving a group of employees will normally take the form of a trust deed and rules. Practice varies as to the content of the deed on the one hand and the rules on the other. Generally however, the trust deed will establish the scheme and will often contain powers to appoint new trustees, and to amend the scheme. The rules normally cover the contributions to be paid and the benefits to be provided.

In recent years it has become the practice for both tax and social security **3–02** legislation affecting pension schemes to be overriding. It is then a matter for decision as to whether the overriding provisions are to be included in the documentation. This is normal practice, in order to ensure as far as possible that the full provisions of the scheme are set out. Care is necessary however to avoid any discrepancy between the legislation and the scheme provisions since, in the event of any inconsistency, the overriding Act of Parliament will prevail.

Within the limits of a book of this nature, which does not pretend to be a **3–03** legal treatise, it is not practicable to discuss all the many matters which might be dealt with in these documents, but it is proposed to comment on some of the main features with particular reference to the requirements of the Inland Revenue.

CHAPTER 10

THE TRUST DEED

3–04 The trust deed will normally start with the date of the deed and set out the parties to the trust. These will generally be the principal company, and the trustees appointed by the employer which may include the trustees (if any) nominated by the employees.

While it is not essential that the employees should be allowed to nominate some of the trustees, many schemes operate on this basis. This is discussed in greater detail in Chapter 17 which deals with member participation in the running of schemes. It is however perhaps worth mentioning here that while it may well be desirable for members to have an involvement in the running of their scheme, it is incorrect to suppose that sectional interests can be represented in this manner. Trustees are bound by law to act in the best interests of beneficiaries as a whole, so that the question of sectional representation does not arise at this level. Indeed trusteeship is incompatible with representation of special interests.

Trustees

3–05 There are three main forms which the appointment of a trustee or trustees can take:

(1) *Personal trustees*

In this case several individuals are appointed as trustees. Usually there will be between three and five people involved.

(2) *In-house trust company*

A special trust company can be created by the employer as a subsidiary or associated company in order to act as trustee of the pension scheme. The individuals who would otherwise have been appointed as personal trustees are instead appointed as directors of the trust company.

The main advantage of a trust company is one of administration. In particular it avoids the administrative difficulties that can occur when an individual is no longer available and someone else has to be appointed to replace him.

(3) *"Outside" trust corporation*

There are several organisations which are prepared to act as trustee for a pension scheme on a fee paying basis. In particular, some merchant banks and some clearing banks own trust companies which will act in this capacity.

If an "outside" corporate trustee is appointed, it is common for a separate in-house committee of management to be set up to liaise between the trustee and the administrators responsible for the day to day running of the scheme.

Whatever form the appointment of the trustee or trustees takes there will usually be a separate clause within the trust deed dealing with the power of appointment and removal of the trustees.

Employer

The deed will usually provide for the holding company in the group to be **3–06** the principal party to the deed and responsible for the appointment of trustees and similar matters, leaving other companies simply as participating companies under the trust, either by the provisions of the trust deed itself or more commonly by the execution of deeds of adherence.

The alternative, of making every participating company a full party to the provisions of the deed, has the administrative disadvantage that any amending deed will have to be sealed by all the participating companies. This may be no great problem with two or three companies, all with their registered offices in the same place, but with a large number of widely spread companies the administrative work could be formidable.

There will be a clause in the deed which states the employer's obligation **3–07** to contribute to the fund. This will usually be drawn in general terms such as "The employer will contribute to the fund from time to time such amounts as the actuary shall recommend."

Sometimes the employer's contributions are more specifically defined but this may result in undesirable rigidity in the face of varying circumstances. The cost of specific benefits can usually only be estimated, rather than determined, in advance so that if contributions are fixed it could well turn out that benefits must be changed, not necessarily for the better, in due course. The distinction between defined benefit schemes which specify the level of employer's contributions, and balance of cost schemes which do not, is made elsewhere. If the employer's contributions are to be closely defined, the clause may specify the basis for current service contributions and also provide for lump sum or periodical payments in respect of service prior to the inauguration of the scheme. If the employer has agreed to pay all costs, charges and expenses in connection with the fund, this will also be stated in this clause. In many cases, the employer pays all expense except investment expenses. However, the current trend is for expenses to be borne by the fund itself, and contributions paid by participating employers include an allowance to cover these.

It is undesirable that employers should be absolutely bound to continue **3–08** contributions to the pension fund in all circumstances, and it is usual to add a proviso somewhat on the following lines:

"Provided always that the company may at any time reduce, suspend or terminate its contributions by giving six months' previous notice in writing to the trustees and upon the expiration of a notice to terminate its payments or upon the dissolution of the scheme all liability on the part of the company to contribute to the scheme shall cease."

If the employer has given a guarantee of solvency or a guarantee of the rate of interest, such a provision will be included in this clause. Such guarantees have little to recommend them; it is not easy to define in quantitative terms exactly what they mean and, in any case, the guarantee can be no stronger than the financial capacity of the employer. Employees must be informed as to whether or not the employer is under any obligation to fund any potential shortfall. In due course, when the relevant provisions become operative, the Social Security Act 1990 will require employers to make good any deficit on the winding-up of a final salary scheme. However, as stated above members will benefit only where funds are available. There is no suggestion that any deficit is to be given priority over other creditors.

Investment powers

3–09 The limitations imposed under the Trustee Investments Act 1961 apply to a pension trust unless other powers are specifically given. Schemes which are contracted-out on a money purchase basis are subject to regulations which restrict the powers of investment of the minimum contributions required, Regulations are to be made shortly restricting the extent to which trustees may invest in the employing companies. The Inland Revenue also in practice restrict investment powers, particularly in relation to residential property, and loans to scheme members. With these exceptions, there are no statutory limitations on the investment powers which may be given to trustees of pension funds.

3–10 The subject of the investment powers of the trustees of a pension fund is dealt with in Chapter 26. In brief, it is desirable that the trust deed and rules should be drawn as flexibly as possible so that the trustees have the widest possible powers of investment. This will include power to insure the scheme benefits by investing in life office contracts.

The trustees would also generally be given power to borrow money for the purposes of the scheme and to make such arrangements for payment of interest and the offering of security as shall seem to them fit, including charging the investments of the fund.

3–11 In exercising their powers of investment trustees must have regard to the Financial Services Act. Under that Act, any persons involved in managing the assets of an occupational pension scheme, where those assets include investments covered by the Act, must be authorised under the Act unless all investment management decisions or all day to day decisions are delegated to an authorised person (FSA 1986 s.191). The Act does not specify what constitutes the activity of management for this purpose, nor the type of decisions which would be classified as day to day.

Authorisation under the Act will normally be obtained by application to the Investment Management Regulatory Organisation (IMRO). The Financial Services Act is explained further in Chapter 41.

Power to delegate

The deed (or, less appropriately, the rules) must contain powers for the **3–12** trustees to delegate some of their functions since it would not be practical for the trustees to involve themselves with every aspect of the running of the scheme. It would be normal for the trustees to delegate some or all of the exercise of their investment powers, the exercise of their discretionary powers in relation to the payment of benefits and the exercise of various routine administrative functions. As indicated above, comprehensive powers of delegation are needed if the trustees are to avoid having to seek authorisation under the Financial Services Act.

It is normal practice for the scheme to provide that majority decisions will prevail.

Trustees' meetings

The deed will deal with the methods by which the trustees shall transact **3–13** their business and exercise their powers. Provision will be made as to what shall constitute a quorum of trustees. When a decision is taken by vote, the chairman of any particular meeting will frequently have a second or casting vote. In practice, however, it is rare that decisions are taken other than unanimously; indeed under general trust law a trustees' decision must be unanimous if it is to be effective, unless the trust instrument specifically provides otherwise.

The trustees will usually appoint a secretary who must keep proper minutes of all meetings, including resolutions, which must be signed by the chairman of the meeting.

Where a sole corporate trustee is appointed the method of operation, including the constitution of a quorum and voting, will depend on the articles of the company.

Membership records and accounts

The trustees will be responsible for making sure that complete records of **3–14** persons becoming entitled to pensions or other allowances are kept and that full records of all deaths and withdrawals of members and all other matters essential to the working of the scheme are maintained. As a rule they will appoint an employee of the principal company to carry out these duties. He will also keep accounts to show the position of the fund and will record the amount contributed by each member. Traditionally it has been normal practice for the deed to provide that these accounts should be audited every year by an auditor appointed for the purpose. Similarly, it was usual for the deed to include power for the trustees (or sometimes the principal company) to appoint such auditors and to appoint an actuary. However, under the disclosure regulations made under amendments introduced by the Social Security Act 1985, there is an overriding obligation to appoint an auditor and an actuary, and to ensure that accounts are audited annually and an actuarial valuation obtained not less frequently than every three and a half years.

Meetings of members

3–15 Many long established schemes provide for periodic meetings of members. Ordinary meetings may or may not be held regularly and there is sometimes power to convene an extraordinary meeting whenever the trustees so direct or in response to a requisition signed by not less than a fixed proportion of members. In some cases, where there is such provision, notices of the meetings must be given to every member while in others it is provided that the posting of a notice in the usual place of business will be sufficient; in the case of pensioners or others not working at the usual place of business, it is usual to notify them by post if they are entitled to attend meetings.

Most modern trust deeds omit provision for meetings of members and give powers to the trustees or a committee to deal with all matters.

Actuarial investigation

3–16 The desirability of periodical actuarial investigations into the position of a privately invested fund is discussed in Chapters 20–23. As stated above the actuarial valuation is now an overriding requirement at intervals not greater than three and a half years. In the past valuations have usually been made at five year intervals but with the rapidly changing financial circumstances during recent years most pension funds are calling for them at shorter intervals so that any surplus or deficiency does not become too large before it is recognised. Frequently, the deed provides that the first valuation shall be made after three years and then at least once every three years thereafter. To give effect to this a clause on the following lines is inserted:

> "The trustees shall from time to time appoint an actuary to the fund. The position of the fund shall be submitted to actuarial investigation on or before . . . and thereafter once at least in every three years and for that purpose all necessary accounts and information shall be furnished by the trustees and the company to the actuary. The actuary shall report to the trustees in writing on the financial position of the pension fund."

3–17   In some long established schemes, the deed provides for action to be taken if the valuation reveals a deficiency or a surplus. In case of a deficiency, provision was made for contributions to be increased, or for benefits to be reduced or for a mixture of both. If a surplus was revealed, the deed provided for contributions to be reduced, or benefits to be increased. In some cases, the action to be taken was decided upon by the trustees, but the consent or agreement of the principal company was often required. Such a scheme is the defined benefit deferred pay scheme referred to in Chapter 1. Modern practice is for the deed to be silent on what is to happen if a deficiency is disclosed, one consequence of which would normally be that increased contributions would become payable by the employer. Where a surplus is revealed above the level prescribed by the Inland Revenue, the trustees are required to produce proposals to correct the position if the investment income and gains are to continue to be fully exempt from tax. Acceptable proposals if the scheme rules permit may include contribution reductions, benefit improvements, or a refund to participating employers. The Social Security Act 1990 will contain provisions requiring benefits to be increased up to a maximum of five per cent. per annum as a priority, if a surplus is revealed. This topic is covered in greater detail in Chapter 24.

Alterations to the trust deed and rules

It is generally provided (and this is essential) that the trustees in agreement **3–18** with the principal company, or vice versa, may amend the trust deed or the rules. There are some trust deeds which provide that no alteration shall be made without the consent of the majority of the members obtained at an extraordinary meeting convened for the purpose or by means of a postal ballot.

Having to obtain the agreement of members to an amendment can create difficulties and, in any case, causes delay. Most modern deeds therefore omit this provision.

It may be provided that no alteration may be made which will substan- **3–19** tially prejudice the rights or interests of any person who is already a member at the date of the alteration, although more usually it is only the accrued rights up to the date of the alteration which are so protected. These rights may be overridden by a specific clause in the trust deed, permitting an alteration under the valuation rule where a reduction is needed to correct an actuarial deficiency or an alteration made under a specific power to reduce pensions consequent upon an increase in social security pensions.

If the alteration provisions effectively protect all rights and interests of **3–20** members at the time of an alteration, it may also be wise to provide that if it is desired to make an alteration which would be otherwise prohibited it may be done by obtaining the consent of a high proportion (say, 90 per cent.) of those affected or likely to be affected. Alternatives of this nature are sometimes necessary where the employer is giving members some *quid pro quo* outside the scheme. Another occasion where this can arise is where it is desired to admit another class of employees to membership and it is impossible to say whether this will substantially prejudice the rights of existing members or improve them, having regard to the possible effect on surpluses or deficiencies. The current trend is for powers of amendment not to contain any restrictions as regards benefits for future service.

The wording of this clause where it relates to alterations which are per- **3–21** missible is important. An illustration of the difficulties which can occur by inadvertently precluding an alteration which might be desirable is a trust deed which, in specifying the alterations which were excluded, used the following words " . . . or alter the main purpose of the fund from that of granting pensions to employees of the company . . . ". Subsequently, the company concerned desired to admit the members of the staff of a subsidiary company to the fund. After taking counsel's opinion, it was decided that under the existing trust this was not possible because the definition of the "company" included only the principal company.

It is generally considered that one should avoid restrictions on powers of alteration which go beyond protecting rights accrued at the date of alteration or which require members' consent. Indeed, the current practice for new schemes is to adopt an alteration power which contains no restrictions.

Winding-up

3–22 It is necessary for the trust deed and the rules to cover the circumstances under which the pension scheme has to be wound up or partially wound up.

Usually, a full winding-up will occur if the employers are unable to continue their contributions to the scheme although in such circumstances provision may be included in the deed for the scheme to continue as a closed fund, if the trustees and the employers so wish.

3–23 A partial winding-up is likely to occur if one of the companies in the group is sold off and so is unable to continue to participate in the scheme. In this case, a modern deed will provide for members in the service of the company which is ceasing to participate to be entitled to benefits as if they had left service. The deed will also allow enhanced transfer values to be paid if members are to be transferred to a scheme of the purchaser, with continuous benefit provision.

3–24 Having covered the circumstances leading to a winding-up, the trust deed and rules will then go on to state what is to be done with the funds in such an event. It is usual in these circumstances to make the first charges on the funds, after paying all expenses, the provision of benefits secured by additional voluntary contributions and the purchase of annuities for existing pensioners. Thereafter the remaining monies are used to purchase annuities or deferred annuities for prospective pensioners. Under proposals expected to come into effect following the Social Security Act 1990, if the funds are insufficient to provide the promised benefits the resulting deficit will form a debt on the employer. A first call on any surplus will be for the provision of limited price indexation.

3–25 The Inland Revenue insist upon the annuities and deferred annuities purchased by the trustees being non-assignable and commutable only to the extent which would not have prejudiced approval by them had the scheme been continuing in existence and had each member left it on the date when winding-up began. Nevertheless, if any annuity to be provided were of trivial amount (and the Inland Revenue lay down limits from time to time, at present £104 per annum, for what can be regarded as "trivial") no objection would be raised to the payment of a lump sum in lieu of the whole of that annuity.

The £104 figure is expected to be increased to £260 shortly.

The trust deed and rules should also provide the alternative of transferring the monies in the fund to another approved fund or funds.

3–26 In the case of a contracted-out scheme (see Chapter 37) the winding-up clause *must* give priority (in whatever order is required) in the event of a winding-up to any liabilities of the scheme in respect of:

— Guaranteed Minimum Pensions;
— Equivalent Pension Benefits (under the National Insurance Act 1965);
— current pensions; and
— State Scheme premiums.

Except that, if required and if the actuary can still give the certificate required by the OPB as to the adequacy of resources on a future winding-up to meet the above four items, any of the following liabilities may rank equally with, or ahead of, those shown above:

— administrative expenses;
— benefits in respect of any period of service before the priority clause took effect;
— benefits to which members who deferred their retirement would become entitled on retirement;
— benefits prospectively payable on the death of a member who has either retired or reached normal pension age; and
— alternatively, a contracted-out scheme may provide for assets relating to additional voluntary contributions (AVC's) to be kept separate in which event such assets may be applied exclusively to secure the AVC liabilities to which they relate.

Finally, it is a condition of Inland Revenue approval that whilst the **3–27** winding-up clause can provide, in the event of a surplus arising on winding-up, for benefits to be augmented within approvable limits, there must then be express provision for the return of any eventual surplus to the employer. The amounts so returned will be liable for tax at 40 per cent. Under the Social Security Act 1990, no refunds to employer's are allowed unless provision is made for all pensions to be increased while in payment by limited price indexation. Although when a scheme is started the question of winding-up may seem remote, it is very important to make proper provision for it in some detail, particularly in view of the many mergers, takeovers and sales or acquisitions of subsidiary companies which now take place.

Multiple schemes

Many employers, frequently though by no means exclusively the larger **3–28** ones, find it desirable to run a number of schemes, for example for non-staff employees, staff employees and executive employees respectively. The need for multiple schemes can also arise in a group of companies whose subsidiaries operate in markedly differing trades with consequent need for benefit and contribution patterns which vary according to the employing subsidiary. Of itself, this need for more than one scheme does not require that there be more than one pension fund. The fund membership could be classified by status and/or by employing subsidiary and each class of member could be covered by a separate set of benefit and contribution scales appended to a single trust deed.

3–29   In these cases, the basic particulars required to be given to members under the disclosure regulations may be restricted to the provisions relating to the group. However, under the regulations members may be entitled to examine the deeds and rules relating to all the group included in the scheme. For complete confidentiality therefore, many employers still run one or more of their schemes by funding it through a trust which is totally separate from any other pension trust or trusts in operation within the group. Neither of these approaches need, in the case of privately invested funds, involve having more than one investment portfolio. Even where there are quite separate funds with separate trustees, a single investment portfolio can be maintained in a common investment fund run on lines closely similar to a unit trust so that the stake of each of the trusts in the common fund is always known.

3–30   For an insured scheme with multiple membership classes and benefit/ contribution patterns, there would probably be one group policy to cover each class of member. Cases exist where there are two membership classes within one pension trust and the benefits for one class are financed by private investment while those for the other class are insured. Nevertheless, on a winding-up of the entire scheme, all the assets may have to be realised and the resulting fund used to satisfy the liabilities in the various priority categories, irrespective of the different classes of membership.

Chapter 11

THE RULES

The exact division of matter between trust deed and rules varies consider- **3–31**
ably according to the way different solicitors draw up their deeds. In some
cases, the trust deed is very short and virtually everything is included in the
rules. It is probably more common to define the administrative provisions
of the trust in the trust deed, and for the rules to give the essential details of
the scheme as it affects employees—that is the contributions and the benefits. The distinction between the two types of provision becomes blurred in
respect of some matters and hence the different division of some matters
between the trust deed and rules in different cases. In Chapter 10 it has
been assumed that the trust deed itself will include a fair amount of detail.

Definitions

At an early stage in the rules it will be necessary to define a number of **3–32**
terms used.

The employer. In the trust deed the principal company will have been a
party to the deed. The term "employer," however, will usually be used to
cover each of the companies which participate in the fund from time to
time, and in relation to an employee will refer to that company by which he
is for the time being employed.

The employee. This definition has to be linked with the rules governing eligibility and membership, and comments are made under the heading "Eligibility and membership" later in this chapter. It is relevant to mention,
however, that it sometimes facilitates drafting to set out some of the eligibility requirements in the definition of "the employees."

Normal pension age. It is essential, in order to meet Revenue requirements
regarding funding, to fix an age at which pensions will normally become
payable. Having fixed the pension at normal pension age, in the majority
of schemes the pensions on retirement before or after normal pension age
are approximately the actuarial equivalent of the normal pension. Following the European Court case of *Barber* v. *G.R.E.*, schemes must have a
common normal pension age for men and women in the same job category.
While the differing state pension ages of 65 for men and 60 for women continue, anomalies are inevitable particularly in contracted-out schemes.
Under employment legislation men and women are protected from unfair
dismissal until the age of 65, unless both men and women in practice retire
at an earlier age which is common to both, usually known as the normal
retirement age.

Salary or Wage. Where pensions, other benefits or contributions are related to salary or wage, the definition is important because it has to be made clear whether it is only basic salary or wages which are to rank, or whether allowance has to be made for some or all of directors' fees, bonus, commission and overtime payments, etc.

Service. Where the amount of a member's pension varies according to his length of service, the definition of such service will directly affect the amount of pension. "Service" may be defined as service whilst a member of the scheme or it may also include service before joining the scheme.

It is often useful to distinguish between "salary" and "wage" or "pensionable salary" and "pensionable wage" or between "service" and "pensionable service" and so on.

There will, of course, be other items to define in most sets of rules.

Eligibility and membership

3–33 Provision will have to be made in the rules as to who is to be eligible for admission to the scheme. This is particularly important where (as is most often the case) not all the employees are to be admitted to the scheme, as it must be made clear from the rules which classes of employee are to be admitted and which not.

Eligibility conditions are discussed in detail in Chapter 4.

However, it is useful to empower the trustees to waive one or more of the limitations on membership, imposing special conditions where necessary as advised by the actuary. This will usually be acceptable to the Inland Revenue. Such a discretion allows the difficult marginal cases to be dealt with sympathetically.

At the start of a scheme, some of the eligibility provisions may be modified, in particular the maximum entry age (if any) may or may not be applied to existing employees.

3–34 The rules will also cover the formalities for joining and the conditions will be stated for subsequent entry of those who at first decline. If the members do not contribute it is unlikely that any eligible person will refuse membership but under a contributory scheme some declinatures are almost inevitable. It is unusual for those declining to be permitted to join subsequently except on less favourable terms than those given to original entrants.

3–35 Membership must now be offered to eligible employees on a voluntary basis. In addition employees must be allowed to opt out at any time if they wish. A reasonable period of notice is often required for opting out, and it is generally assumed that the legislation permits this. In contributory schemes care should be taken to ensure that an appropriate authority to deduct contributions from pay has been obtained for employees. Such authority could be incorporated into an application for membership, but is more frequently contained in the contract of employment. A specific authority is required under the Wages Act 1986.

A statement concerning the availability of a pension scheme has to be included in the written statement of the terms of employment which an employer is required to give his employees, under the employment protection legislation.

Discontinuance of membership while an employee remains in the service **3–36** of the employer can be considered under two cases. The first of these is where promotion or demotion makes the employee no longer eligible for the scheme of which he has hitherto been a member.

The second case is where the employee seeks to opt out of membership while remaining eligible. In both cases the member will normally become entitled to preserved benefits under the rules as if he had left service. The statutory right to have the cash equivalent of his accrued benefits transferred to a buy-out policy or a personal pension scheme will also be available. Where the period of pensionable service completed is less than two years a refund of employee's contributions can be offered, as an alternative.

Another point which needs consideration is the question of broken ser- **3–37** vice. In times of trade depression especially, a number of employees leave and are subsequently re-engaged. Should they be re-admitted to the scheme without any rights in respect of their previous spell of service? Many employers take the view that where any contributions paid by the employee during the previous spell of employment have been refunded on his leaving, entirely new membership is the only proper course. Others, however, are agreeable to giving full rights for the previous spell provided the employee is prepared to repay the amount refunded to him with interest to the date of such repayment. If any rights are given for previous service it should be provided in the rules that the actuary shall certify the amount to be paid to the fund to cover the cost. Analogous problems arise when an employee is directed overseas, to be employed for a limited period by a foreign subsidiary. For obvious reasons it is common that cases of this type are treated as generously as possible on their return.

The question of broken service also has implications relevant to preservation of benefits as required by the Social Security Act 1973 (see Chapter 35).

Contributions

The method of calculation of employee's contributions must be stated in **3–38** precise terms so that there is no room for doubt or dispute.

The contribution rule will usually specify that the employer will deduct the contributions from salaries or wages and pay them to the trustees. The rule will also indicate when contributions will cease; this is usually at normal pension age but in the case of an insured scheme it may be on the policy anniversary preceding normal pension age. Further contributions after normal pension age can be made if the scheme so provides but in such cases provision has to be made for contributions to cease once a member's pension reaches the Inland Revenue maximum. There are considerable practical drawbacks to providing for such further contributions, so that the usual practice (cessation at normal pension age) is to be preferred. However, this practice will have to be modified where normal pension age is different for men and women, to avoid any question of discrimination—see Chapter 42.

3–39   Under current legislation members must be offered the right to pay additional voluntary contributions. It is normal practice for such contributions to be a fixed percentage of pay in each scheme year. However, more flexible provisions may be incorporated if the employer is prepared to cope with the additional administration involved. If approval is to be obtained, the total of a member's contributions in any one year must be limited in such a way that he does not, in total, pay more than 15 per cent. of his remuneration. This includes any contributions the member is required to pay under the rules, and also any contributions he has elected to pay either under the scheme on to a free standing additional voluntary contribution scheme he may be contributing to. Such schemes are now offered by, for example, insurance companies.

3–40   Under a money purchase scheme, the basis for the employer's contributions will also be set out in the rules. In most other cases, the employer meets the balance of the cost after allowing for employees' contributions. The employer's commitment will probably be expressed in general terms, although reference may be specifically made to payments for pre-scheme service.

Benefits

3–41 As with the rules dealing with contributions it is important that those setting out the benefits should leave no doubt in the minds of the members as to the benefits payable in any given circumstances. Any disappointment arising out of confusion on these points can do a great deal to militate against that sense of security among employees which should be expected to emerge from the existence of a pension scheme.

Except with money purchase schemes, members' pensions will usually be defined in relation to the pension payable from normal pension age. The rule will set the method of calculating the normal pension, the frequency of payment and any period for which it is guaranteed. Separate rules will govern early and late retirement.

3–42   In the case of early retirement, if any special benefits are to be provided on retirement on account of ill-health these should be indicated.

If, as is usually the case, the member has an option at retirement to take part of his pension in the form of a lump sum, this should be covered along with details of whether or not the trustees' and/or the employer's consent is required, the method of calculating the maximum amount of lump sum, and the basis for determining the amount of pension to be foregone.

3–43   A rule allowing for the augmentation of a benefit, subject to Inland Revenue limits, should always be included because it can be of great practical use on many occasions. Such a rule should normally provide for the payment by the employer of the cost of any additional benefit provided, as advised by the actuary.

In respect of voluntary contributions an appropriate rule must be included covering the terms on which the emerging benefits are payable and the winding-up provisions should be so drawn as to ensure that, before the general funds of the scheme are apportioned, the particular assets deriving from each member's AVC's are allocated to that member.

Where it is possible that a benefit payable, whether as a normal benefit or by reason of augmentation, can increase to a point where it would exceed an Inland Revenue limit, provision must be made to apply that limit. For the purpose of this limit, special definitions of final "salary" or "wage" laid down by the Commissioners, must be included in the provision.

If the scheme provides widows' pensions or lump sum death benefits, **3–44** appropriate rules governing these benefits must also be included. Similarly, if a widow's pension option is available, the terms of the option must be set out.

In addition to indicating the lump sum benefit on death, the rules should stipulate to whom the benefit is to be paid. The way these provisions are framed will largely determine whether inheritance tax liability adheres to that benefit. In an approved scheme no liability to inheritance tax will arise if the trustees have complete discretion as to the distribution of the benefit among a defined class of possible beneficiaries.

The rules will cover the benefit to be allowed on a member leaving the service and in particular must satisfy the preservation requirements of the Social Security Act 1973 (see Chapters 8 and 35), the requirement to revalue accrued benefits in the period up to normal pension age, and the right to a transfer or buy-out.

Contracted-out schemes

For a scheme to be contracted-out, members must have an entitlement to **3–45** "guaranteed minimum pension" as defined in the legislation and a specimen rule to this effect is given in Appendix 1 of Memorandum No. 77 issued by the Occupational Pensions Board. The rules will also normally include provisions for the payment of State Scheme premiums to be made in the event of employees leaving or the scheme winding-up, and for deductions from refunds of contributions for leaving members to be allowed in respect of their share of their contributions equivalent premium.

As an alternative to the provision of a guaranteed minimum pension for **3–46** members, widows and widowers, a scheme may adopt a money purchase test. Under this arrangement contributions equal to the National Insurance contacting-out rebate must be applied to secure "protected rights" pensions. Whilst clearly appropriate in a money purchase scheme, this test could also be adopted in a hybrid scheme providing, for example, money purchase benefits with a final pay guarantee.

Memorandum No. 77 mentioned above sets out full details of the many **3–47** points which need to be covered in the rules of a contracted-out scheme and is a highly comprehensive and well indexed document. It includes a number of other specimen rules together with an appropriate check list.

For more details on contracted-out schemes, the reader is referred to Chapters 37–39.

Miscellaneous

3–48 There are a number of points which can usefully be covered in the rules such as the following.

(i) The formalities of proving the continued existence of a pensioner before making pension payments may occasionally be important. While a signature on a receipt may be some evidence it is as well to have this supported by periodical checks, such as a declaration by the pensioner's bank manager or doctor. These periodical checks should be provided for in the rules to prevent any subsequent charge of officiousness on the part of the fund secretary.

(ii) In the common case where premature retirement due to ill-health involves a higher pension than that available in normally good health, it is wise to provide (a) that the trustees may call for periodic evidence that the state of ill-health continues and (b) that, if such evidence cannot be given, the trustees may review the case and, if they think fit, modify or extinguish the pension payable until the pensioner attains the normal retirement age,

(iii) A useful addition to the pension rules is to provide that:
"if the pensioner is, in the opinion of the trustees, suffering from any disease or other incapacity rendering him unable to manage his affairs or to give a proper receipt, they may at their discretion pay the pension to the spouse or any relatives or dependents of the pensioner or to any bank or institution to be applied for his benefit and the receipt of the person, bank or institution so paid shall be a complete discharge to the trustees for money paid and they shall not be under any liability to see to the application thereof."

3–51 (iv) The employer's purpose in establishing a pension scheme has been to provide a reasonable standard of living for his employees during old age, and yet it was not unknown in the past for a pensioner's creditors in bankruptcy to seize the whole of the pension payments to satisfy debts. In order to prevent this situation, the following words should be added to the rules.
"The retirement pension to which a member shall or may become entitled under these rules shall cease to be paid or payable if such member shall become bankrupt, execute any assignment for the benefit of creditors or attempt to alienate charge or anticipate the same or any part thereof. In any such case as aforesaid and whether the pension has begun to be payable or otherwise the trustees may apply such forfeited pension for the personal support and maintenance or otherwise for the benefit of the member or his wife and children."

3–52 (v) It should be provided that nothing in the deed shall restrict the right of an employer to dispense with the service of an employee and that the benefits conferred shall not be used to increase damages in respect of dismissal although, clearly, such provision would be subordinate to statutory employment provisions.

(vi) The trustees should have the right to production of evidence of date **3–53** of birth and to adjust benefits as appropriate if the age given at the time of entry should subsequently be proved to have been incorrect.

(vii) Provision can be included for the employer to be able to exercise a **3–54** charge or right of set off against the member's benefits (in excess of his guaranteed minimum pension or protected rights if he is contracted-out of the State Scheme) if there is a debt to the employer arising out of a criminal, negligent or fraudulent act or omission by the member. Any such provision must comply with the preservation legislation, and its application in practice must be carefully considered by the trustees in conjunction with their advisers.

(viii) The commutation in full of a member's pension on retirement if the **3–55** pension is "trivial" (and the Inland Revenue lay down limits for trivial pensions from time to time) or if the member is in "exceptionally serious ill-health" should be provided for.

(ix) If on leaving, a member opts for a refund of contributions (assuming **3–56** such option is available to him), then the trustees are liable to tax, currently at the rate of 20 per cent. on such a payment. It is usual to empower the trustees to reduce the member's refund by the amount of any tax due.

(x) Finally, it is sensible to cover in the rules the arbitration procedure **3–57** in the event of a dispute as to the meaning of any part of the trust deed and rules.

Conclusion

As was stated earlier, this and the preceding chapter do not purport to be **3–58** an exhaustive treatise on the trust deed and rules of a pension scheme but are intended merely to give a greater idea of their contents. In practice, and this is always to be recommended, these documents will be drawn up, or at least finalised, by a solicitor who may well work on the drafting in conjunction with the scheme's actuary or other advisers.

PART 4

RUNNING A PENSION SCHEME

RUNNING A PENSION SCHEME

In this Part we consider the general responsibilities of the employer and the **4–01** scheme trustees. We also consider the involvement of the members, their need for adequate information and their participation in running the scheme.

CHAPTER 12

THE EMPLOYER'S RESPONSIBILITIES

4–02 Pension advisers distinguish very succinctly between the two main designs of pension schemes by calling them "defined benefit" schemes and "defined contribution" schemes. Under a scheme of the first type, the legal document constituting the scheme defines the benefits to be paid (and, in fact, the contributions, if any, which are to be made by the members) but, when it comes to describing the contributions payable by the employer, the substance of the document is in effect that the employer shall contribute to the scheme at such rate or rates as may be necessary from time to time having regard to the liabilities of the scheme to members. There is then some amplification of this so as to guide those construing the document as to where they should look for informed advice as to what is "necessary." In the case of a privately invested scheme this will usually refer to the actuary to the scheme. Where a scheme is insured the reference will probably be to the insuring life office.

4–03   The unknown factor, it will be noted, is the level of the employer's contribution from time to time. By contrast, under a defined contribution scheme the employer and each member contribute a defined amount (probably a percentage of pay). The unknown factor here is the size of the emerging benefit because this will depend (a) upon the result of accumulating defined contributions, by each member and by the employer in respect of him, until the member retires and (b) upon the terms on which, at that time, the trustees are willing (on advice) to turn an accumulated lump sum into an equivalent pension.

4–04   The majority of United Kingdom occupational pension schemes are of the "defined benefit" type. In sponsoring such a scheme the employer is therefore assuming a responsibility which cannot be defined in advance; his safeguard is that he will always be empowered in the scheme constitution to reduce or suspend his contributions. Moreover, nearly all these defined benefit schemes are on a "final salary" basis: that is to say, the main benefit (the retirement pension) directly depends upon the member's salary at, or near, the date of his retirement.

It will be seen that, though subject to the safeguard described above, an employer assumes greater financial responsibility under a defined benefit scheme and especially so when it is on a "final salary" basis. Note also that following the Social Security Act 1990 the employer will be required to make good any deficit disclosed on the wind–up of a defined benefit scheme.

4–05   Responsibility for selection and supervision of pension fund investment advisers will, in the legal documents, be allocated to the trustees and we discuss this in more detail in Chapter 13. However, the investment return secured can have an enormous effect upon the cost of benefits under a defined benefit scheme or upon the emerging benefits under a defined contribution scheme. This is illustrated by the following table which indicates, at various assumed rates of interest:

(a) the amount to which an annual contribution of £1,000 will accumulate over 40 years,

(b) the annual contribution necessary to provide £100,000 at the end of 40 years.

Rate of Compound Interest	Accumulation of £1,000 p.a. for 40 years	Annual Amount to produce £100,000 at the end of 40 years
% p.a.	£	£
5	120,800	830
6	154,800	650
7	199,600	500
8	259,100	390
9	337,900	300
10	442,600	230
11	581,800	170
12	767,100	130
13	1,013,700	100
14	1,342,000	80
15	1,779,100	60

It is therefore essential that the employer should take a vital interest in the investment function whether the invested assets consist of direct investments or indirect investments through a collective vehicle such as a unit trust or policies with a life office.

The employer must also inevitably take a prominent part in reaching **4–06** decisions about the granting of discretionary benefit increases (over and above those required by statute) in times of inflation to those retired on pension and to members formerly employed by him who have left the scheme with the right to a deferred pension to start at pension age.

In addition, the employer must take important decisions as to the form and extent of the information to be provided to scheme members having regard to the disclosure requirements imposed under social security legislation and as to the method of scheme administration (including the degree of involvement of the members in this last function). Both these matters affect the total cost of having the pension scheme and (except possibly in a defined contribution scheme) the burden of increased cost usually falls upon the employer.

It is interesting to note that while the cost element involved in running a pension scheme is clearly the province of the corporate finance executive, the matters mentioned in the preceding paragraph fall, in the main, more naturally within the personnel function.

CHAPTER 13

THE TRUSTEES' RESPONSIBILITIES

4–07 The fundamental responsibility of the trustees of any pension scheme is to administer it in accordance with its trust deed and rules and to exercise vigilant stewardship over its assets.

Put at its simplest a trust is where property is held by trustees for the benefit of others. Upon appointment as trustees individuals become joint legal owners of the trust property, which they hold for the benefit of the scheme members.

4–08 United Kingdom approved pension schemes are invariably established under trust. There are two very good reasons for this. Firstly, the assets are segregated from the employer's business and accordingly will survive if the employing company finds itself in financial difficulties as the trust funds will not be available to satisfy its creditors, at least not until all of the scheme's liabilities have been met and post-retirement limited price indexation has been provided. Secondly, a trust is essential if full advantage is to be taken of the tax reliefs available for approved schemes.

4–09 As mentioned earlier in chapter 10, in many schemes employees are themselves appointed as individual trustees. In other cases a corporate trustee may be appointed, either solely or jointly. The corporate trustee may be a company in business for this purpose, or it may be established by the employing company simply to fulfil the trustee role. Some schemes operate on the basis that a corporate trustee will be responsible for custodianship of the assets, and possibly their investment, whilst the day to day management of the scheme would be vested in a committee.

4–10 The constitution of the trustee body is in practice to a large extent dependent upon the size of the scheme. In the insured scheme for one individual the employing company may itself be sole trustee. Small schemes catering for a group of employees will often be administered by individual trustees. As schemes increase in size it is common practice for a corporate trustee to be appointed and this is frequently the case in respect of very large schemes.

A corporate trustee has the advantage of limited liability. This is not to say, however, that the individuals concerned as directors of a corporate trustee will always be absolved from liability should things go wrong. Whilst there are no decided cases on the issue, it is generally considered that the corporate shield will not protect individuals from a deliberate breach of trust. It may however be useful as a shield in the event of an error in scheme administration which might otherwise expose them to liability.

4–11 For schemes established in England, the statute governing the activities of trustees is the Trustee Act of 1925. This was amended in 1961 by the

Trustee Investments Act of that year, to give trustees wider powers of investment. It is however important to remember that the Trustee Act only applies generally in the absence of specific provisions in the trust deed and rules. Equally important are cases which have been decided in the Courts. Generally these cases will not have arisen in the context of pension schemes but in respect of family trusts. It is clear that pension schemes are subject to the ordinary law of trust and accordingly many of the principles establishing how trustees are expected to operate will derive from long established case law relating to trusts generally.

As stated above the provisions of the trust deed and rules will generally **4–12** override the Trustee Act of 1925. Under that Act new trustees would be appointed by the trustees themselves, who would therefore be in a position to determine their own successors. It is normal practice for pension scheme documentation to provide that new trustees will be appointed by the principal company. This does not preclude the appointment of individuals from various sectors of the workforce, including trade union representatives, and this is normal practice, particularly in large schemes. Again, it is a fundamental principle of trust law that the trustees' decisions must be unanimous. In practice this too is overruled by scheme documentation which normally provides for a majority decision to prevail.

On the question of investments, the Trustee Act of 1925 as amended in **4–13** 1961 contains powers of investment which are generally regarded as much too restrictive for a modern pension scheme. The powers involve dividing the fund into two parts, one of which can be invested in "narrow range" investments, and the other in specific "wide range" investments. All contributions paid into the scheme would similarly have to be split into two parts. Because of the restrictive nature of these provisions, and the complexity of administration, it is normal practice for trustees to be given investment powers which are virtually unrestricted.

The scheme documentation is clearly very important. As stated in **4–14** Chapters 10 and 11, this will set out the basic trust provisions and also any division of responsibilities between, for example, a corporate trustee and a committee of management. The document will contain detailed provisions concerning entitlement to benefits and the contributions payable by employers and employees. Of necessity, in the case of approved schemes the Inland Revenue requirements will be specified in some detail. The documentation will also be influenced by the social security legislation, particularly affecting early leavers. If the scheme is contracted-out of the State earnings related scheme, the rules will also contain overriding provisions to ensure that scheme members and their surviving spouses become entitled to guaranteed minimum pensions as required by the legislation related to contracting-out.

The position of the trustees is now further complicated by the current **4–15** trend towards legislation which is overriding. We now have a position where the trust deed and rules will themselves be overriding as regards basic trust law, but will be overridden by the social security and tax legislation. It is necessary therefore for trustees to be clear that the scheme documentation must be looked at in the context of the relevant Acts of

Parliament. This is particularly important where the scheme documentation is out of date, as in many cases in practice it will be.

4–16   Perhaps the most important duty of the trustee is to carry out his functions in good faith in the best interests of the scheme beneficiaries. In a pension scheme context this will generally mean their best financial interests. The trustee is under a duty to familiarise himself with the trust and to give effect to its provisions. As stated above, the function is one of stewardship, and there are important duties regarding investment.

It is also incumbent upon the trustee to maintain accounts and records and to give information. Whilst trust law has always required trustees to divulge full information concerning their dealings with the trust fund, legislation relating specifically to occupational pension schemes now imposes upon them overriding specific disclosure requirements.

4–17   The duty to act in good faith in the best interests of the members involves impartiality. The role of steward must be contrasted with the negotiating function, in which the individuals involved as trustees may also be concerned. It is no part of the function of trustees, when acting as such, to negotiate improvements in the pension scheme. Such negotiation will be quite a separate matter to be resolved between employees and the employing companies.

4–18   When exercising their powers of investment the trustees should have careful regard to the investment powers conferred upon them. They must also have regard to the provisions of the Financial Services Act which requires trustees to be authorised unless investment decisions are delegated to an investment professional. Where the powers of investment are very wide it is incumbent upon trustees to examine all the investment opportunities available to them and to proceeding accordingly. They may nevertheless, in accordance with modern portfolio theory, adopt a different approach where this would appear more beneficial. Thus where trustees have determined to ensure that their performance does not fall behind one of the investment performance indices, the fund may be invested in proportion in the investments included in the index.

4–19   The trustee is under a duty to take such care as an ordinary prudent man would take if he were minded to make an investment for the benefit of other people for whom he felt morally bound to provide. He is under a duty to exercise his powers in the best interests of present and future scheme members, and these powers should not be used for ulterior motives. Where a trustee exercises his power in good faith his decision, if consistent with the scheme documentation, cannot as a general rule be successfully challenged.

4–20   In most cases in the exercise of his powers, for example in respect of augmentation of scheme benefits, or the granting of an early retirement pension in circumstances of ill-health, there will be little if any conflict of interest. However, such a conflict could arise if the trustee is requested to invest a part of the trust fund in the business of the employer. Such investment may be best avoided, but any such proposal should be considered only with the benefit of independent advice as to its merits. Difficulties will also arise in relation to any proposal that any surplus funds in the scheme should be returned to participating employers. Whilst some modern schemes may impose a duty upon trustees to return such surplus, where this is not the case the interests of the scheme beneficiaries will have to be very carefully considered before trustees proceed. Following the Social Security Act 1990, "surplus" here is after fulfilling the statutory requirements regarding post-retirement pensions indexation.

It must always be remembered that trustees are personally liable for **4–21** breaches of trust. This fundamental principle may be modified in practice by provisions in the scheme documentation which afford the trustees a measure of indemnity. They may be indemnified out of the fund, which in a continuing scheme usually means that any loss will in practice be borne by the employer. They may also in some cases be indemnified separately by the employing company itself. Before accepting an appointment as trustee, the individual should ensure that these aspects are clarified.

One area in which trustees will become involved in very difficult **4–22** decisions concerns the disposal of lump sum death benefits, where these are payable at the discretion of trustees. The first point to be made in this context is that the trustees must be absolutely certain that the person to whom they propose a payment should be made is in fact included in the class of persons to whom such benefits may be paid. In the case of the surviving spouse this will normally cause no difficulty since he or she will invariably be included among the possible recipients. Difficulty arises in the case of a common law wife or husband. Whilst he or she may not be expressly included, in some cases such a person may qualify as a dependant.

Having decided that the proposed recipient is within the trustees' dis- **4–23** cretion, any decision reached by the trustees in good faith as to how the lump sum should be distributed cannot normally be successfully challenged. This is not to say that no complaints will be received. In practice they will be and trustees may be put under considerable moral pressure by relatives and their advisers. Having made their decision in good faith, the trustees are not expected to give their reasons for making the distribution in a particular way and in practice should not do so. Best practice of course requires that as much information as possible regarding the personal circumstances of the deceased is put before the trustees so that as complete a picture as possible can be built up to enable them to make the right decision.

They may in some cases be guided by an expression of wish given by the deceased. Whilst in most cases this will not be binding on the trustees, the normal practice will be to follow the deceased's wishes unless there are very good reasons for not doing so.

In practice many duties and discretions of the trustees will be delegated **4–24** to others. This is particularly so in the case of powers of investment since the Financial Services Act requires it unless the trustees themselves are to seek authorisation.

Statutory Rights

4-25 In the course of pension scheme administration, trustees must now have particular regard to social security legislation, which confers important rights upon employees, and restricts the powers of trustees.

In many cases, the legislation is overriding, and accordingly applies irrespective of any provision to the contrary in the deed or rules relating to the scheme.

4-26 The principal modifications imposed by statute are as follows:—

1. Preservation.
2. Revaluation of preserved benefits for early leavers. Where pensionable service ends on or after January 1, 1986, preserved benefits for employees must be revalued, from the date of cessation, up to scheme normal pension age. The rate of revaluation is geared to increases in the Retail Price Index, subject to a limit of five per cent. compound, over the whole period.

   When originally introduced, the right applied only to benefits accrued after January 1, 1985, but this is to be extended to cover all preserved benefits, where pensionable service ends following the coming into force of the relevant overriding provisions of the Social Security Act 1990.

   The revaluation increases apply to benefits in excess of any guaranteed minimum pension, where the scheme is contracted-out.

   The increases apply to final salary schemes, irrespective of the reason pensionable service ends. They thus apply to an employee leaving service, and also to an employee who decides to opt-out of membership of the scheme.

   Preserved benefits under money purchase schemes must continue to participate in investment proceeds, on the same basis as for members whose pensionable service continues.
3. Transfer rights. Again, where pensionable service ends on or after January 1, 1986, members have a statutory right to transfer the "cash equivalent" of their accrued benefits. The transfer may be made to a personal pension scheme, to another occupational pension scheme, or to a "buy-out" policy with an Insurance Company.
4. Post-retirement pension increases. Following the coming into force of the relevant part of the Social Security Act 1990, pensions accrued for subsequent service must be subject to limited price indexation. Also, the first call on scheme surplus will be to extend similar revaluation to pensions accrued for earlier service.

4-27 Where an employee opts out of membership, the rights only applies to the cash equivalent of benefits accrued after April 6, 1988. There is however nothing to prevent schemes from offering the cash equivalent of all benefits in these circumstances. The automatic right does not apply where pensionable service ends within one year of normal pension age.

No special form is required for exercising the option, and where the requirements are complied with, the trustees are discharged from their obligation to provide the benefits to which the cash equivalent related.

CHAPTER 14

DAY TO DAY ADMINISTRATION
AND SCHEME ACCOUNTS

Though ultimately the responsibility of the trustees, day to day administra- **4–28** tion will in practice be delegated by them. For a sizeable scheme this delegation will be to a pensions manager who in turn will have his own staff. He and they may be employees of the pension scheme itself, in the very largest of cases, although more usually they will be employees of the sponsoring employer. In smaller schemes the duties of, in effect, a part-time pensions manager may well be assumed by the company secretary with or without clerical assistance, depending upon the size and nature of the scheme.

In a growing number of cases, smaller schemes (and not so small **4–29** schemes) delegate the administration, made growingly complex by successive waves of legislation, to an outside agency. This external agency may be an insurance company (for an insured scheme, usually but not necessarily with the insurance company which provides the investment) or the administration services may be provided by a firm of actuaries or pension consultants. Such external administration services may vary from record keeping to the provision of a full administrative service including the payment of benefits.

A number of computer software houses can supply pension administra- **4–30** tion packages adapted, where necessary, to the requirements of the particular scheme.

The day to day administrative functions involve the following.

  (i) The maintenance, with updating, of individual records in respect of each member, pensioner and deferred pensioner (*i.e.* former member not yet on pension).

 (ii) The collection of members' and employer's contributions, in accordance with the scheme rules and actuarial recommendations, and the receipt of transfer-in payments from other schemes.

(iii) The payment of pensions to retired members and widows, widowers and other dependants, subject to PAYE.

(iv) The payment when due of benefits other than pensions, *e.g.* lump sums on death or retirement, refunds of contributions to leavers where permissible, transfer payments to other schemes in respect of some leavers.

 (v) The purchase and sale of investments, the collection of dividends and interest and the reclaim of income tax suffered at source thereon.

(vi) The periodic provision of membership data for actuarial valuations and other reviews, and the provision of benefit and other data to members as required by the disclosure regulations.

(vii) The production of membership and other statistics required for the trustees' annual report to members (see the next chapter).

(viii) Correspondence and liaison as necessary with insurance companies, financial institutions, the Department of Social Security (DSS), Occupational Pensions Board, Superannuation Funds Office and the local inspector of taxes.

Membership

4–31 As mentioned in Chapter 4, one can go about establishing scheme membership in one of two ways. One can have the contract of employment state that the eligible employee is a member of the given scheme, as soon as he becomes eligible, until he opts out, or one can have the eligible employee apply to join the given scheme. When a scheme is started, and all the eligible employees are in service with existing employment contracts, it is usual to have initial eligible employees apply to join, irrespective of the practice to be adopted for employees joining service after the scheme has started.

4–31A For automatic membership the following is an example of an opting out form. Some of the detail may need changing for a given scheme.

THE ACME RETIREMENT BENEFITS SCHEME
NOTICE OF WITHDRAWAL FROM SCHEME ("OPTING OUT")
(without leaving the service of the Company)

Surname: ....Title: ....
First Names:
....
National Insurance No. ..../............./............./............./............
I hereby give notice that I wish to terminate my membership of the ACME Retirement Benefits Scheme with effect from the date this Notice expires.

I acknowledge and understand that:
1. In the event of my death, the lump sum life assurance benefit will reduce to .... times salary and be payable along with a refund of the contributions I have paid to the Scheme (unless previously refunded).
2. My service with the Company after I cease to be a member will be non-pensionable so that, when I retire, no pension or other benefits will be payable to me or to my dependants from the Scheme in respect of that non-pensionable service.
3. My employment will not be contracted-out of the State Earnings-Related Pension Scheme, and my National Insurance contributions will be increased accordingly—see Note (b).
4. I will not be re-admitted to membership of the Scheme at a later date.
5. I will receive a refund of my contributions, less deductions paid during my membership, so that no benefits will be payable from the Scheme to me or my dependants in respect of that membership.
*OR
 The benefits earned by my membership of the Scheme will be held for me and my dependants under the Scheme in accordance with the Scheme Rules.

Signature of employee: ....
Date of Notice: ..../............./............
Date Notice expires [see Note (a)]: ..../............./............

NOTES:
(a) The Notice Expiry Date is the end of the pay period next following the pay period in which Notice of Withdrawal is given.
(b) The increase in the employee's NI contribution rate will be effective from the first pay day following the Notice Expiry Date
  *Alternative paragraph 5 depending on period of qualifying service completed by the member

---

The following specimen may be useful where the alternative procedure, **4–32** of having eligible employees apply for scheme membership, is adopted. Incidentally, in this case a form like the one above will still be required, for the individual who having joined the scheme subsequently decides to opt out of it while still in the Company's service.

THE ACME RETIREMENT BENEFITS SCHEME
MEMBERSHIP APPLICATION/REFUSAL FORM

Please complete the details below, using BLOCK CAPITALS and return to PERSON-NEL DEPARTMENT:

Surname: .... Title: ....

First Names ....

Please indicate your decision on whether you will be joining the Scheme by completing Section I or II below:—

I (1) I hereby apply to join the Scheme, acknowledge receipt of the explanatory literature and authorise the deduction from my pay of the amount of my contributions in accordance with the provisions of the Scheme. I shall produce a birth certificate or such other evidence of age as may be required.

*Details of retirement benefits to which I am entitled from my membership of Schemes with previous arrangements are attached. (If no documents available of previous benefits please list on the reverse of this form, information of benefits secured).

*I am not entitled to any other retirement benefits.

(2) I confirm that I am not contributing to any other pension arrangement.

*Delete as appropriate.

Signed _____ by the employee Date _____

OR

II I do not wish to join the Scheme. I understand that, by not joining:

(1) In the event of my death, lump sum life assurance benefit will be restricted to .... times Pensionable Salary and no pension benefits will be payable to my dependants from the Scheme.

(2) My service with the Company will be non-pensionable so that, when I retire, no pension or other benefits will be payable to me or to my dependants from the Scheme.

(3) My employment will not be contracted-out of the State Earnings-Related Pension Scheme, and thus my National Insurance contributions will be at the higher (not contracted-out) rate.

(4) By not joining the Scheme now, it is unlikely that I will be allowed to do so at a later date.

Whether or not you join the Scheme you should also complete the "NOMI-NATION FORM", enclosed with the Scheme Explanatory Booklet.

Signed .... Date ....

FOR COMPLETION BY EMPLOYER

Employee's birth certificate examined	YES/NO*
Employee's marriage certificate examined (for married women)	YES/NO*

National Insurance No: ..../............/............/............/............

Sex: MALE/FEMALE*

Date of birth ..../............/.
    ....

Date joined Company ..../............/.
    ....

Date of entry into
Pensionable Service ..../............/.
    ....

Basic annual salary £ _____

*Delete as appropriate

SIGNED .... for the Company. DATE ....

4–33 Where eligible employees are required to apply for scheme membership it will be necessary to have a system in place for ensuring that they receive the application form, and the scheme's explanatory booklet or other descriptive literature, in good time. This material should be accompanied by a note emphasising the importance of joining the scheme when first eligible.

With this approach of requiring eligible employees to apply for membership, it is important for the avoidance of possible dispute to try to ensure that those eligible employees who do not join sign the alternative statement.

4–34 A separate form is suggested for members to pay AVCs. A form separate from the application form will in any case be necessary for the existing member who wants to start paying AVCs or who wishes to amend his existing payment rate. The following is a specimen.

THE ACME RETIREMENT BENEFITS SCHEME
APPLICATION TO PAY/AMEND AVCS
FOR COMPLETION BY EMPLOYEE
Full Name (surname) ————————————————————————
(first name) ———————————————— (second name) ————————————
(third name) ————————————————————
I hereby apply to start payment of Additional Voluntary Contributions to be invested with:

——
I authorise deductions of contributions from my earnings starting at the rate of ——————— per cent £——————— month* with effect from ——————— or as soon as possible thereafter.
This cancels any previous application.
Signature ....   Date ....
*Complete/Delete as appropriate.

FOR COMPLETION BY COMPANY   STAFF NO ————————
We confirm the deductions will be made with effect from ——————— in accordance with the above instructions and that we will notify you each month of the amount(s) deducted from this employee for each investment medium.
Signature: ....   for the Company
Date: ....

Birth and Marriage Certificates

4–35 A scheme member who leaves service, or opts out, after two years' membership will have the right to choose a preserved pension, to transfer the value of that preserved pension to his new employer's scheme (assuming the trustees of that scheme will accept it) or have the trustees apply the value in the purchase of an appropriate policy from an insurance company or as a transfer to a personal pension scheme. The value will depend on, among other things, the individual's age (unless the scheme is a cash accumulation money purchase scheme). It will be necessary for the scheme administrators, on behalf of the trustees, to be assured of the member's correct date of birth before paying out a transfer value or starting a pension or paying a death benefit. Any insurance company involved in any underwriting of any of the benefits will similarly want proof of age.

It is usual to request the employee to produce his or her birth certificate **4–36** (and in the case of a married woman her marriage certificate) at the time the individual is joining the scheme, or is automatically included in it, rather than wait until a benefit becomes payable from the scheme. It should be easier to obtain birth and marriage certificates while employees are in service rather than after they have left. In any case, the scheme rules should give the trustees power to withhold the payment of any benefit until evidence of age satisfactory to the trustees has been provided to them.

Lump sum death benefit nomination

When an employee becomes a member, if not shortly before, he should be **4–37** asked to complete a nomination form, indicating his wishes as to the recipient of any lump sum death benefit. Such a completed form could be of considerable help to the trustees where, as is usually the case, the lump sum death benefit is payable under a discretionary trust. Members should be reminded from time to time that they may change such nominations as their personal circumstances change. The following is a specimen.

THE ACME RETIREMENT BENEFITS SCHEME
NOMINATION FORM
TO: THE TRUSTEES OF THE ACME RETIREMENT BENEFITS SCHEME

Whilst I understand the application of certain lump sums arising on my death is at the complete discretion of the Trustees, I should like the person or persons names below to be considered as possible recipients:—

		FRACTION OF
NAME	**ADDRESS**	**BENEFIT**

Signed ....   Date ....

Name (in BLOCK CAPITALS) ....

NOTES:

(1) This form should be completed and returned in a sealed envelope to:
    The Trustees of the ACME Retirement Benefits Scheme
    c/o

(2) The envelope should be clearly marked with your name (BLOCK CAPITALS) and the words "ACME Retirement Benefits Scheme in respect of Death Benefits". This will only be opened in the event of your death.

(3) If you wish to alter any details given here, you should ask for and complete a new form. Your earlier form will be returned to you. If applicable, this form will be regarded as cancelling any previous form which the Trustees might hold.

Membership records

The records to be maintained for each in-service member may include the **4 38** following.

       Full name, sex, marital status.

       National Insurance number.

       Date of birth, and whether appropriate evidence of it has been accepted.

Date of entry to group service.

Date of entry to scheme.

A year by year record of the member's contributions, with AVCs shown separately (for money purchase schemes a more detailed contribution record will probably be required; where a scheme is contracted-out a record of the second tier National Insurance earnings needs to be maintained; where contracting-out is on a money purchase basis then in addition it is necessary to maintain a record of the cumulative fund from protected rights contributions—see Chapter 38).

Year by year record of salary.

Transfer in data.

4–39 Cases have been known of, for instance, employees who have had a contribution return coming back at retirement age and requesting their alleged pension rights. When the employee ceases to be a member it is important to retain appropriate evidence of what benefits were paid out (*e.g.* return of contributions, transfer to a personal pension scheme) in the form of, for example, a copy of the cheque and covering letter. It should also be possible to reproduce how the benefits paid out or being paid were calculated, if only because the Inland Revenue may demand to know, as part of one of its audits.

4–40 The administration of a pension in payment is similar to that involved in paying, and deducting PAYE from, salaries and wages. National Insurance contributions are not deductible from pensions.

Accounts

4–41 We describe below the essential requirements. As we remarked earlier, these requirements will in many cases be met by means of a mechanised or computerised system. In the case of investment items the records will normally be kept by an investment manager authorised under the Financial Services Act.

Cash book

4–42 For a small fund a single-column cash book of the normal type is sufficient and all items can be posted individually to the appropriate ledger accounts. Where, however, there are a large number of entries, an appropriately analysed cash book is a great simplification. On the debit side separate columns may be provided for members' contributions, employer's contributions, interest and dividends received (gross and tax credit), investments sold or redeemed as well as a bank column. On the credit side one column could usefully be devoted to pension payments, three to withdrawal benefit payments (contributions with or without interest; the certified amount (part of the contribution equivalent premium, see chapter 37) and tax deducted at 20 per cent.), one to income tax and social security payments, one to death benefits, one to retirement lump sums, one to investments purchased, possibly a sundry column and, finally, a bank column.

If such an analysed cash book is used, monthly or even yearly postings can be made to ledger accounts except in the case of investment and dividend items which would have to be posted to their own ledger account. Nevertheless, total investments purchased and sold each month or year can usefully be posted to an investment control account.

An investment journal will probably be necessary, as the cheque paid to **4–43** or received from the stockbroker at the end of each stock exchange account will be a net amount for investments bought and sold. A rather unorthodox way of avoiding the use of a journal is to enter investments sold in red on the credit side, crediting the net cheque in black or red, as the case may be.

Ledger

Whether an analysed cash book is used or not, ledger accounts will be **4–44** opened for each of the items mentioned above. Individual accounts for each investment will be opened, with separate columns for nominal amount purchased or sold, total cost of realisation and interest or dividends received. Drafts received from the Inland Revenue (for refund of tax deducted at source from interest or dividends less amounts owing on withdrawal benefits paid) may have to be journalised so as to post them to the appropriate investment ledger accounts as dividends or to the withdrawal benefit ledger account.

The income tax ledger account will, of course, contain entries for tax **4–45** deducted from benefits, tax deducted from interest or dividends received and amounts paid to or received from the Inland Revenue. The interest or dividend tax deduction certificates will provide the material for the appropriate claim on the Inland Revenue and a check is obtained from the tax deduction column in the cash book and also from the dividend warrants. If this check is to be effective the amount of any income tax not recoverable must also be recorded.

Annual accounts

These should follow the practice recommended by the Accounting Stan- **4–46** dards Committee in its SORP1 (Statement of Recommended Practice, 1). Copies of SORP1 can be obtained from Chartac Books, PO Box 620, Central Milton Keynes MK9 2JX. If the annual accounts do not follow the recommendations of SORP1 then the trustees' annual report, required by law to be made available to members, will have to record that fact.

The trustees' annual report to members is discussed briefly in the next chapter. It should be made available to the auditors of the pension scheme's accounts. Most auditors will not complete their audit of the accounts and sign them off without a sight of the trustees' annual report in its final signed form.

The accounting year of the scheme may coincide with the employer's **4–47** financial year but need not do so. In fact, to have a different accounting year enables the pension scheme accounts to be prepared at different times from the company accounts and, if the same staff prepare both, it spreads the work load. Many contributory schemes make the pension scheme year correspond with the tax year, as this enables the same figures to be used in the pension scheme records for employees' contributions for the year as has to be used for PAYE purposes.

4–48   With a final salary scheme, what the employer contributes to it in any given year may not be the same as the amount entered in the company's accounts as the cost of the scheme for that year. The subject of accounting for pension costs in the company's accounts is covered in Chapter 25.

Claims for benefit

Pension benefit

4–49 When pension age is reached and such age has been proved either at the time of joining the scheme or subsequently, the amount of the member's pension benefit will be calculated in accordance with the rules. The PAYE rules apply to pension payments in much the same way as for salary or wage payments. Note however that, unlike pay, pensions are liable to income tax on an accruals basis (*i.e.* for any given tax year, on the pension payments due in that year rather than on the payments received).

Pensions arising out of employment are taxed in the same way as salary. If refunds of tax are involved, an appropriate settlement must be reached between the scheme, the employer and the Inspector of Taxes.

4–50   If the member is to retire before normal pension age on the grounds of ill-health, the administrator must obtain evidence of ill-health. For the rest the procedure is the same as for pensions at normal pension age, except that it is important to obtain regular evidence to the trustees' satisfaction, until the pensioner reaches the normal pension age, that the pensioner remains significantly disabled. As mentioned in chapter 9, it is not unknown, in the absence of such procedure, for a person to be an ill-health pensioner of one company while holding down a full time job with another.

Death benefit

4–51 A certified copy of the death certificate must be produced to the administrator, who will calculate the amount of the benefit and give this information to the executor or administrator of the estate. Where, under the rules, death benefits are payable under discretionary trusts, full payment of the benefit may be made without undue delay. Where, under the rules, benefits are payable to the member's estate, they should not be paid until probate or letters of administration are produced.

Withdrawal benefit

4–52 If a refund of employee contributions is payable on withdrawal from membership of an approved fund, tax at the special rate of 20 per cent. of the amount is a debt due from the trustees to the Inland Revenue. It is not a liability of the member and he cannot recover any part of it even if he is not liable to tax. Nevertheless, the rules of most pension schemes give the trustees power to recoup themselves wholly or partly from the benefit otherwise payable.

Under some approved schemes, the rules allow the whole pension to be **4–53** commuted for a lump sum at retirement, either because the pension is trivial or because of the serious ill-health of the member. Any part of the resulting lump sum which exceeds what the member could in normal circumstances have taken in commuted lump sum form involves the trustees in liability to tax at the 20 per cent. rate, as in the case of a refund of contributions on withdrawal.

Periodically a return must be made to the Inspector of Taxes of refunds of contributions and special commutation of pensions paid and the appropriate amount of tax must be forwarded on request. Generally, it is arranged for the passage of a net amount of tax as between tax recoverable by the fund and tax due on refunds and special commutations.

Where the employer makes a deduction designed to meet part of the cost **4–54** of preserving guaranteed minimum benefits or of paying a "contributions equivalent premium" (one of which will arise if the withdrawing employee has been contracted-out under the Social Security Pensions Act 1975, see Chapter 37), called the certified amount, the tax is calculated only on the amount actually being paid to the withdrawing employee.

No tax is payable where a transfer payment is made to another approved fund.

Miscellaneous

The administrator of a scheme, whether insured or directly invested, will **4–55** have sundry other duties. It is most important, whether one is dealing with an insured or directly invested scheme, that at an early stage a bank account is opened in the name of the scheme or trustees. The bank will need to be provided with specimens of the signatures which are to be valid on cheques and the administrator will need to ensure that all cheques are signed in accordance with the scheme's rules.

With regard to obtaining approval for a new pension scheme the Super- **4–56** annuation Funds Office of the Inland Revenue has said in one of their publications

> "Applications which are not made on the appropriate form fully and accurately completed and accompanied by the appropriate undertaking and documentation will not be accepted as valid for approval . . . In that event, the SFO may return the submitted material to the practitioner under cover of a printed note which will indicate why the application is deficient . . . . Employers' contributions will not be automatically allowed under Schedule D or for corporation tax, nor will it be possible to authorise provisional relief on employees' contri-

butions until a fully completed application on the prescribed form is supplied."

There is no backdating before that time.

It is essential to obtain experienced advice in the design of one's pension scheme and to delegate to such an adviser the obtaining of approval from the Inland Revenue and, if contracting-out is to apply, the Occupational Pensions Board. Experienced advice should also be obtained prior to making any changes to one's scheme.

4–57   In connection with the investments of a directly invested fund, the administrator will generally deal with the investment manager who will normally ensure that stock and share certificates and title deeds are duly received and placed in safe custody. If the investments are registered in the names of individuals who are trustees, the necessary alterations must be effected on a change of trustees. Registration in the name of a corporate trustee avoids the necessity for such periodical alterations. The due receipt of all contributions, interest and dividends must be watched.

Valuation data

4–58 The scheme rules will provide for periodic actuarial investigations. The present tendency is to have an investigation made every two or three years, because of changing financial conditions. On each occasion the actuary of the fund will notify the administrator as to what information is required in order to enable him to carry out such investigation.

This will include an up-to-date copy of the trust deed and rules, the audited accounts for the inter-valuation period, a list of investments at the valuation date and details of each person who has been in membership at any time during the inter-valuation period. These latter details are usually obtained from the membership record cards already described or, more commonly nowadays, from the equivalent computer stored data.

To a greater or lesser extent, depending upon the type of insured scheme involved, data along the same lines is required by an insurer.

4–59   Note that the actuary will also need to be involved with the production of pension scheme costs in the company's accounts, unless the scheme is a money purchase scheme.

Cost of administration

4–60 Before a true estimate could be made of the cost of administering a pension scheme an accurate costing system would have to be in operation—a true picture can be obtained only after making appropriate allowance for office accommodation, lighting, heating, etc., as well as salaries, printing, stationery, etc. This detailed information is not available in every case but indications are that the total expenses of a large scheme will be in the range of three to five per cent. of the contribution income. For a smaller scheme the expenses will, of course, be a somewhat higher percentage of the con-tribution income, rising perhaps to 10 per cent. and even higher in some cases.

A life office scheme

Once a scheme is established through a life office the employer will receive **4–61** full instructions as to his part in the administration, which in many respects will follow the same lines as that for a privately invested scheme. The employer's main responsibility will be that of deducting the appropriate amounts of contribution week by week or month by month from the wages or salaries of his employees and paying these, together with his own contributions, to the life office.

In addition to the above the employer will have to notify the life office of new entrants to the scheme and any withdrawals through death, leaving service or retirement. In the case of ill-health retirements, appropriate evidence of ill-health may have to be supplied.

If at any time it is desired to make a change in the scheme, the employer **4–62** will need to enter into negotiations with the life office. Before starting a life office scheme with a given office, the employer should make himself aware of any penalties that may apply should he decide at some time in the future to discontinue the scheme, or switch to some other office or form of investment. He should also know what penalties if any would apply if at some time he wanted to separate the investment aspects of running the scheme from the rest of its administration.

It is sometimes thought that insuring a scheme with a life office elimi- **4–63** nates nearly all the clerical work of administering a pension scheme. In practice this does not generally prove to be so. It is true that the life office carries out the whole of the work in connection with the investment of the funds and the actuarial valuation, but the collection of contributions and the keeping of individual records is almost identical for a contributory scheme, whether it is insured with a life office or not. The various decisions as to the entitlement of members to benefit in special circumstances must also be the province of the trustees and the employer and not that of an outside party.

CHAPTER 15

INFORMATION TO MEMBERS

4–64 It will be appreciated from what has been said earlier that the running of a pension scheme involves a considerable annual investment by the company, and possibly also by the participating employees. The funds thus built up can become very sizeable and in many cases can exceed the net worth of the company itself. Moreover, as a member with long service approaches retirement, the reserves built up in respect of him for the payment of his retirement benefits can perhaps represent the most important potential asset he has. In all these circumstances, it is desirable that the trustees should make it clear to the members and to the pensioners that they are carrying out their custody of the scheme on a financially sound basis, and that the scheme is being administered in accordance with its rules.

4–65 Quite apart from its substantial payment to the pension scheme over the years, it is in the company's interests, in promoting good staff relations, that the company ensures the members understand and appreciate what the scheme is providing for them. Yet judging by the work which the Occupational Pensions Advisory Service (OPAS) gets involved in, ignorance, misunderstanding and mistrust are more common than they should be.

In addition there are comprehensive legislative requirements governing the disclosure of scheme information to members (and to recognised trade unions with union members in the scheme).

Documents constituting the scheme

4–66 The trust deed governing the scheme, the formal rules and all amending documents must be available for inspection by any member, prospective member, member's and prospective member's spouse, beneficiaries and recognised trade unions with members in the scheme. Also, copies must be made available, on request, at reasonable charge.

Explanatory booklet

4–67 The disclosure regulations include an extensive list of basic information about the scheme which must be passed to members (automatically to new members, on request to existing members but not necessarily more frequently than every three years). It is usual to have this information set out in an explanatory booklet.

4–68 The following are the items of basic information required to be disclosed by the regulations.

(i) Who is eligible for scheme membership and the conditions of membership.

(ii) How the members' *and* employers' contributions are calculated.
(iii) Whether the scheme is a tax approved one, and if not whether an application for tax approval has been submitted to the Inland Revenue. Whether the scheme is set up, and the rate or amount of the benefits is determined, under a statute.
(iv) Which categories of member are contracted-out from the State earnings related pension scheme.
(v) What the scheme benefits are, how they are calculated and the conditions on which they are paid. Which benefits, if any, are payable only at the trustees' discretion.
(vi) Which of the benefits are and which are not funded.
(vii) Which of the benefits if any are guaranteed by means of one or more insurance policies.
(viii) Whether the employer has entered into an obligation to pay the benefits if the scheme's resources are insufficient to do so. This particular regulation is redundant given that the Social Security Act 1990 requires the employer to make up any deficits emerging on a scheme wind-up.
(ix) Information about pension increases after they have started and the extent to which such increases are discretionary.
(x) Information about contribution refunds, preservation of benefits and transfer of accrued rights for a member whose pensionable service stops before he or she reaches normal pension age (for example, on opting out or leaving service).
(xi) The address to which enquiries about the scheme and requests for benefit statements should be sent.

Regular benefit statements

The regulations require for a defined benefit scheme that any member in **4–69** service should be told, in writing, annually if requested, how the scheme benefits are calculated together with sufficient information for the member to calculate them. Alternatively, individual benefit statements can be issued and many schemes do this on an annual basis, for all members, unasked.

Whether or not it is requested, a member of a scheme providing only **4–70** money purchase benefits (or only money purchase benefits and salary related death benefits) must receive an annual benefit statement. *Member* here is not restricted to *active member*. In brief, this must show the member's fund and the contributions paid into it during the year. If protected rights are involved (they arise if the member is contracted-out on a money purchase basis) they must be shown separately.

Option statements

Clearly, members leaving or retiring need to know what their benefit **4–71** entitlements are and what options are available. When a member dies the legal personal representatives need to know what if any benefits are pay-

able to the estate. These information needs are covered by detailed regulations.

Thus a leaver must be given a statement of rights and options available at
the time. An in-service member, or an ex-member with a preserved benefit, must be supplied on request with an estimated buy-out/transfer value
statement in relation to accrued or preserved benefits. Any member has a
right to know whether he or she can have a contribution return.

Trustees' annual reports and accounts

4–72 Scheme accounts must be prepared and audited each year. The relevant
regulations (part of The Occupational Pension Schemes (Disclosure of
Information) Regulations, 1986 Statutory Instrument No. 1046) set down
in some detail what the accounts must include. This is also covered in the
accounting profession's Statement of Recommended Practice 1, mentioned
in chapter 14 under the heading *Annual accounts*.

4–73 The trustees must also have available for supply to members, and recognised trade unions with members in the scheme, an annual report on the
operation of the scheme. The disclosure regulations do not apply to one
member schemes, but they do to schemes with two or more. Some trustees
of very small schemes, with more than a single member, are disinclined to
prepare the annual report until a request for it is made. Note however that
most auditors will not feel they can complete the scheme's audit until they
have had a sight of the trustees' report. And if the scheme is contracted-out
the Occupational Pensions Board will require confirmation that the
accounts have been audited.

4–74 The minimum contents of the trustees' annual report are laid down in
the regulations and are fairly detailed. The items of information required
include such things as the names of the trustees, the address to which
scheme enquiries should be sent, information about pension increases
made during the year, numbers of members, and who has managed the
scheme's investments. In addition the report must be accompanied by a
copy of the audited accounts, an investment report (including among other
things a review of the investment performance of the scheme's fund) and
an actuarial statement (see below) unless the pension benefits are solely on
a money purchase basis.

4–75 All defined benefit schemes must have an actuarial valuation not less frequently than every three and a half years. The common frequency is every
three years although, since investment and other relevant factors can
change so quickly, annual actuarial reviews if not full scale valuations are
common among medium to larger sized schemes. The valuation must be
accompanied by a statement made by the actuary in relation to the
scheme's funding level and record the actuary's opinion that in respect of
prospective rights "the resources of the scheme are likely in the normal
course of events to meet in full the liabilities of the scheme as they fall
due," or record a qualified statement instead.

4–76 It is a copy of this statement that must accompany the trustees' annual
report. The form of the statement is prescribed in the regulations and it

must include a summary of the method and assumptions used in the valuation. A copy of the valuation report must be made available for inspection by members, beneficiaries, prospective members and recognised trade unions with members in the scheme.

The trustees' annual report and its accompanying documents can be **4–77** somewhat daunting for most members. In fact, the majority do not ask for a copy, although the trustees are required by the regulations to take reasonable steps to draw the attention of members, prospective members, etc., to the availability of the annual report and accompanying documents. In addition to supplying the full documents to those who ask for it, some schemes send all members an abbreviated report, highlighting the more interesting and important aspects of the full report and accounts. This can be an important annual piece of communication aimed at making members properly aware of the scheme.

CHAPTER 16

INDIVIDUAL COUNSELLING FOR MEMBERS

4–78 Pensions are for people and the fact that pension rights are basically money rights should never be allowed to obscure the personal nature of the work involved. There is an almost infinite variety in the circumstances of any group of people, even though they work for the same company. Communication is nowadays an overworked word, but the concept is vitally important. In a well run scheme a certain amount of individual counselling for members is essential from time to time.

On joining the scheme

4–79 A young person joining a pension scheme is unlikely to be particularly receptive to the details of the pension scheme. However, whether one operates the opting out or opting in systems described in Chapter 4, the individual must be given the necessary explanatory literature. The member who is joining, or the automatic member who is not opting out, should be encouraged to complete a death benefit nomination form for the trustees. An individual joining later in his career may well require individual advice in two areas. First, he may want help in deciding what to do about the options available to him under the pension scheme of his previous employer and whether it is possible and, if so, advisable to bring a transfer payment across into his new scheme. Secondly, the facility to pay additional voluntary contributions to increase his benefits at retirement should be drawn to his attention. This is so particularly if the pension rights he has earned during a previous employment are not as favourable as those which he would have earned had he been in the new scheme during that period—in other words if there is a shortfall which he might want to consider making good.

On leaving the scheme before retirement

4–80 Clearly, if a member leaves before retirement it will be necessary to give him or her details of the options available. Ideally advice on the implication of the various options should be made available although such advice is almost certain to include advice which is investment advice under the Financial Services Act. It should not be provided by the trustees if they are not authorised under the Act to give such advice.

On death before retirement

4–81 If a member dies before retirement then the dependants and, in the case of a married person, the surviving spouse, will need to be given advice on what benefits are due to them under the scheme. If there is a substantial lump sum payment then the beneficiary may well want help in deciding how to make the best use of it. Where the beneficiary of the lump sum is a minor it will be necessary to set up a trust.

On retirement

If those responsible for running a pension scheme are to take into account **4–82** the wider welfare of members on retirement, the most usual first step is discussion with each individual member of his or her particular circumstances, the benefits due and the options open. This may well lead to the establishment of pre-retirement courses taken at any time within two or three years before retirement. Such courses vary widely from employer to employer but they should all serve the important purpose of drawing the member's attention to the problems of retirement while there is still time to plan to meet them.

In particular, as more and more members reach retirement age entitled to draw a substantial tax free lump sum, advice should be available in one form or another just before retirement as to whether or not the lump sum should be taken (assuming it is an option) and, if it is, as to how the lump sum should be used to best effect.

After retirement

Finally, whatever can be done to help pensioners in retirement is always **4–83** greatly appreciated. Many larger schemes have a system of pensioner visiting with the visits being made by the younger, more able pensioners themselves. They can then report back to the company or those responsible for running the scheme if there are any serious cases of difficulty. This can be a very cost effective way of providing a service in that those visiting will usually be prepared to do so in return for no more than their expenses being met. This service, which in some cases includes advice on tax problems, can be particularly valuable when a married pensioner dies leaving a surviving spouse who may need some help initially in sorting out routine financial matters.

Chapter 17

MEMBER PARTICIPATION IN RUNNING THE SCHEME

Committee of management

4-84 A committee of management would usually be catered for in a scheme's rules which provide for a custodian trustee, whose duties are confined to holding the scheme assets. To all intents and purposes, the committee of management is the same as the trustee in schemes which do not have asset holding custodian trustees. We use the word trustees in the rest of this chapter to include individual trustees, directors of a trustee company and members of a committee of management. The advantages and disadvantages of individual and corporate trustees are discussed in Chapter 10.

General principles

4-85 Member participation in running the scheme, if it is to have any real meaning, usually entails having some of the trustees, or trustee directors, elected by the members from among their number.

4-86 Where scheme members are not represented among the trustees it is in some cases found useful to have a pensions consultative committee. Such a committee has no operational or executive powers but in substantial organisations it can provide a useful forum for communication and the airing of complaints or queries. It is clear from the enquiries that the Occupational Pensions Advisory Service receives that pension scheme administration departments and external administrators do not always communicate effectively enough with all scheme members.

4-87 Having elected representatives among the trustees from the scheme members is not a legal obligation. Whether or not to have members as trustees should be determined in large part by the type of scheme being operated. In a pensioneer trustee scheme (less than 12 members) it is probably wise to have all the members as trustees—see Chapter 29.

4-88 A money purchase scheme, with its accumulation of individual accounts, can be most clearly accepted by both management and employees as a deferred pay scheme and the individual's eventual retirement benefits will depend not only on the amount of contribution input but also on how well the contributions have been invested. Accordingly, member participation in the operation of money purchase schemes, by means of trustee representation, is generally accepted as beneficial, if not essential.

The same point can be made about final pay schemes in which the employer's contribution rates are fixed in the rules (see Chapter 1 under the heading *Deferred Pay*).

4-89 The greater majority of final pay schemes are of the balance of cost type, in which under-funding is in effect a liability of the employer (see Chapter

1). If, for example, the investments perform well then the benefit of that will in due course, if not immediately, accrue to the company in smaller company contributions, unless the company decides that scheme benefits should be increased in some way or unless some indexation is required as a result of the Social Security Act 1990—see Chapter 6. To have member trustees with such a scheme could therefore be a cause of friction and misunderstanding, unless great care is exercised.

In one instance, for example, the member trustees complained bitterly that they did not see it as a function of the trustees to produce good investment results for the purpose of reducing the company's costs (they meant the good investment results produced by the investment house selected by the trustees on the advice of the actuary who, at the request of the company, had produced a comprehensive analysis of the investment management available). Unless a thorough programme of explanation is put into effect with every new member trustee, in a balance of cost scheme, there is a very real possibility that the member trustees will come to believe that the balance of cost scheme is in fact a deferred pay scheme—at least during periods when the scheme is over-funded or in surplus.

Practicalities

Where there are to be member trustees, the idea of a 50/50 split, between **4–90** those selected by the employer and those elected by the members, has certain attractions and was first put forward as long ago as 1975 as a recommendation in a report from the Occupational Pensions Board.

Because a trustee's duties are so clearly defined, and because he must act **4–91** in the best interests of all the members, it would be wrong to think that differences of opinion would always divide the trustees according to whether they are members' representatives or employer representatives. They may well vary according to some other basis and for this reason it is also important to make sure that trustees represent a sensible cross section of the membership in other ways—for instance that a reasonable proportion are women (bearing in mind, of course, the ratio of men to women in the scheme itself).

There is no single correct answer for the method of appointment of member representatives. The best solution will almost certainly vary from company to company depending on the structure of the pension scheme membership, the extent to which members are unionised, geographical locations and so on.

For practical purposes the number of trustees must be limited and it is **4–92** unusual for it to be more than, say, 12. In schemes other than pensioneer trustee schemes the number will usually be much smaller, with a minimum usually of three. Furthermore, because a pension scheme is such a specialised subject, one in which misconceptions and misunderstandings can easily arise, it can often make sense for the members serving as trustees to do so for some time. For all but the smallest of schemes, this means that proportionately few members will ever have the opportunity to become a trustee and as a result a system of local consultative committees, or pension councils, are often operated in conjunction with member representation on the trustee body. As indicated earlier local consultative committees or pension councils provide a forum in which views on pensions matters may be heard from many more members and information exchanged.

4–93   Incidentally, if there are to be member trustees then these should include a representative of the pensioners except perhaps in the early history of the scheme when there are very few pensioners.

CHAPTER 18

INDUSTRIAL RELATIONS

General

The importance of pension schemes from an industrial relations viewpoint **4–94** can be judged from the following two facts.

  (i) Assuming it not to be a minimal contracting-out scheme, the pension from the scheme will be the most valuable benefit an employer provides for his employees after their take home pay. Accordingly, pensions can no more be divorced from the normal industrial relations system than can pay.

  (ii) There has been industrial unrest, there have been strikes and court cases over pension schemes, mainly over the way any over-funding has been corrected.

The trade union movement is fully aware of the value of pensions and of **4–95** the need to be involved with them. Although anxious to promote substantial improvements in the State pension system, the trade union movement is reasonably well disposed to the idea of occupational pension schemes fulfilling the role of supplementing the State provision. In addition to a wish to see pension schemes improved generally, the trade unions' main aims are to retain employees in occupational schemes (as opposed to encouraging them into personal pension scheme membership); to extend membership to part-timers; and to influence the use of any scheme over-funding or surplus.

The trade unions are of course keen to be involved in the running of the **4–96** schemes, as described in the previous chapter, through acting as trustees, serving on investment panels and so on. However, they recognise that the question of negotiating benefit improvements is an entirely separate matter which we see as taking place in much the same way as negotiations on pay. In the case of contracted-out schemes unions have the force of law behind them, in that section 31 of the Social Security Pensions Act 1975 provides for consultation with recognised trade unions regarding the issue, variation or surrender of a contracting-out certificate except where the variation will not affect the scope of the certificate, or is minor and has little or no effect on the membership. (See also Chapter 15 on the right of recognised trade unions to receive information about the pension scheme.)

Difficulties with surpluses

Most of the industrial unrest which has arisen in connection with pension **4–97** schemes has occurred with final pay schemes. The majority of it has arisen in connection with the disposal of scheme surpluses, as members and their representatives would see it, or with the correction of the over-funding of its promises as the employer would see it. Some of the few court cases which have occurred between companies on pension matters arose similarly: following the sale and purchase of a subsidiary litigation has on occasion arisen, in effect, on whether the bulk transfer value should be on a share of the fund or on a past service basis (see Chapter 19).

4–98   The industrial unrest in these cases has probably occurred through a lack of understanding of just what type of scheme is involved. The final pay scheme was probably regarded as a balance of cost scheme by the employer (see Chapter 1). That view may well have been supported by the company's having paid increased contributions at a period in the past to correct a deficit or a measure of under-funding which had emerged. The trade unions involved, at least when it is in surplus, will see every final salary scheme as a deferred pay scheme. That there has been some justice in this viewpoint can be argued as follows.

4–99   Until the advent of the 1990 Social Security Act, nearly all defined benefit schemes were written on the basis that if the scheme were wound-up in deficit then the benefits would be appropriately reduced. Thus, the argument might go, if the deficit belonged to the members on wind-up then the surplus, whether the scheme has been wound-up or not, should also belong to the members. Whether these points of view will change following the Social Security Act 1990 (see Chapter 1) remains to be seen.

4–100   What seems clear is that if a company has to meet the cost of any underfunding of benefit promises while the scheme is being continued and when it is wound-up, then in equity it should be entitled to the benefits of any over-funding. What then remains is for the company to ensure that the scheme rules are appropriately written and, just as important, that an effective communication policy is implemented. Note that, following the Social Security Act 1990, over-funding cannot in effect arise until all accrued pensions and pensions in payment have the RPI, 5 per cent. limited, indexation attaching to them.

4–101   A useful type of final pay scheme is where surpluses (and deficits, except on wind-up) are shared on, say, a 50/50 basis between employer and scheme members. Such a scheme does not preclude the employer helping the members with their half when the scheme gets into deficit but the facts of such a scheme, its fundamental sharing philosophy and the way it works must be adequately explained.

4–102   As with a scheme where the surpluses and deficits (except on wind-up) belong wholly to the members, a scheme in which a proportion belonged to the members results in the employer having perhaps less flexibility. For example, the augmentation of the pension of an individual retiring early in good health (particularly the early retirement pension of a member of senior staff) should not be done without the full added contribution from the employer to meet the additional liability, whether or not the scheme is in surplus at the time.

Negotiating improved schemes

Negotiating with trade unions on the terms and conditions and benefits of a **4–103** pension scheme may prove unhelpful if central pay negotiation is not in force at the same time. The point is that the pension scheme will be a central operation applying to all eligible employees across the company whereas pay may be negotiated locally. Central pension negotiations can only increase pressure for central pay negotiations.

CHAPTER 19

MERGERS, ACQUISITIONS AND DISPOSALS

Introduction

4–104 The importance of this chapter can be gauged from the following examples. They are extreme ones but in more normal cases the sums of money involved can still be significant and substantial. The first example we have in mind is where a company sold a subsidiary in the late 1970s and agreed that the purchaser's scheme would receive a transfer value from the vendor's scheme to provide full past service pension rights. It turned out that the vendor's scheme was substantially under-funded and its rules precluded a transfer greater than an appropriately calculated proportion of its funds. The vendor had to pay the purchaser a sum additional to the inadequate transfer value, an additional sum almost the size of the price previously agreed for the company. The other example occurred in the late 1980s. Here the vendor's scheme was over-funded and the purchaser's scheme received far more than was necessary for full past service pension rights, by a margin approaching the size of the purchase price previously fixed. Both eventualities could have been allowed for.

The sale and purchase agreement

4–105 When one company is selling and another buying a subsidiary or undertaking there will of course be a sale and purchase agreement. And among the matters the agreement will cover there will be the subject of pensions. Consider the case where a subsidiary is being sold and bought, with that subsidiary's participation, prior to the sale, in a final pay pension scheme operated by the vendor group of companies. All scheme members in the company being sold will have pension rights, at least in respect of service to date, and they will probably all have pension expectations in relation to any continuing service in the subsidiary. But once the sale has been effected the subsidiary will no longer be able to participate in the vendor's group scheme.

4–106 The purchaser might set up an identical scheme to that of the vendor, and invite the new employees to transfer to it on the understanding that an appropriate transfer value will be paid. More likely the transfer value will be paid to the purchaser's scheme for those employees who agree to transfer to it.

4–107 Now, what should be transferred from the vendor's scheme? In the mid 1970s the vendor's scheme could well have been significantly underfunded. In the late 1980s the vendor's scheme could well have been substantially over-funded. What is transferred might be governed strictly by the rules of the vendor's scheme and the sum involved might not bear a great deal of relation to what the purchaser (and vendor) might believe to be the correct sum, say sufficient to provide a pension accrual equal to that in the vendor's scheme for service to date of sale but based on salaries to future retirement or earlier leaving service.

It is unlikely that it will be possible to determine at the time that the sale/ **4–108** purchase price of the subsidiary is being agreed whether "too much" or "too little" will be provided by way of transfer value from the vendor's scheme. But whichever it is it should affect the sale/purchase price of the company or undertaking being sold and bought. The sale and purchase agreement should provide for a subsequent adjustment to the price. And for that to be possible the sale and purchase agreement must provide for how the transfer value, agreed between vendor and purchaser, is to be calculated. The agreement may well provide for the vendor to exercise his best endeavours to procure such a transfer value from the trustees of his group scheme. However, the trustees of the vendor's scheme are independent of the vendor and cannot transfer more than is allowed by the scheme's rules—hence the need for the sale and purchase agreement to provide for an adjustment, either way, to the sale/purchase price.

Thus not only should the sale and purchase agreement allow for adjustment to the sale/purchase price of the company or enterprise being sold, but it should also set out how the transfer value is to be calculated by reference to which the sale/purchase price is to be adjusted having regard to what is actually transferred.

How should the transfer value be calculated?

We are referring here to the sum to be agreed to between the purchaser **4–109** and vendor, not to the sum actually paid by the trustees of the vendor's scheme. In fact, the sum we are concerned with here will be substantially affected by the type of scheme which is to pay the transfer value.

Where the vendor's scheme is a money purchase scheme, then the sum **4–110** agreed in the sale and purchase agreement should not be less than the total value of the accounts in respect of the individuals transferring. If the money purchase scheme is an insurance company scheme then, to avoid possible surrender value losses, it may be necessary to arrange a policy assignment and, in some cases, for the acquiring company to continue with a similar scheme (with premiums paid to the insurance company) for at least a limited period in respect of the acquired company. Where the money purchase scheme is directly invested in stock exchange and other securities, the question arises as to the date when the relevant assets should be valued, and what adjustment should be made in respect of the period between the valuation date and the actual cash transfer date. We consider this point later, in relation also to other types of directly invested scheme.

Where the vendor's scheme is a final pay scheme, the sale and purchase **4–111** agreement might provide for one of the following.

(i) A share of the fund—that is, an equitable proportion of the vendor's scheme's total assets, the division to be made by a method and using actuarial assumptions as agreed and laid down in the sale and purchase agreement. We would suggest that a share of the fund is the correct sum for transfer where the vendor's final pay scheme is a fixed contribution scheme and surpluses and liabilities belong to the members. However, in arriving at the company's purchase price, the purchaser ought to take account of the fact, if it is a fact, that the vendor's scheme is significantly under-funded. The point is that although the vendor's scheme may be such that deficits, as well as surpluses, belong to the members, nevertheless the purchaser in due course could come under pressure to help make good the deficit in respect of the members who come across with the subsidiary. Also, following the Social Security Act 1990, the purchaser would be liable should he at any time wind-up a scheme of his while it is in deficit.

4–112   (ii) The past service reserve—that is, a sum calculated on agreed assumptions as sufficient to provide the final pay pensions under the vendor's scheme formula, for service to date of sale and related to salaries projected to retirement or earlier leaving. This is the correct sum, we would suggest, where the vendor's scheme is a final pay pension scheme of the balance of cost type (see Chapter 1).

4–113   (iii) The cash equivalent rights' total—that is, the total of the sums the vendor's scheme would pay out if all the individual scheme members involved in the sale left service and elected a buy-out. The vendor might seek to argue that this is the correct sum when the sale of an undertaking is involved, rather than a subsidiary. The point is that the employees involved in the sale of the undertaking will have to leave the service of the relevant company participating in the vendor's scheme, if they are to retain their jobs. Given that there is continuity of employment, and having regard to the employees' expectations, the purchaser would want the vendor and his scheme to provide sufficient to fund pensions for service to date and projected salaries. Having regard to the industrial relations repercussions if the employees concerned are pensioned to a lesser degree, the purchaser should bear in mind what is involved in negotiating the price to be paid for the undertaking and the wording of the sale and purchase agreement.

Some other points to watch

4–114 The purchaser should scrutinise with particular care any proposal for an upward adjustment of the purchase price on account of any surplus transferred by the vendor's scheme. From the purchaser's viewpoint, the ideal is for the purchase price to be adjusted downwards if the sum transferred is insufficient for the pensions accrued to date, based on projected salaries, and carrying post-retirement indexation at least at the RPI, five per cent. limited, rate. The vendor may argue to the contrary, particularly if he considers his scheme is insufficiently in surplus.

4–115 The vendor will usually want the scheme members that go with the sale out of his scheme as soon after the completion date as possible. However, an immediate transfer may just not be possible, having regard to the time necessary to decide what offer to make the members in respect of their transfer, and the communication of that offer. Also, if the numbers involved are substantial, incorporating them into the administrative systems of the purchaser's pension arrangements cannot be achieved overnight.

A period of continued membership of the vendor's scheme will need to **4–116** be mutually agreed between vendor and purchaser. With an approved pension scheme, the Inland Revenue will usually allow the employees concerned to continue as full members of the vendor's scheme for up to the balance of the scheme year plus a further year.

The sale and purchase agreement will need to cover a number of techni- **4–117** cal pension matters. Although technical, if overlooked the possible costs could be substantial, or give rise to dispute, or both. For example, it must be assumed that the transfer value calculation date and the date the transfer value is actually paid over will not coincide. This must be allowed for in the sale and purchase agreement (consider a "Black Monday" on the stock exchange like that of 1987 falling between the two dates). The points involved need to be carefully considered since the scope for the mismatching of investments and liabilities can be substantial.

Acquiring a company and its pension scheme

Here it will not be necessary for the members to leave the scheme once a **4–118** change of company ownership has occurred. The purchaser will be able to give a more leisurely consideration to the points for and against a possible transfer and what terms to offer for a transfer to his scheme. However, as purchaser he needs to be aware, in advance of agreeing a purchase price, of any possible unfunded liabilities.

An important conclusion

In buying and selling companies and undertakings, both parties will no **4–119** doubt be relying substantially on their financial and legal advisers. Given the possibly substantial sums involved, both parties would be well advised to call in their actuarial advisers before agreeing the terms and conditions of the sale and purchase and, in particular, the pensions detail in the sale and purchase agreement.

Finally, the purchaser should avoid making promises to the effect that **4–120** "no one will be any worse off in their pensions expectations," without first having obtained actuarial advice on just what the implications of such a promise might be. One of the most difficult aspects of pension planning is the merging of two schemes to the satisfaction of both sets of members, without ending up with a costly mix consisting of the more generous aspects of each original scheme.

PART 5

FUNDING AND EXPENSING

FUNDING AND EXPENSING

Funding means making advance provision for retirement benefits separate **5–01** from the general assets involved in the employer's main business. Normally this involves setting up a separate pension fund trust alienated from the employer's normal finances.

Pension expensing is concerned with how much the employer's declared **5–02** profits should be reduced each year to allow for the cost of the pension benefits promised in relation to that trading year or accrued during that trading year. Historically in the United Kingdom the pension expense has been the employer's contribution paid to the approved pension scheme plus any ancillary benefits paid directly. As will be seen from later on in Part 5, with the introduction of the Statement of Standard Accounting Practice No. 24—Accounting for Pension Costs (SSAP-24) this has changed, with effect for company years starting after June 30, 1988.

As approved pension schemes are not subject to tax on their investment **5–03** income, the Inland Revenue has an interest in controlling the size of funds and hence the tax reliefs received. Chapter 24 deals with the Inland Revenue's restrictions on the size of pension fund surpluses.

A company could decide quite separately how much to contribute to its **5–04** pension fund and by how much to reduce its declared profits in respect of its pension promises. However any decision made concerning one of the matters has implications for the other. For example, if the company decides to pay into its pension scheme more or less than the calculated pension costs by which profits are reduced then it generates or changes any pension provision or pre–payment in the company balance sheet. For this reason the two matters are often considered together: we discuss both in this Part.

CHAPTER 20

FUNDING OBJECTIVES

5–05 There are four factors affecting the decision to fund a pension scheme or otherwise. They are the cost, the timing of the cost, the security afforded to the pension promise and the influence of legislation including tax law.

Ultimate cost of the benefits

5–06 Apart from the amount of the benefits paid and the tax reliefs obtained for their expenditure, a major factor affecting the ultimate cost of the benefit is the investment return obtained by the funding medium (or if the unfunded route has been followed, the general rate of return earned on the company's assets after corporation tax). In the United Kingdom, there are many companies where the net internal rate of return after corporation tax exceeds that which can be obtained gross before tax by direct investment in the stock markets. In these instances it is cheaper for a company ultimately to provide its pension benefits on an unfunded basis than to fund them via an approved pension scheme. However there are many instances where the converse is true, where a funded approved pension scheme would be the cheaper route. If the pension scheme is unapproved and it is funded then it is the rate of investment return after tax which should be compared with the company's net internal rate of return after corporation tax, to see which is the cheaper long term alternative.

5–07 If a company has substantial borrowings, the choice between funding and paying cash to the pension scheme and not funding may mean that the cash that would otherwise be paid to the pension scheme is retained in the company and the company's borrowings would be reduced. In this instance it may be that a decision is based purely on the cost difference between funding and not funding (based on a comparison of the investment returns obtained by pension schemes generally against the net marginal cost of the company's borrowings). There are, however, the insecurity and industrial relations aspects of not funding to consider (see below).

Timing for cash payments

5–08 An individual's economic effort on behalf of his employer is aimed ultimately at producing some net cash receipt from which the employer can meet his expenses and contribute to profits. One of these expenses is the cash cost of the individual's pension arrangements. The cash generation of an employer's business, and the timing of that cash generation, may be a reason for delaying or advancing the meeting in cash terms of the cost of the employee's pension benefits.

In theory the cash cost at the time of payment of an employee's benefits could be met by borrowing. However, since for most types of economic activity an employee generates cash on behalf of his employer throughout his working lifetime, borrowing to meet the cost of income during an individual's retirement would not be satisfactory. Accordingly most employers aim to meet the cash cost of an individual's benefits at least by the time the individual has retired or the benefit is paid.

Depending on the other cashflow demands of the employer there can be 5–09 reasons for advancing or delaying the meeting of this cash cost throughout the individual's working lifetime. The rate at which this cash cost is met is quite often referred to as the pace of funding. By meeting the cash cost sooner one would be increasing the pace of funding and by postponing the payment of the cash cost decreasing the pace of funding. We give later a few simple examples of different extremes of pace of funding.

Security

Funding provides a separate pool of assets on which the only charge is the 5–10 provision of pension, retirement or death benefits for employees. The resulting asset, the "fund," gives the employees security concerning the future receipt of the benefits promised. If the pension promise were not funded and were to be met from within the general assets of the company then, should the company go into liquidation, the individual's pension promises would rank only with other general creditors.

Clearly a funded scheme provides greater security than a non-funded arrangement. This is especially so in a business world where company takeovers and mergers and company reconstructions are common. These quite often involve changes in a company's senior management. A new management may not place the same importance on any pension promises made by its predecessors.

Legislation/Taxation

The legislation of a particular country may require a scheme to be funded 5–11 for certain advantages to be obtained. For example in the United Kingdom, if a corporate body or individual employer wishes to contract his employees out of the State earnings related pension scheme, the occupational scheme used to provide the contracting-out vehicle has to be a funded one. In the United Kingdom a scheme has to be funded for that scheme to gain Inland Revenue approval. In the United States a minimum level of funding has to exist for tax reliefs to be obtained.

Reasons for non-funded schemes

Traditionally non-funded schemes have been used where the lack of secur- 5–12 ity involved is not a problem. Such a case would be the United Kingdom State pension schemes or the occupational schemes offered for civil service employees. There is the further argument in these instances that if a funded scheme existed it would be of such a considerable size that it would have a dominating effect on stock markets.

Funding, pace of funding and funding objectives

5–13 There is an infinite number of ways of arranging the incidence of contributions over the working lifetime of a pension scheme member. For example, there are several options even if we have the object of having sufficient in reserve on the day of the individual's retirement to pay the pension thereafter. By way of illustration, suppose that a male member aged 30 has been promised a pension of £5,000 per annum payable from the age of 65. On the assumption that money invested earns eight per cent. per annum, a once and for all lump sum of £2,700 paid into the fund at the age of 30 will be sufficient to meet the promised benefit. There are many alternatives. One would be to pay £232 per annum for 35 years from the age of 30 to the age of 65. Another would be to pay £40,000 into the fund on the employee's 65th birthday.

5–14   These three examples illustrate three different possibilities as to "the pace of funding." The first is faster than the second which is faster than the third. It should be clear that in between the first and last example there is an unlimited number of alternatives. However we hope that even our simple example shows why it is inappropriate for an employer to try to judge the relative merits of several pension scheme proposals for the same group of members by looking at the recommended first year "cost." In the three simplified examples above the initial "costs" are £2,700, £252 and nil respectively.

5–15   Some criteria are needed for deciding between the numerous alternatives for funding the scheme. One way of defining the pace of funding is to have a funding objective. The funding objective is the reason or target behind the particular pattern of funding chosen. For example, a company could have a funding objective which is related to maintaining a particular size of fund defined in a particular manner, or relating to the form the pattern of contributions would take (*e.g.* an even percentage of pensionable salaries) or of maintaining the fund held within a particular band and the contribution rate within a particular band. It is not possible to control both the precise level of the fund and the precise contribution rate. One or both must vary.

5–16   Here are some examples of funding level objectives (*i.e.* related to a target size of fund). One is to maintain a fund equal to the value of pensions in payment plus the value of deferred pensions in respect of previous early leavers plus the value of benefits accrued to date for in-service members based on their accrued service and current pensionable salary. A variation on this would be to include the value of future revaluations due pre-retirement under the revaluation provisions of the Social Security Act 1985. The second objective is to base the value of the benefits for active members on their salaries projected with expected increases to date of retirement or earlier death or withdrawal. The variation on the first objective, and the second objective, would increase the size of the target fund and therefore increase the pace of funding. In all three cases the benefits ultimately provided are the same and hence the ultimate cost to the employer is the same. All that varies is the timing of the meeting of this cost.

Other examples of funding are those which relate to a contribution **5–17** objective. The employer could seek to maintain a payment into the scheme each year equal to a percentage of the salary bill appropriate to the cost of providing benefits for new entrants to the scheme at a typical age. Alternatively the employer could seek to maintain a contribution rate appropriate to the value of benefits accruing in the future based on the average age of the current membership of the scheme.

We have discussed above one or two simple funding objectives. It will be **5–18** seen later that the funding objective the employer chooses after discussion with the actuary will affect the actuarial method chosen for funding and possibly also the actuarial assumptions chosen.

Some employers have left both the choice of the funding objective and the actuarial method to the scheme's actuary. However these have such a fundamental effect on the employer's contribution level or the pace of funding (and hence important implications for the employer's business) that we believe it is best if he is very much involved in these decisions.

CHAPTER 21

ACTUARIAL CONSIDERATIONS

Economic and demographic assumptions and actuarial methods

5–19 In the last chapter we described funding and set out the reasons for funding an occupational pension scheme. To arrive at a funding rate one needs to make some assumptions about both demographic and economic factors, the actuarial assumptions for the valuation, and one needs to have an actuarial method to complete the calculations. The actuarial method is concerned with which benefits are valued for comparison against the actual fund, *i.e.* those based on accrued or prospective service. It is also concerned with calculating the normal contribution rate. The choice of actuarial assumptions and actuarial methods very much affects the pace of funding as described in the previous chapter. It should always be remembered that neither the assumptions nor the actuarial method affect the benefits that are ultimately paid from a continuing scheme as required by the trust deed and rules. Thus the actuarial assumptions and method do not affect the ultimate cost to the employer. they affect the pace at which the cost is met. Stronger or less optimistic assumptions result in the cost of benefits being met sooner rather than later. A similar comment applies to the strength of the actuarial method adopted, some methods producing a quicker pace of funding than others.

DEMOGRAPHIC ASSUMPTIONS

Mortality

5–20 It will readily be recognised that the cost of the pensions provided will depend on the number of members who survive to retirement and how long they live thereafter. When considering a normal healthy person it is impossible to make any forecasts as to when he or she will die. There is often a misconception that the expectation of life can be used in this connection. However, although not related to any one life, if the expectation is based on suitable mortality rates it is possible to forecast within reasonably narrow limits the average future lifetime of a large group of persons of the same age, sex and general background. It is this average future lifetime that is known as the expectation of life. Nevertheless, it is of little value in pension fund calculations, as is seen from the following example.

5–21 Suppose that it is required to calculate the annual contribution to be made to a pension fund to support a pension of £100 per annum from the age of 65 for a person now aged 50. There is a great variety of mortality tables giving different expectations of life, but setting that problem aside and taking the expectation at the age of 50 as 20 years (*i.e.* to the age of 70) we might come to the conclusion that on average the pension will be payable for five years, *i.e.* from the ages of 65 to 70, and that the contributions of those now aged 50 must be paid for 15 years or until preceding death in order to support total payments of £500. At first sight this appears to be a reasonable statement, but that there is a fallacy becomes apparent if we consider pensions from the age of 65 to persons who are now aged 20; for the expectation of life at that age according to the same mortality table is 44 years and we should, if we followed the same line of argument, conclude that the pensions would never become payable and that the annual contribution is therefore zero.

5–22 While the expectation of life as such gives fallacious results if used in this way, the mortality table on which it is based can be most helpful. A brief explanation is therefore given of what a mortality table is and how it is constructed.

Studies are made of statistics derived from national population and other records of the proportion of persons of a certain age, sex and class of life who die within a year. It is generally found that the proportions vary within narrow limits from year to year for persons of the same age, sex and class of life. Accordingly from the records of a large group of lives, the average proportion of persons at each age who die within a year can be calculated and since the proportions are reasonably stable, the results can be used to predict the future. It is therefore possible to draw up a table showing the number of persons who out of say, 100,000 births may be expected to survive to each age up to the limit of life. The limit of life is normally just beyond a 100 but as few reach such a high age mortality statistics there are more variable. It should be noted that however large the group being investigated, random fluctuations will be revealed from year to year and it will be necessary to smooth these out before preparing the table.

5–23 As medical knowledge and standards of living have improved so have mortality rates reduced. Some mortality tables are therefore constructed which attempt to forecast future mortality rates assuming that the past trend to reduced rates continues in the future. This principle is very useful. There has been a significant reduction in death rates over the past 80 years. In the graphs on page 108 (figure 3) we compare typical mortality rates in the first 20 years of this century (table a(m)) with typical present rates (table PA(90)).

5–24 Until the middle of the 20th century many deaths occurred at younger ages especially in early childhood. Since the Second World War death rates at the older ages, previously remarkably stable, have also reduced somewhat as medical science has increased the ability to keep people alive. This increased scientific knowledge has offset the increased incidence of heart disease and cancer. The scope for further improvements at the younger ages is limited. Death rates at these ages are already very small although the effect of AIDS may be to increase death rates at the younger ages. In theory the scope for improvement at older ages remains as medical science and technology continue to advance.

5–25 When completed, the mortality table will enable forecasts to be made. If the mortality table is based on suitable data these forecasts will be suf-

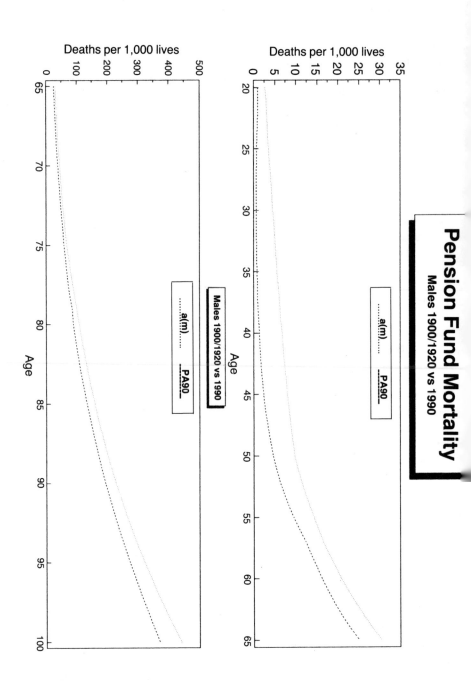

Figure 3

ficiently reliable to form the basis of the pension fund calculations. In this country very few pension funds are large enough to provide mortality experience stable enough for the table used to be based purely on the experience of pensioners and active members of that fund. It is more common for actuaries to base their calculations on mortality statistics derived from the population as a whole (for a particular class of life or occupation relating to overall population statistics) or on a table based on the data of several large insurance companies related to their experience of the mortality of pensioners in schemes for which they provide insured benefits.

It is, however desirable to test the suitability of the particular table used **5–26** at each actuarial review by comparing the number of deaths which have actually occurred with the number which was expected to occur according to the table. For this test any future forecast element might be removed. When doing this test it must always be remembered there must be some element of random fluctuation from year to year.

The form the mortality table basically takes shows the number of mem- **5–27** bers of a fund at a particular age who are expected to survive to a later age, *i.e.* for example those who are aged 20 who are expected to survive to the age of 21, 22 and every age thereafter. From the table therefore can be seen for each age the proportion of members who are expected to survive to age 65 then to age 66, 67, etc. It can thus be calculated how many of them are expected to draw a pension for one year, two years, etc. From these statistics a more accurate costing of the pension fund can be done.

As well as making assumptions for the mortality rates of those members **5–28** of the fund who are currently in service the actuary will need to make mortality assumptions for those whose pensions are currently in payment, for deferred pensioners in the pre-retirement period and for the spouses of the different types of member. A different mortality table may be used for pensioners who retired in good health compared with those who retired from the scheme with ill-health pensions. Alternatively those with ill-health pensions may be assumed in practice to have mortality akin to an individual several years older.

Other demographic factors

Mortality is not the only demographic factor an actuary needs to make **5–29** assumptions about. The other demographic factors involved also affect the ultimate size or timing of benefits paid out. They include the rate of turnover of in-service membership, rates of ill-health and good health early retirement, the proportions of members who are married and possibly remarriage rates. This latter factor will only be necessary if spouses' pensions cease on remarriage.

Before making comments about these different assumptions we must **5–30** mention a principle which the actuary will have to consider when deciding exactly what assumptions to adopt irrespective of the type of demographic decrement. Irrespective of whether it is withdrawal, ill-health mortality or a proportion married, any variations in them will affect the costings produced. The actuary normally considers how a small increase or decrease in a particular decrement will affect the cost produced. Sometimes for example an increase in the withdrawal decrement can increase the contribution rate produced. Sometimes the reverse can happen. The particular result will depend on the interaction of the withdrawal decrements with the other assumptions, the type and nature of the benefits promised and possibly the actuarial method adopted. If an actuary is over-cautious in assumptions the client will be contributing or expensing too much. If the actuary is over-optimistic there will be a further cost or further expense to be met later. It is therefore common for actuaries to set their assumptions so they are just on the prudent or cautious side. Whether this means adopting a rate which is slightly lighter or heavier than that suggested by past experience will depend on the effect of the change in the particular decrement. As with mortality, few funds are large enough for the demographic assumptions to be based solely on their own experience. Actuaries generally use sets of assumptions derived across the experience of many similar funds.

Withdrawal rates

5–31 The rate of withdrawal from service is one of the most difficult factors to forecast. Not only does it vary from firm to firm, industry to industry, location to location but it will often vary depending on the general state of the economy and the labour market. And sometimes the introduction of a pension scheme can have a stabilising effect on the turnover of a workforce.

5–32 Historically a high turnover of membership has contributed to pension scheme surpluses. As legislation has improved the benefits provided for early leavers, the financial effect of a high turnover has decreased. However for most schemes if the actuary assumes too low a rate of withdrawal he is still normally being conservative and the higher turnover will contribute to over-funding. This is because the value of a reserve for the member as a deferred pensioner is still quite often less than the value of the reserve as an active member. There may be other factors but an actuary's assumption for the rate of earnings inflation, including promotional increases, is normally significantly higher than the guaranteed level or assumed rate for discretionary increases for deferred pensioners. However with valuation methods which take into account both past and future service (see later) the opposite can often be true. If for a particular scheme the cost of the older members' benefits is being met by paying a percentage of payroll expressed across the whole membership, then under those particular valuation methods a high assumption regarding the turnover of younger members may serve to increase the calculated contribution rates.

5–33 Sometimes the withdrawal decrement will be split between the different types of benefits taken by an early leaver, *i.e.* refund of contributions, deferred pension or transfer value. This is only worth doing if there is a considerably different financial value attached to these various options. Even then if economic circumstances vary it is hard to predict accurately the rate of withdrawal, and so the extra refinement may not be worthwhile.

Ill-health retirements

The provision of an augmented pension on retirement in ill-health can be a **5–34** valuable benefit from a pension scheme. If it is to be offered it is prudent for the employer to make advance financial provision (with the actuary including an ill-health decrement in his valuation assumptions). However it can be one of the most difficult decrements to predict in advance. Past experience of the employer may offer a poor guide. The actual introduction of the benefit will mean more individuals will be able to retire in ill-health with a resulting increase in the rate of ill-health retirement. For an established scheme, the employer and trustees quite often have discretion over who is granted ill-health retirement, and their judgment in this area can vary considerably from employer to employer. Sometimes the facility is used as a manpower planning facility, to retire early those employees whose ability or desire to work has reduced.

Good health early retirement decrement

In the late 1970s and early 1980s in the United Kingdom, we had a period **5–35** of good real investment returns, generating surpluses at a time when some employers wished to reduce the size of their workforce. It became common for many schemes to offer members in good health the option to take retirement before normal pension age without their accrued pension being actuarially reduced or with a generous early retirement factor being used. To assess the cost of such benefits the actuary has to assume a good health early retirement decrement. This might be quite heavy at the first age the augmentation is offered, falling off just after that age then steadily increasing up to the original normal retirement age. Again this is a decrement where the actual experience can be very much affected by general economic conditions.

Proportions married and remarriage rates

These generally will be based on population statistics. However the actuary **5–36** should always be aware of recent social trends and how these may affect experience in the future.

New entrants

As will be seen later from the chapter on valuation methods, the actuary in **5–37** deciding on his recommendations, costings or expensing may be looking several years into the future. Over this period the membership of the pension scheme will be changing and assumptions will have been made about the withdrawal, mortality and retirement rates. The scheme will also have a flow of new members. The actuary may decide to ignore this flow and just check that his recommended contribution rates are sufficient to provide the new entrants' benefits based on the likely ages of joining. An alternative would be to make an implicit assumption about new entrants to the effect that the membership of the pension fund retains a stable distribution with regard to age and salaries. A further option would be to discuss with the client's personnel department the likely age and salary profile of new employees and to make assumptions based on the advice obtained.

5–38 Whichever of these routes is followed regarding new entrant assumptions, the actuary should now consider the effect of the recent introduction to the UK of voluntary scheme membership. Employers have reacted to this in different ways. Some require members positively to opt out of the scheme while others require employees positively to opt in. Which is done affects considerably the actual experience on numbers joining schemes and should therefore be reflected in the actuary's assumptions about new entrants.

ECONOMIC ASSUMPTIONS

5–39 Let us suppose we hold £100 today. If we earn an investment return of nine per cent. per annum compound, that £100 would grow after 10 years to just under £237. Conversely if we know we have to make a payment of £100 in 10 years' time and we can earn in the meantime nine per cent. per annum compound over that 10 year period the amount of money we need to hold or reserve now is £100 divided by 2.37, *i.e.* £42. Alternatively if the investment return we felt confident of obtaining over the 10 year period was 12 per cent. per annum this amount would reduce to £32. Clearly, the investment return obtained has an effect on the ultimate cost of the benefits. Assumptions about future rates of investment return along with assumptions about future inflation and the level of pension increases (the economic assumptions) have a major importance in the actuarial calculations for a pension fund.

5–40 If the pension benefit were to be based on some form of final remuneration (for example, the final year's earnings, the average of earnings over the final three years, the best average three consecutive years out of the final ten) it is not so much the investment return obtained that affects the ultimate cost of the benefits but rather the real rate of investment return; that is, the rate of investment return obtained in excess of the rates of earnings or salary inflation experienced. Similarly, if post retirement pension increases are granted, it is the excess of the investment return obtained above the level of post retirement pension increase that is material.

5–41 Experience shows that, over the periods of time with which pension schemes are involved, there is some correlation between the rate of investment return obtained, the rate of earnings inflation and the rate of retail price increases. So in general the actuary's assumptions about investment return, earnings inflation and pension increases are interrelated. The general experience, with economic progress and growth, is that standards of living increase and that earnings increases exceed price increases. Importantly, one argument for funding a pension scheme is that if a real rate of return is obtained it is cheaper to meet one's pension costs in today's money rather than tomorrow's. If a real rate of return were not obtained, it would be cheaper for companies to meet the cash cost of the pension benefits when they arise rather than fund for them in advance. Most actuarial bases assume an excess of investment return above earnings inflation and an excess of earnings inflation above price inflation. It is not the absolute rates of these assumptions that matter but the differences between the three components.

Even for one particular investment medium, for example equities, the **5–42** real rate of return obtained has varied widely from year to year. Over long periods the average rate obtained depends very much on the start and end points of the period over which one is calculating the average. In times of very low inflation deposit interest rates have been as low as two per cent. To be attractive more risky investments must offer higher real yields long term. A typical real yield above price inflation would vary from say $2\frac{1}{2}$ per cent. to 5 per cent. per annum. A real yield above general earnings inflation would be lower to take into account economic growth. Typical assumptions for yields in excess of general earnings inflation lie in the band $1\frac{1}{2}$ per cent. to three per cent. per annum. Exceptionally, the upper figure might be as high as four per cent. per annum. The graph on page 114 (figure 4) shows past experience has varied but nevertheless supports assumptions of this order. When final salary pension schemes first started, a common assumption for the real rate of return was four per cent. per annum with no allowance for salary increases.

In periods like the early 1970s, of high inflation and comparatively low **5–43** investment returns, actuaries reduced the real rate of return assumption. For example, the Government Actuary's calculations for the rebate for contracting–out on a GMP basis when first available in 1978 were based on a real rate of return of one per cent. with a margin in his calculations which in practice reduced it to $\frac{1}{2}$ per cent. per annum. Recently there has been a slight trend for higher real rate of returns to be adopted. At the present time (September 1990) a typical real rate of return above earnings inflation would be about two per cent. per annum and above price inflation of the order of $3\frac{1}{2}$ per cent. to 4 per cent. per annum.

When considering earnings inflation it must be remembered that **5–44** employees in general, at least in staff schemes, receive promotional increases as their experience increases their economic worth to their employer and as they gain additional responsibilities. Actuaries allow for this by narrowing the real earnings gap, possibly by one per cent. per annum, or by adopting a specific promotional salary scale. The latter has the advantage that most promotional increases are weighted towards the earlier parts of an individual's career and a specific promotional salary scale can allow for this. Such a salary scale may be a general one or client or industry derived.

Asset Valuation Methods

If the scheme is an established one the actuary will need to value existing **5–45** assets. There are different ways of doing this and we discuss them in the rest of this chapter.

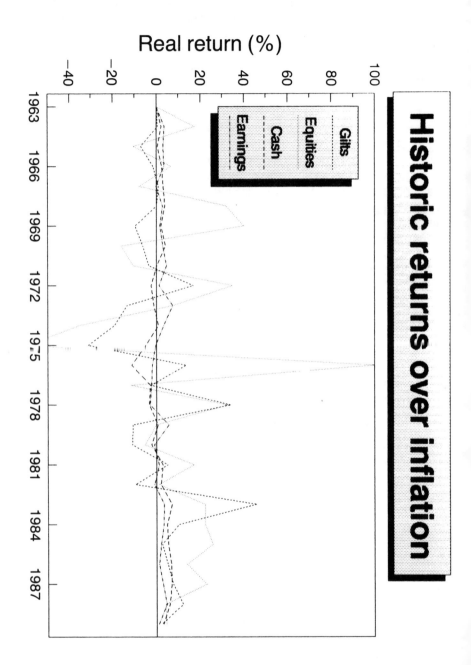

Figure 4

Book value

Some actuaries have in the past valued assets at their book value *i.e.* price **5–46** paid plus any realised capital appreciation net of realised depreciation. This value is not in any way connected with the future proceeds or future income receipts. It is a historical value. Most actuaries today adopt a method of valuing assets which is consistent with the method used for valuing the liabilities of the scheme. This will not apply to book values which have largely fallen into disuse as a method of valuing assets.

Market values

Another option would be to place a value on the investments equal to their **5–47** estimated or actual market value at the valuation. If this method of valuing assets is adopted the actuary is assuming that the market's judgment as to value is correct. The market for a particular type of investment is made up of many different investors; for example, individuals, financial houses, insurance companies, pension funds. These investors will all have different tax positions and different priorities. The market value of an investment is just the balance in the price for the buyers and sellers of that particular stock on a particular day. Some actuaries would therefore argue it has no connection with the investment's long term value. Others argue that in reality the market value progresses, admittedly in an unstable fashion, along the investment's true underlying value.

If this latter concept is accepted there are two possible approaches. One **5–48** would be to use the market value of the investments unadjusted. In this case the actuary would in theory adjust his assumptions used for valuing the liabilities from valuation to valuation, in order to reflect the implied judgment of the market concerning real yields, earnings inflation and prices. If this is done it can then be argued there is some consistency between the valuation of assets and the valuation of liabilities. The other approach is to remove some of the inherent instability in market values and smooth the change in market value over a period, possibly from three to five years. When using a smoothed market value approach the actuary would maintain basically the same actuarial assumptions from valuation to valuation. Nevertheless if other factors dictated a change in the assumptions, a change would still be made.

Discounted cash flow values/compound interest values

This is now the most common method adopted by United Kingdom **5–49** actuaries for the valuation of pension fund assets. The theory behind the method is that the actuary should adopt the same underlying valuation process for assets as he does for liabilities. For the liabilities he discounts the flow of future pension and benefit outgo using his actuarial assumptions. The pension fund investments held will produce a flow of future income and possibly future capital receipts. A consistent method of valuation of assets is therefore to value this future flow of income and capital receipts using the assumptions decided on for the valuation.

5–50   The expected income from Government fixed interest securities and other corporate fixed interest stock is known and no further assumptions are necessary other than the valuation rate of interest or discount. However company dividends in general increase as company profits increase from time to time. The rents from property are also expected to increase. The proceeds from index linked gilts increase with inflation. So for consistency between the valuation of assets and liabilities the same rate of RPI increase implied by the valuation assumptions for liabilities will be used to value the income from index linked gilts.

5–51   An assumption is needed for the rate of increase in equity dividends and rents from properties. The assumptions the actuary makes here will typically be in the range of 1 per cent. less or more than the general implied rate of price inflation in his actuarial basis. Company dividends and rents from properties tend to change in a steady manner and this method of valuation is reasonably stable as well as consistent with the valuation of liabilities. It is also the method required by the over-funding regulations issued under the provisions of the Finance Act 1986 for testing whether there is an excessive statutory surplus or not (see Chapter 24). That is another factor which has led to the increasing use of this method for valuing pension scheme assets in actuarial valuations.

5–52   The method requires the actuary to ensure that his assumptions are consistent one with another. He also needs to have an eye to the particular portfolio of the pension fund. For example it could be inappropriate to use the same rate of dividend growth for a portfolio containing low yielding high growth equities as for a portfolio containing mainly non-growth stocks in mature industries.

5–53   The graph opposite (figure 5) compares the values produced by using a particular compound interest value of assets against both unadjusted market value and market value smoothed over five years.

Expenses

5–54 Before we move on to the main actuarial valuation methods we must mention a further assumption the actuary may need to make in his assumptions for the valuation. If the fund bears the expenses of its administration, investment and professional fees the actuary will need to make assumptions about their future levels. They will normally be based on their past level with some allowance for inflation. The total expense may be expressed as a percentage of the contributions to the scheme or related to the size of the fund.

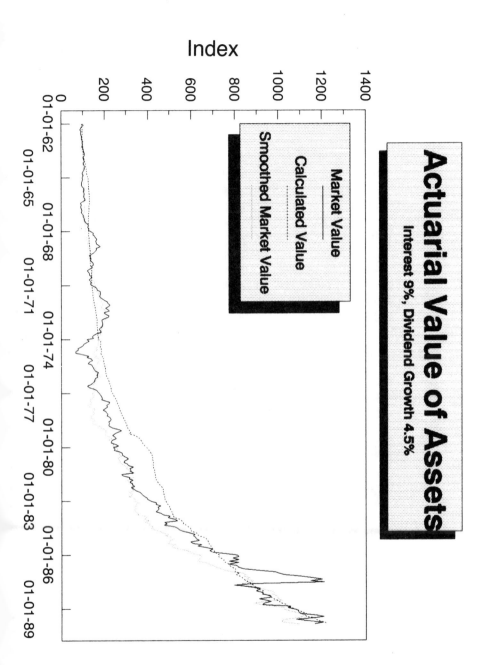

Figure 5

CHAPTER 22

ACTUARIAL FUNDING METHODS

5–55 In this chapter we describe the main actuarial valuation methods used by actuaries for calculating funding or contribution rates for final salary/ defined benefit occupational pension schemes. There are five main methods used. They can be divided into two groups, the accrued benefit methods and the prospective benefit methods.

5–56 The accrued benefit methods have a target fund (see Chapter 20) which is decided on by reference to just the accrued liabilities of the scheme up to the date of the valuation. In the prospective benefit methods the target fund is arrived at as a balancing item between the value of total prospective liabilities over past and future service and the value of future contributions payable at the intended long term or normal rate. Under the prospective benefit methods this normal contribution rate is usually related to the value of benefit accruing in the future throughout the rest of the scheme membership's working lifetime, or since the members joined the scheme. We will describe first the two main accrued benefit methods, the current unit method and the prospective unit method.

ACCRUED BENEFIT METHODS

Current unit method

5–57 Under this method the value of the target fund is the total value of the actuarial liabilities for pensioners, for deferred pensioners, and for active members based on their accrued service to the date of the valuation and their then current earnings. Under the strict current unit method no allowance is made in the target fund for any increase in benefits to active members due to future salary increases. A variation of the method is to include an allowance for future increases at the rate that would be granted if the active members were deferred pensioners. The target fund therefore only covers the bare minimum accrued liabilities. The method aims to produce a fund equal to that required on the actuarial basis to provide the benefits that have accrued to date if the scheme were to be wound up. It provides a target fund which offers the bare minimum level of security to members. Where the variation is not employed there is no protection via the level of the target fund towards maintaining the real purchasing power of benefits pre-retirement.

5–58 Under the current unit method the normal contribution in a given year is the contribution required in that year to provide the benefit accruing in that year for active members, again based on their current earnings, plus the increase in the fund required to provide their current year salary increase on the value of their benefit accrued up to the end of the previous year.

If the actual fund is higher or lower than the bare minimum accrued liability, the actual contribution recommended will be the normal contribution adjusted for the over or under funding that has occurred. The adjustment may be spread over a period longer than a year.

The current unit method is appropriate if the employer's objective is to maintain a fund that offers the minimum level of security to members equivalent to what they have already accrued based on their current salaries.

The projected unit method

The projected unit method is in concept similar to the current unit method, **5–59** except that when deciding both the target fund and the normal contribution rate for the year account is taken of the members' prospective increases in pensionable earnings from the date of the valuation up to their projected exits from the scheme whether by retirement, death or withdrawal. Accordingly the target fund is normally higher than that of the current unit method. The pace of funding is therefore quicker than the current unit method.

The normal contribution for a given year is equal to the value of the **5–60** benefits accruing in that year but based on the members' earnings projected to their future exit from the scheme due to retirement, death or withdrawal. As salary increases are funded in advance there is no need to adjust the normal contribution rate for the effect of the year's salary increase on accrued benefits.

It can be argued that this funding method is the one method that is con- **5–61** sistent with the accruals concept of accounting. Under the accruals concept of accounting the amounts charged to the profit and loss account are supposed to be those related to trading in that particular year. If an employer offers a final salary pension scheme the normal contribution rate produced by the projected unit method is directly comparable with the actual value of the prospective benefit payable but accrued in the particular year. For this reason the projected unit method is that adopted in some of the overseas pension accounting standards. As will be seen later the United Kingdom accountancy standards body took a slightly different view.

On the basis that the assumptions made are borne out in practice, the **5–62** projected unit method offers a reasonable degree of security to the member. At any particular time his rights accrued to date are fully funded but the employer does not aim to hold any assets in the scheme in relation to service beyond that date. For this reason it is often argued that the projected unit method combines an adequate level of security with good business practice. If a company is profitable it will quite often obtain a higher rate of return by investing internally. Companies quite often require further capital and it represents good business practice to fund the pension scheme to an adequate level but not beyond. Excess over-funding of the pension scheme could increase the need to borrow or to obtain capital from internal investments.

Control periods

5–63 A control period is used sometimes under both the current unit method and the projected unit method. As described above the normal contribution rate is usually based on one year's accrual. If the age/salary profile of the scheme is changing or the scheme has a small number of members the contribution rate produced by considering one year's accrual may not be too stable. Using a control period introduces more stability into this normal contribution rate. Rather than basing the normal contribution rate just on one year's accrual of benefit one would base it on the value of benefits accruing over the control period, divided by the length of the control period. In making this calculation any likely new entrants into the scheme may also be considered.

PROSPECTIVE BENEFIT METHODS

Entry age method

5–64 Under the entry age method, the normal contribution rate is decided first. This is fixed as the contribution rate required over the whole of his service life to produce the benefits of the average new entrant to the scheme. The entry age can be taken as the average of the entry ages of the current membership, or as the expected age of entry on average of future new entrants. As the entry age to most schemes is fairly young, the normal contribution rate produced by the entry age method is usually fairly low compared with that of other methods. However, the contribution rate does allow for the increasing cost of benefits as the new entrant ages throughout his expected working lifetime.

5–65 Under the entry age method the target fund is established as follows. First all benefits are valued (both those accrued in the past and those accruing in the future including those related to future salary increases). This value is then reduced by the value of future normal contributions throughout the remaining working lifetime of the current membership. Thus the target fund in practice funds the increase in cost due to the fact that the current age of the membership is higher than that assumed in calculating the new entrant contribution rate. The target fund under the entry age method is normally quite high compared with that produced by other methods.

Any surplus or deficit of the funds held against the target is corrected by subtraction from or addition to the normal contribution rate over a chosen period. This period would not normally exceed the expected working lifetime of the current membership.

The entry age method is appropriate when the employer's funding objective is to maintain a fairly high target fund or when he wishes to aim for a normal contribution which is below or equal in value to the long term cost of the scheme for new entrants.

The attained age method

This method is similar in concept to the entry age method except that the **5–66** normal contribution is based on the average age of the current membership rather than that of the typical new entrant. It is the contribution required to provide the benefits for all future service for the current membership spread over their future working lifetime. In arriving at the contribution rate account is taken of future increases in salaries.

The target fund under the attained age method is exactly the same as the **5–67** target fund under the projected unit method. Its value is the total value of current pensions, deferred pensions and benefits for active members based on their accrued service but with salaries projected to retirement, death or withdrawal.

With the attained age method the normal contribution rate is usually **5–68** higher than that of the entry age method, but the target fund lower. Compared with the projected unit credit method the attained age method usually produces a higher normal contribution rate. This is because, in using this method, one is funding in advance the increasing cost of benefits for the current membership as it ages.

The attained age method is normally considered to be appropriate for **5–69** funding the benefits of members of a scheme closed to new entrants. It avoids the steadily rising contribution rate as the scheme ages that would be produced by adopting an accrued benefit method. However, for a scheme in which the membership is fairly stable as to its age and salary profile, or which is open to a substantial supply of new entrants, the attained age method will generate surplus in the normal course of events. This is because the target fund is the same as that required by the projected unit method but the contribution rate is normally higher due to the assumption of an ageing population.

The aggregate method

Historically this method was the one most commonly adopted by consult- **5–70** ing actuaries in the United Kingdom. The method has neither a target fund nor a normal contribution rate. Under the aggregate method, the value of the total benefits for existing members (for both past and expected future service, with allowance for future salary increase) is first obtained. The value of the actual fund held is subtracted to produce a net liability value. The contribution rate is then calculated as that which, when applied to the expected future salaries of the existing members, produces a contribution income flow having the same value as the net liability.

The method does not make any explicit allowance for new entrants. In **5–71** many cases the contribution rate produced is higher than that necessary to provide for the benefits of new entrants and if the scheme is open to new entrants, surpluses may be automatically generated. It can be shown that if the actuarial assumptions used are borne out in practice the contribution rates produced by the aggregate method ultimately tend to be that of the entry age method. Accordingly the use of the aggregate method implies the employer wishes to maintain a high target fund.

5–72   As the presentation of results under the aggregate method is not normally split between the funding of past and future benefits it is difficult for the employer and trustees to follow the progress the fund is making. As soon as the actuary splits past and future service so as to aid understanding, the actuary is no longer using the aggregate method and technically has adopted the attained age method. As the high level of surpluses generated in the early 1980s became apparent, due in part to the previous use of the aggregate method, some actuaries switched from using this method to using the projected unit credit method. The use of the projected unit credit method was also encouraged by the Government Actuary's adoption of it for controlling surpluses under the Finance Act 1986 (see Chapter 24).

5–73   The following two graphs (figures 6 and 7) illustrate the effect of differing funding methods. The first compares theoretical contribution rates under the current unit, projected unit, entry age and attained age methods. Note the theoretical stability produced by the entry age method. At the younger ages the projected unit and current unit rates are lower but are higher at the older ages. Across the whole scheme membership however, given a suitable supply of new entrants, the rates produced by the unit methods can remain stable.

5–74   We also show a graph of the relative funding levels of the current unit, projected unit, and entry age methods for given ages of members. Note that at normal pension age (age 65 in this case) all methods produce the same target fund. All that differs is the pace at which this target is achieved. The entry age method has the higher target funding level at all other ages.

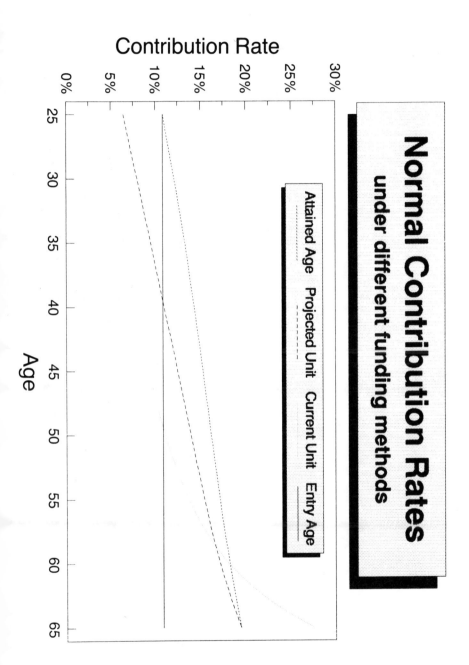

Figure 6

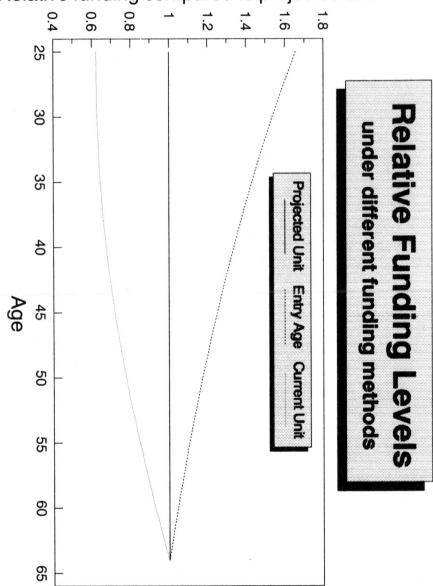

Figure 7

CHAPTER 23

THE PROCESS OF AN ACTUARIAL VALUATION

The process of an actuarial valuation is much the same whether it is the **5-75** first funding rate calculation or the first or subsequent valuation of the scheme which is involved. The only difference for the first funding rate calculation is that if the scheme is completely new there may be no existing assets to value. However, quite often new schemes are established after takeovers, mergers or management buy-outs and there will be a transfer value or asset available from an existing scheme of another employer or holding company.

The first stage of the valuation is quite often a preliminary meeting **5-76** between the actuary and employer and trustees to decide on priorities. Questions might arise concerning the company's interest in increasing or reducing the rate of funding, whether there is need for improved benefits, the company's likely future employment policy, and whether any redundancy or early retirement exercises are likely. The purpose of the meeting is to supply advance knowledge to the actuary of the employer's current thinking so that the actuary's initial calculations are those required. A preliminary meeting can save time and unnecessary work and hence save unnecessary expense. The actuary is less likely to waste time producing figures which are not ultimately required.

Prior to or shortly after the preliminary meeting the actuary will receive **5-77** the valuation data from the employer's payroll department or pension administrator. This data may require punching for entry into a computer or may, as is more common these days, be in the form of computer tape transferable to the actuary's computer and valuation systems. The data needs to be checked and validated to ensure that the results of the actuarial valuation are not spurious. It will be compared with the data used in the previous valuation for its age and salary profile. An attempt will be made to reconcile the membership movements over the inter-valuation period. Summarised data will be produced in order that the actual contributions paid in the inter-valuation period can be compared with that expected from the current data. Similar comparative checks will be made with pensions valued against pensions paid. Validation checks will be made with the eligibility conditions of the scheme against the age of employees at commencement of pensionable service under the current valuation. Before these checks can be made the actuary will need to receive draft accounts but at this stage, although preferable, there is no actual need for the accounts to have been audited.

Typically in the United Kingdom at the present time most companies **5-78** obtain an actuarial valuation at least once every three years. There was a time when the usual inter-valuation period was five years. Some companies obtain annual valuations, others every two years. The shorter the period the more frequent is the assessment of the progress of the pension fund and at any time the employer's knowledge is more up to date. An argument in favour of longer valuation periods is that any experience must be subject to random fluctuations and the longer period between valuations gives more time for the experience to stabilise itself, with less of a chance of a spurious correction being made to the funding process. In general three years is thought to be a reasonable period but, when experience is very favourable and surpluses are being generated, it is in the interest of companies to correct these items sooner rather than later. This is especially so in today's competitive business environment. Assets placed in the pension fund could be usefully employed elsewhere. A favourable valuation result can have an effect on declared profits and offer protection in a takeover and merger situation. For these reasons annual valuations have become more common.

5–79   Having checked the data the actuary will start his more detailed valuation calculations. The experience of the scheme regarding mortality and demographic factors over the inter-valuation period may be analysed. Initial values of assets and liabilities will be produced using the assumptions and valuation method of the last valuation and using any new valuation method and assumptions the actuary and his client are considering. The cost of any changes in scheme benefits that are under consideration will also be established.

5–80   The actuary will normally send his client, as a discussion document, a preliminary paper setting out a brief summary of his initial calculations. The discussion with the employer and trustees may show that no further calculations are necessary or that other figures will be required.

5–81   As part of the valuation process the actuary will reconcile, perhaps approximately, the results of the current valuation with those of the previous one. This provides a further check on the data and will help in the understanding of the scheme's operation. It is known technically as an analysis of surplus. If a surplus has been generated is it due to excess investment performance, high withdrawal or turnover experience, or low increases in earnings?

5–82   The valuation process involves other matters in addition to being the time for reviewing the progress of the scheme's funding. These will usually include producing an estimate of the scheme's position were it to be wound-up. The actuary will also inform the employer on the data and annual calculations necessary under any accountancy standard on pensions costs which is in force. In the United Kingdom this is the Statement of Standard Accounting Practice No. 24 (SSAP-24). However, if the company is quoted on the American Stock Exchange, or is American owned, figures will also be required on an annual basis under the U.S. Financial Accounting Statement No. 87 (FAS 87).

5–83   At the time of the periodic valuations the actuary gains a great deal of knowledge of the operation of the scheme. As a result he can often provide useful advice on day to day matters concerning the scheme over the period to the next valuation.

If the scheme is used to contract-out employees from the State earnings related pension scheme the actuary will take the opportunity to effect any calculations necessary to review or complete the actuarial certificate required by the Occupational Pensions Board. Also at the time of the actuarial valuation, if the scheme is directly invested, the Inland Revenue will require the completion of a funding certificate under the provisions of the Finance Act 1986. This is required every time a valuation is done but not less often than $3\frac{1}{2}$ years since the last time or the establishment of the scheme. We discuss these matters in more detail later.

Solvency Valuations

Normally as part of the actuarial valuation the actuary will report to the **5–84** employer and trustees on the solvency position of the scheme. In a solvency valuation the actuary compares the value of the assets, normally for this purpose the market value, with the value of the benefits promised under the deed if the scheme were to wind up at the valuation date. For many schemes, these would be the pensions currently in payment plus contingent widows' and widowers' pensions for current pensioners, deferred pensions and benefits for active members based on their service to the present date and their current pensionable salary. Some schemes may give a guaranteed increase to deferred pensioners over and above that required by statute. Under the Social Security Act 1990 a first charge on any winding-up surplus will be to provide RPI, (five per cent. limited) indexation on all pensions, current and future, in the post-retirement period.

Depending on the wording of the deed, the actuary might also report on how any surplus in the winding-up position could be distributed by way of further increases.

Normally the solvency valuation is only of major interest if it shows an **5–85** insolvent position. Solvency valuations can be completed on market related assumptions which try to estimate the cost of purchasing in the market the benefits promised. These assumptions would include the yields underlying immediate and deferred annuity rates. Alternatively the valuation can be completed using the main actuarial valuation assumptions. If this route is followed the ratio of assets to liabilities is in practice what is known as the current funding level. The Institute and Faculty of Actuaries' Guidance Note GN9 requires the actuary to comment on the current funding level in the actuarial valuation report and also requires a statement from him as to whether in his opinion the assets were sufficient at the valuation date to cover the liabilities arising (including any dependants' contingent benefits) in respect of pensions in payment, the preserved benefits of members whose pensionable service has ceased, and the accrued benefits for members in pensionable service (which will normally be related to pensionable service up to and pensionable earnings at the date of the valuation, including revaluation on the statutory basis or on such higher basis as may have been promised). GN9 then requires the actuary to give an indication of any shortfall if there is one. In his comments on a shortfall the actuary should have regard to the priorities attaching to the various categories of benefits under the scheme's winding-up rule.

5–86   If a scheme shows a current funding level of less than 100 per cent. the auditor to the company might provide some comment to this effect in the company's main accounts. SSAP-24 (see Chapter 25) requires a current funding level of less than 100 per cent. to be mentioned and requires disclosure of any action being taken to correct such a funding level.

Actuarial statement for the purpose of the disclosure regulations

5–87 Under the disclosure regulations of the Social Security Act 1986 the trustees of the scheme have to obtain an actuarial valuation report and an actuarial statement once every three and half years. These documents only have to be provided for final salary/defined benefit schemes or schemes which involve such an element. They do not have to be obtained for pure money purchase schemes.

5–88   The form of the actuarial statement is prescribed in the disclosure regulations. The statement must give the current salaries funding level if it is less than 100 per cent. for any benefits and, if so, what measures are being taken to bring the level up to 100 per cent. If the current salaries funding level of all benefits is over 100 per cent. then actual percentage figures are not required. The actuarial guidance note GN9 states that for the purpose of the actuarial statement the calculation of the current salaries funding level may be less rigorous than that required formally for the main actuarial valuation. The difference is that for the purposes of the actuarial statement the benefits to be valued are those provided on leaving service. For a member who has not qualified for preservation these benefits may be less in value than accrued pensions based on current pensionable earnings and current accrued service.

5–89   A further opinion is required in the actuarial statement. The actuary must express an opinion that in respect of the prospective rights "the resources of the scheme are likely in the normal course of events to meet in full the liabilities of the scheme as they fall due." If this statement cannot be given he must qualify the statement and provide some explanation. Finally, the actuarial statement must give a summary of the valuation method and assumptions used by the actuary in giving his statement. These will normally be those used for the main actuarial funding valuation.

CHAPTER 24

STATUTORY SURPLUSES

Provisions of the Finance Act 1986
The Inland Revenue's control of pension scheme over-funding

In the early 1980s earnings inflation was reducing and coming under con- **5–90** trol and stock markets experienced a period of fairly steadily rising values. In the manufacturing industry overmanning was being reduced with a consequential turnover in pension scheme membership. Pension scheme surpluses were generated while industrial surplus capacity was reduced. At the same time many companies had high cash demands on their liquidity. For some companies the pension scheme was in a better financial condition than the company itself. A natural demand was therefore created for the continuing pension scheme to refund some surplus to the employer.

Under "Old Code" Inland Revenue approval, refunds of pension **5–91** scheme monies to the employer were prohibited. Under New Code approval (in force from 1970) a condition of approval was introduced that on the winding-up of the scheme any surplus, after augmenting benefits to the Inland Revenue maximum, should be returned to the employer and be taxed. In practice, under the winding-up rules, many new code schemes allowed for the surplus to be refunded to an employer once benefits promised on winding-up had been provided. In some schemes increases for members out of such surpluses were at the discretion of the trustees or employer. No deeds however permitted a refund of pension scheme monies to the employer whilst the scheme was continuing. Indeed many deeds specifically prohibited a rule amendment permitting such a refund.

With employers' profits and any investment return on retained profits **5–92** being taxed at corporation tax rates, and the investment returns in approved pension schemes being untaxed, the Inland Revenue has an interest in controlling the amount of money in pension schemes and the size of pension schemes surpluses. If pension scheme surpluses were not restricted in any way employers could use the pension scheme as a gross investment vehicle for any cash they did not require within the business. Employers could even boost profits at the expense of the Inland Revenue by borrowing and then depositing that money in the pension scheme.

Because of their interest in controlling surpluses and wishing for their **5–93** correction earlier rather than later, the Inland Revenue agreed in a few special cases submitted to the Superannuation Funds Office to a refund of surplus from a scheme which was not winding-up but continuing. However as the number of requests for such refunds increased it became clear there was a need to establish some consistency in the Superannuation Funds Office's rulings. If repayment to the employer of a pension scheme surplus was to be generally permitted, subject to the trust deed and rules of the scheme, then the Inland Revenue would need to control funding more tightly than previously in order to stop employers abusing the system. Employers could abuse the system by making large cash payments to a scheme in years when profits were high, obtaining a gross investment return via the pension scheme, and then refunding the money in a year when the company was making a loss. The practical effect would be for the company to receive corporation tax relief on its contributions while the return when received would not be taxed.

5–94   The factors described above were behind the introduction of the control of surpluses legislation contained in the Finance Act 1986. This legislation was later consolidated into the Income and Corporation Taxes Act 1988. Much of the detail of the legislation is contained within regulations.

The main features of the legislation

5–95 An actuarial valuation report should be submitted to the Superannuation Funds Office of the Inland Revenue, on the establishment of a scheme, and at least every three and a half years thereafter. This valuation report could be on the basis of the actuarial method described below. If it is not, a separate actuarial certificate should be submitted to the Inland Revenue. This certificate would state whether on the prescribed basis and method the assets of the pension scheme exceed the liabilities by more than five per cent.

5–96   If assets exceed liabilities by five per cent., corrective action must be taken to reduce the excess to no more than five per cent. if the scheme is to retain full tax exemptions on its investments. This action must normally correct the position within a five year period. Where it produces a longer period, a scheme can take corrective action over the period until it has been in existence for 15 years, provided it was not established to replace a previous scheme. If the appropriate corrective action, over the permitted period, is not taken then the scheme will lose part of its tax exemption on investment income and capital gains.

5–97   Three possible methods of correcting statutory surplus are allowed. Each method can be used on its own or in combination with the others. Which corrective action is used will be a matter for the trustees and the employer to decide and will also be subject to what the trust deed and rules of the scheme permit. The methods available are as follows.

1. A reduction or suspension of contributions by the employer and/or the employees for up to five years (15 years for new schemes as described above).
2. Improving the benefits within Inland Revenue limits.
3. A cash refund of surplus to the employer. No refund will be permitted which on its own or in combination with 1 or 2 above would reduce the surplus to below five per cent. of the liabilities. The legislation does not override scheme rules and a refund to the employer will only be permitted if it is allowed by the scheme rules. Note also that, under the Social Security Act 1990, no refund to the employer

is permitted unless provision is made in the scheme for all pensions to increase in payment by limited price indexation.

Unlike the position before the legislation was introduced, cash refunds **5–98** to the employer are not included in the employer's taxable profits but are subject to corporation tax or income tax as appropriate at a flat stand alone rate of 40 per cent. It is not possible to reduce this liability for tax by any offset whatsoever. The administrator is required to deduct the tax directly from the refund before payment is made to the employer.

Schemes affected

All directly invested schemes with more than 12 members have to satisfy **5–99** the requirements of the legislation. However schemes which are the sole scheme of an employer and have less than 30 members may reduce any excessive surplus over a period ending with the active service of the youngest member. Insured schemes whose provisions allow for the automatic correction of surplus do not have to submit valuation reports to the Inland Revenue. In practice this includes schemes where the employer is required to pay contributions as recommended by the insurance company actuary. These schemes are not required to satisfy the statutory surplus procedures. Another exemption exists for directly invested schemes which are set up as simplified defined contribution schemes.

However should a directly invested scheme with less than 12 members, **5–100** or an insured scheme, wish to refund money to the employer then it will still be subject to the 40 per cent. rate of tax. Technically, surpluses should not occur in simplified defined contribution schemes so that refunds should not be possible.

Statutory surplus regulations
Actuarial valuation method and basis

The actuarial method and basis are set out in the regulations. Both the **5–101** method and the basis could in theory be changed from time to time. It would normally take a substantial change in economic conditions before the basis would be changed.

The actuarial method to be used is a projected accrued benefit method which in practice is the past service test of the projected unit method. Essentially, surplus is defined as the positive difference between the value of the scheme's assets at the valuation date and the value of the benefits accrued to the valuation date based on projected salaries.

Rate of interest

The valuation rate of interest is $8\frac{1}{2}$ per cent. per annum.   **5–102**

Salary/earnings inflation

The margin between the valuation rate of interest and the rate of general **5–103** increase in salaries or earnings must be assumed to be $1\frac{1}{2}$ per cent. per annum, *i.e.* the level of general salary or earnings inflation to be assumed is seven per cent. per annum. Unless a change can be justified and is appropriate, any allowance for career escalation in salaries should be appropriate and consistent with the previous valuation. Alternatively allowance can be made by reducing the net investment yield pre-retirement by one per cent. (thus using an overall rate of salary/earnings increase of eight per cent. per annum). Which allowance for promotional increases, if any, is used has to be consistent from valuation to valuation.

Pension increases
Guaranteed or discretionary

5–104 Pension increases which are guaranteed under the rules must be included in the benefits valued.

5–105   If the scheme rules provide for regular reviews of pensions in payment and for increases to be made at the trustees' or employer's discretion, then provision for discretionary increases may be made in the valuation of the liabilities. The level of increase allowed for must be the average level of increase given over the previous three years. This level of increase may be measured absolutely or relative to the level of inflation. Provision may be made for a higher level of increase provided the employer and the trustees make a joint declaration of intent to the Superannuation Funds Office to pay increases at the higher rate subject to the availability of funds. This declaration of intent has to be disclosed to the members. As an overriding limit, the net difference in the valuation rate of interest and the rate of pension increases (whether guaranteed or discretionary) must not be less than three per cent. per annum, *i.e.* the maximum rate of pension increase that can be allowed for is $5\frac{1}{2}$ per cent. per annum. There is one exception to this. If the scheme rules include a commitment linking pension increases to the retail price index, the net investment yield must be two per cent. per annum, *i.e.* the implied increase valued would be $6\frac{1}{2}$ per cent. per annum. However an appropriately higher net yield or lower rate of increase must be used where the commitment is subject to a stated maximum.

Pensioner's mortality

5–106 Unless based on the experience of the scheme or other schemes where mortality is not expected to be different, the mortality assumption (including allowance for future mortality improvements) should be the PA(90) table rated down by one year. This is a table of mortality rates published by the Institute of Actuaries appropriate to pensioners due to retire in the year 1990. The rating down by one year allows for possible future mortality improvements in later years.

Other assumptions

5–107 Other allowances, (for example for withdrawals, ill-health retirements, good health retirements) should be appropriate and consistent with the previous valuation unless a change can be justified. Any change has to be notified by the actuary in his certificate to the SFO.

Valuation of assets

For the purpose of the statutory surplus test, the value of existing assets is **5–108** to be arrived at by discounting the expected future income from the investments at the valuation rate of interest of $8\frac{1}{2}$ per cent. per annum. Variable income from investments other than indexed linked gilts must be assumed to increase at $3\frac{1}{2}$ per cent. per annum. The income and capital from index linked gilts should be assumed to increase at the rate of 5.3 per cent. per annum. The income values may be those generated by the actual assets held or those generated by an appropriate standardised portfolio. Which of the two methods used has to be consistent from valuation to valuation unless a change is appropriate.

The tax charge

Tax exempt bodies such as charities are not liable to the 40 per cent. charge **5–109** on any repayment from their schemes. However if appropriate corrective action is not taken then, as with any other employer, the scheme will lose part of its tax exemptions on investment income and capital gains.

If no corrective action is taken
or a statutory surplus is not fully corrected

If no action is taken to correct an excess statutory surplus or the corrective **5–110** action is not expected to bring the surplus down to five per cent. at the end of the required 5 or 15 year period (whichever is applicable), then a proportion of the scheme's investment income and realised capital gains will be taxed. The proportion is the ratio of surplus in excess of five per cent. to total assets. The income tax and capital gains tax charge is at the rate of 25 per cent. If the pension scheme is a trust, as would normally be the case, the capital gains tax exemption for trusts would apply. This is £2,500 and real capital gains (after RPI indexation in excess of this amount) would be taxed at the 25 per cent. rate.

Refund of surplus on winding-up of the scheme

The treatment of surplus depends on whether or not the scheme is being **5–111** replaced. If the scheme is being replaced by another scheme of the same employer, or of an associated employer, or of an unassociated employer after a takeover and merger, any refund will have to be justified by a valuation using the statutory method and assumptions. If the scheme is not being replaced, and limited price indexation applies post retirement, any surplus could be repaid to the employer, subject to the scheme's rules. In either instance any surplus repaid is subject to the 40 per cent. tax charge and should not be repaid without the prior agreement of the Superannuation Funds Office.

General comments

5–112 The statutory method and basis are intended to be conservative. For an employer wishing to operate a funded scheme providing a reasonable level of security the provisions of the statutory surplus legislation should not present a problem. However at the time the proposals were introduced there were many schemes with excessive surpluses and they were forced to take corrective action to avoid the tax charge on income and realised capital gains.

CHAPTER 25

ACCOUNTING FOR PENSION COSTS

For company years starting before July 1, 1988, there was no standard on **5–113** accounting for pension costs in the United Kingdom. The general practice had been for the contribution paid in a given year to be taken as the pension cost in the company's accounts for that year. As indicated in earlier chapters, there is a large number of choices for the actuarial methods and assumptions used for funding a pension scheme. Also a surplus or deficiency can be corrected in many ways and over different periods of time. Standards on accounting for pension costs attempt to reduce these options and put the amount taken off company profits in respect of pension costs on a more scientific and consistent basis. The idea is to make the reported pension costs of different companies more comparable.

For instance, two companies could have identical pension schemes **5–114** funded to the same level of surplus. One company could decide to correct that surplus by a short term contribution holiday producing a pension cost of zero over that period. The other company could decide to correct its surplus by taking a long term reduction in company contributions spread over the remaining working lifetime of employees then in the scheme. In this latter case there would be a charge to company profits but at a reduced rate. Without an accounting standard and a disclosure standard on pension costs, it might not be possible to see which of these alternatives had been adopted and investors in the stock market could place a wrong value on the different true worth of the two companies. As another example, one company could be funding its scheme on pessimistic actuarial assumptions using small real rates of investment return above salary and price inflation. The other company could be using optimistic and larger real rates of return. Their contributions to their schemes, their "pension costs'," could differ substantially.

In 1983 the International Accounting Standards Committee published **5–115** the International Accounting Standard No. 19, "Accounting for Retirement Benefits in the Financial Statements of Employers." This international standard is very flexible. It requires the cost of retirement benefits for defined benefit/final salary schemes to be actuarially accessed. It permits the use of both accrued service and prospective service actuarial valuation methods. A principle requirement is that the cost of pension benefits be spread systematically over the expected remaining working lifetime of employees covered by the retirement benefit scheme and that past service surpluses and deficiencies are adjusted over a period no longer than that. There are then some quite simple disclosure rules. The United Kingdom Accounting Standard SSAP-24, the American Accounting Standards FAS87 and FAS88 and the Canadian Standard are all interpretations of the

International Standard. The U.S. and Canadian standards impose far tighter conditions. The United Kingdom standard to all intents and purposes is very similar to the International Standard.

SSAP-24

The accounting objective

5–116 The accounting objective contained within SSAP-24 is that the employer should charge against profits the expected costs of providing pensions, on a systematic and rational basis over the period during which he derived benefit from the employees' services.

Application

5–117 The standard applies to all financial statements relating to accounting periods beginning on or after July 1, 1988. There is an exemption for companies registered in the Republic of Ireland which are not quoted on the United Kingdom and Ireland international stock exchange. Here the provisions for defined benefit schemes do not have to take effect until January 1, 1993.

5–118 The statement applies to all pension arrangements where the employer has promised to provide retirement benefits. It also applies if there is an established practice of providing retirement benefits but no explicit promise to do so. The standard applies irrespective of whether a scheme is funded, partly funded or not funded. The statement applies both to final salary and money purchase schemes. In the SSAP-24 booklet it is recorded that the principles of the Statement may be equally applicable to the cost of providing other post-retirement benefits. The Accounting Standards Committee has offered guidance to the effect that the Statement does not yet have to be applied to post-retirement medical cover. The Statement does not specifically mention death-benefit-only-schemes or the separate treatment of death in service benefits. The principles of the statement apply to post-retirement benefits, so death in service benefits can be accounted for separately. However as many of these benefits are often insured, their separate cost accounting would make little difference. If the cost of death benefits were accounted for as they were paid it would (compared with applying SSAP-24) have the effect of introducing more volatility to the company's profit declarations, except possibly where substantial companies and schemes are involved.

If the death benefits are provided through the pension scheme the correct treatment is to account for their costs under the principles of SSAP-24.

It is generally accepted that the Statement does not apply to the State social security contributions or to redundancy benefits.

Money purchase/defined contribution schemes

5–119 For defined contribution schemes, the standard introduced few changes. The amount of pension cost to be charged against profits should be the amount of the contributions due to be paid to the pension scheme during the accounting period. In addition the disclosure requirements for a money purchase scheme are far simpler than for final salary schemes. The following disclosures should be made.

    (1) the nature of the scheme, *i.e.* it is a money purchase/defined contribution scheme
    (2) the accounting policy (which is just to charge the amount of contributions due)
    (3) the actual pension cost charge for the period (the contributions due) and
    (4) any outstanding or pre-paid contributions.

For hybrid schemes (see Chapter 3) the Statement implies that the costs **5–120** should be accounted for in accordance with the method required for the dominating benefit. For example, if the final salary guarantee dominates the money purchase benefit, or is normally expected to do, then for SSAP-24 purposes the scheme should be treated primarily as a final salary scheme.

Defined benefit/final salary schemes

In a final salary scheme the employer has made a long term commitment to **5–121** provide a given level of retirement benefit. Normally this level of benefit is related to earnings at, or averaged over a period near to retirement. The exact cost of retirement benefits depends therefore on the eventual outcome of a series of unknown future events. A cost assessed during the employee's working lifetime is subject to review as over or under expensing develops and is corrected. There is therefore some choice about the calculation of the pension cost.

SSAP-24 states that the pension cost should be calculated using actuarial **5–122** valuation methods and assumptions which are consistent with the requirements and the accounting objective of the statement. The Statement requires the pension cost to be spread over the service life of the employees in the scheme. The actuarial methods and assumptions as a whole should be such as to produce the actuary's best estimate of the cost of providing the pension benefits promised. The statement then goes on to require that the regular cost (that part of the cost that is independent of any previous over or under-expensing) should be a substantially level percentage of the current and expected future pensionable payroll. This expected pensionable payroll should be worked out in the light of the actuarial assumptions used. These assumptions will include the usual ones but also the likely supply of future new entrants to the scheme.

The calculation of the regular pension cost should include the cost of any **5–123** benefit promised or which is implicitly promised. This will include unfunded pension promises and could include unfunded pension increases. Where a guaranteed rate of pension increase is included in the scheme rules this should be expensed for in advance over the employees' working lives. The Statement's preferred treatment for discretionary increases is that they are similarly accounted for in advance. If this is done they would be included in the calculation of regular cost. However the statement offers a choice. As an alternative, discretionary increases could be costed and charged against profits in the year they are granted. The Statement does say that ad hoc non-recurring increases or benefits which are purely *ex gratia* should be costed and charged against profits in the year in which they are granted (unless their cost is covered by, *i.e.* being met from, a surplus).

Variations from regular costs

5–124 As previously stated the exact cost of pensions depends on the eventual outcome of a series of unknown future events and should be subject to review as over or under expensing develops. These variations from regular costs can arise for the following reasons.

The scheme is or becomes over or under-funded.

The actuarial methods or assumptions are changed.

Benefits or conditions of membership are changed.

The level of increases to pensions or deferred pensions is changed from that previously promised or provided for.

5 125 Deficiencies or surpluses due to variations in the experience from what was assumed in calculating the funding rate are inevitable. In order to correct the earlier cost estimate, surpluses or deficiencies should be spread for accounting purposes (as a deduction or addition to the regular cost) over the expected average remaining working service life of the current employees in the scheme. This period will vary from scheme to scheme and from time to time and should be determined by the actuary. The actuary should use a method of calculation which is consistent with his main actuarial method and assumptions. The period to be used could be a weighted average of the expected future service of the current members of the scheme up to their normal retirement date or expected earlier date of withdrawal or death in service. The actuary would decide the appropriate weightings to use.

5–126 SSAP-24 does not lay down any guidelines in this area other than that variations in cost should be spread in a rational and systematic manner over the remaining working lifetimes or their average. One method is to spread any surplus or deficiency as a percentage of pensionable payroll. Another method is to spread it in equal annual instalments (which like mortgage repayments include interest). A third is to use the spread method adopted by the American accounting standard FAS87. This is to spread the surplus or deficiency as an equal capital instalment and then to charge or credit interest as appropriate on the reducing balance of the pension surplus or deficiency. These three methods do not exhaust all the possibilities. If the accountant or actuary can produce another method which is rational and systematic it would be acceptable under the standard. There is therefore a considerable choice of spreading methods. However, once the spreading method has been decided on first adoption of SSAP-24, or later, the accountancy principle of consistency requires that in general it should continue to be used in future years, unless it becomes inappropriate for some reason. Such a reason is hard to foresee.

Apart from the transitional provisions available when the standard was **5–127** first adopted, two exceptions are permitted to the above principle of spreading surpluses or deficits. The accountancy principle of prudence may some times introduce a third exception. The exceptions permitted by the standard lie outside the normal actuarial assumptions, methods and running of the scheme. They are therefore expected to arise infrequently. They are as follows:

1. When there is a significant reduction in the number of employees covered by the company's pension arrangements.
2. When a surplus is corrected by a repayment to the company.

In both these instances the surplus or deficit can be charged to the profit and loss account in the year in which the event occurs. In the case of surpluses the cash contribution saving from the surplus should not be anticipated. Accordingly in the case of contribution holidays, as well as repayment of surpluses from the above causes, the sums should be accounted for on a cash receipts basis.

In certain very limited circumstances the accountancy principle of pru- **5–128** dence might require a deficit to be recognised over a period shorter than the expected remaining service lives of the current employees. The standard limits these circumstances to where an extraordinary event has occurred which has not been allowed for in the actuarial assumptions, which would normally be outside the scope of those assumptions and which necessitated the payment of significant additional contributions to the pension scheme. For example, one such circumstance could be a significant market crash affecting the solvency of the scheme in respect of its contracting-out certificate. Another example is where a substantial pre-payment has built up in the balance sheet from previous pension expensing, the pension scheme then suffers a dramatically worse experience and the surplus might as a result no longer exist or the scheme is in substantial deficit. In these circumstances it might be considered prudent to write down the prepayment to zero, or to the remaining surplus, via an exceptional charge to the profit and loss account.

Effect on the profit and loss account and balance sheet in company accounts

Each year the total of regular costs for that year plus or minus any variation **5 129** should be charged against company profits for that year. If this cost is not completely discharged by the payment of contributions and by pensions paid by the company, the difference should increase any existing pension provision in the company balance sheet or reduce any existing prepayment. The converse applies if there is an excess of contributions paid plus pensions paid by the company, over the pension cost charged. The difference in this case should increase any existing pension pre-payment or reduce any existing pension provision. The existence of pension pre-payments or provisions can have a significant effect on a company's borrowing powers.

Actuarial methods and assumptions

5–130 SSAP-24 requires that the actuarial methods and assumptions used for calculating the pension costs satisfy the requirements of the statement. These are that in aggregate they produce the actuary's best estimate of pension costs and that the regular cost remains at a substantially level percentage of payroll. These requirements determine which actuarial methods are acceptable for SSAP-24 expensing. The disclosure requirements and the need to split pension costs between regular cost and variation rule out the aggregate method.

5–131 Many actuaries would argue that there is a range of acceptable economic and demographic assumptions for use in calculating a pension scheme's future costs. No one can foretell future economic experience and investment returns. Some would argue that it is therefore unreasonable for SSAP-24 to ask the actuary to produce a single best estimate figure. Other actuaries would argue that an economic model can be fitted to past experience and this produces definite guidelines as to best estimate assumptions. However experience over past decades has varied widely and there is no reason to believe that it will not vary over future periods as short as 15 or 20 years (a typical future average working lifetime for a current pension scheme membership).

5–132 Currently (1990) typical assumptions used under SSAP-24 would be for a real rate of return above general earnings inflation varying between $1\frac{1}{2}$ per cent. and 3 per cent. and real returns above price inflation varying between 3 per cent. and 5 per cent. It must be stressed however that SSAP-24 does not require best estimate assumptions but that the assumptions and method in aggregate produce the actuary's best estimate of the pension cost. One alternative is to decide the best estimate assumptions and best method separately, the other is to make an overall judgment.

5–133 If the pension scheme membership is judged likely to maintain a stable profile with respect to age and salaries then the projected unit method produces a regular cost which meets the requirement of being a substantially level percentage of payroll. If it is expected that the entry age will remain stable the entry age method also meets this requirement.

5–134 In the opinion of the authors the attained age method does not meet the requirements of SSAP-24 either for a closed scheme or for a scheme open to new entrants. This comment is subject to the method producing materially different answers in a particular case compared with those produced by a more suitable method.

5–135 The current unit method may satisfy the requirements of the standard but several projections may be necessary to show that the requirement for a substantially level percentage regular cost is met. It may be necessary to introduce a control period to introduce some stability or a substantial level of pre-retirement salary increases. In this latter instance the method is very nearly akin to the projected unit method.

Deferred tax liabilities

The tax relief the Inland Revenue grants against profits for corporation tax **5–136** purposes is related to the pension contributions paid. The pension expense charge made to the profit and loss account under SSAP-24 may be different. So the under or over-payment of contributions compared with the pension expense will have deferred taxation effects. To the extent that the company contributes less than the pension expense it charges there might be a deferred tax credit. In simplistic form this would be equal to the value of tax on the current underpayment. The converse applies. If a company contributes more than the pension expense charge it will be due to receive less tax relief in the future (when, to balance the earlier difference, the expense will be greater than the contribution): there would be a deferred tax liability. SSAP-24 requires that such deferred tax effects are accounted for under SSAP-15, Accounting for Deferred Tax. In brief, the standards require that deferred tax should be provided for to the extent that it is probable that a tax charge will ultimately arise. But for tax credits to be taken into account only those that are expected to arise within the next three or four years are to be counted. SSAP-15 also requires that deferred tax effects are considered across all items involved, not just the pension cost. There might therefore be some cancellation against other deferred tax items.

The deferred tax treatment has an unfortunate effect when considering **5–137** non-funded unapproved schemes and their tax treatment under the provisions of the Income and Corporation Taxes Act 1988 as amended by the 1989 Finance Act. Corporation tax relief against profits is not available until the non-funded benefit is ultimately paid and the member is taxed on that benefit. However SSAP-24 would require that such schemes are expensed in advance. Because the deferred tax credit is expected substantially beyond the end of a three or four year period (for a typical executive in mid-career), the effect is that the full gross cost of the accruing pension promise is charged immediately against net profits while the deferred tax is credited to net profits many years later. However, most accountants now agree that this treatment is unjustified and will allow the immediate credit for a company with a stable record of profits.

Interest

Invariably, when actuaries effect calculations for pension costing or fund **5 138** ing, allowance is made for the different value of money paid at different times. The actuary takes account of interest on reserves held, and discounts expected payments of contributions back to the costing date. In company accounts it is not usual to make allowance for interest where payments are expected in different years. SSAP-24 states that where the periods of payment are short no allowance for interest need be made.

However, when the periods are long term and a substantial provision or expensing deficit exists then the standard requires that interest is charged and passed through the profit and loss account as a reduction to profits. It can be argued that for consistency when a substantial pre-payment exists, interest should be credited and passed through the profit and loss accounts as an increase in profits. It can also be argued that if interest is not passed through the profit and loss account on pension provisions and pre-payments then the actuary's arithmetic will not work out and his best estimate of pension cost will not have been charged.

PART 6

INVESTMENT

INVESTMENT

GENERAL INVESTMENT PRINCIPLES

In any funded pension scheme the employer generally pays contributions **6–01** into the scheme throughout the members' term of employment. The members themselves may also be contributing. At a later date the benefits under the rules of the scheme are paid out. The time between the scheme receiving a contribution and the benefit being paid out can be very long, in the extreme possibly as long as 80 years. When a stable funding position is achieved and in real terms the fund remains constant (with contributions in a year plus the investment income being equal to the benefits paid in that year) there is a large fund of investments earning income and contributing to a reduction in the employer's outgo. In general after the collection of contributions and before the payment of benefits there arises a long period, and decisions must be made on how to invest the resulting substantial monies held in the scheme.

If the scheme is exempt approved by the Inland Revenue, investment **6–02** income and capital gains on realisation of the investments held, or in the case of insurance policies the underlying investments, will be free of income and capital gains tax. The trustees will not therefore be influenced by tax planning. In most cases they will be concerned primarily with choosing investments to give the highest return consistent with the degree of risk they wish to adopt. In deciding on the degree of risk they wish to adopt, the trustees should give consideration to the form and nature of the liabilities of the scheme.

In this part we discuss the various types of investment available, both **6–03** direct investment such as stock exchange securities and property, and financial vehicles such as insurance policies. We consider each type in turn, commenting on their suitability for the pension scheme and the type and degree of risk involved.

Historically some trustees have considered that by handing all the **6–04** scheme monies to an insurance company they are delegating their investment decisions. This is not completely true. The decision to select an insured vehicle in the first place is an investment decision. The trustees should consider before deciding on an insurance policy whether the guarantees are appropriate to the nature of the scheme's liabilities.

Ultimately the return on an insurance policy should depend on the return on the underlying investments. An insurance policy may smooth this investment return and may or may not offer some form of capital guarantee. The trustees need to consider whether such smoothing or guarantees are worthwhile. It should always be remembered that the insurance company is itself a commercial operation needing to offer returns to its with-profit policyholders or shareholders. By following the insured route a third party is being introduced between the trustees and the investments which underlie the operation of the scheme. This is not done without cost.

We consider first the types of direct investment available and then the various insurance policies most frequently used for pension provision.

CHAPTER 26

TYPES OF DIRECT INVESTMENT

Direct investment can be split into two basic types. One is where the pro- **6–05** ceeds of both income and capital are known. The other is where the proceeds, either income or capital, or both, vary. The income may be a function of the profitability of the commercial operation offering the investment or linked in some way to some Government index. The capital value could be subject to similar variations or possibly to the judgment of world stock markets. Even with the first type of investment, with income and capital at a known date guaranteed, the day to day market value of the investment will fluctuate as underlying interest rates vary. However, within each of the two basic categories there can be a considerable difference in the degree of security offered to the investor.

Investments which fall into the first category are: **6–06**

Central and local Government fixed interest/gilt edged securities;

Commercial and industrial prior charge stock exchange securities;

Mortgages.

Investments falling into the second category include: **6–07**

Index linked Government securities;

United Kingdom and overseas equities;

Property.

There are other financial vehicles like options or warrants which pension **6–08** funds may use as part of their investment operations. These are sometimes used on a short term basis to protect a capital value or to achieve another particular short term investment objective. We consider each of the main types of investment in turn.

Conventional gilt edged securities

The essential feature of these securities is that they are considered to be **6–09** completely (or almost completely) secure. Accordingly the value of such securities depends entirely on the rate of interest which the investor requires.

Gilt edged securities consist primarily of British Government stocks but **6–10** include some Commonwealth and local government stocks which have a stock exchange quotation. Some Government guaranteed issues and public board stocks are also included. Conventional fixed interest gilt edged securities offer a fixed income payment, normally twice a year. If the securities are redeemable there will be a date at which the nominal value of the capital will be returned. In the meantime the market value depends primarily on the underlying interest rates in the market.

6–11   Gilt edged stocks were once the Government's prime source of funding its shortfall of income over expenditure. With the recent public surpluses few such stocks have been issued and in fact some have been bought back before their redemption dates. In the past they have been issued at widely differing coupon rates (coupon rate being the interest rate paid on the nominal value of the stock). It is quite common for the coupon rate to be just above the interest rate ruling in the market at the time of issue for the same particular term.

6–12   Since interest rates on fixed securities have varied widely over the last 60 or 70 years, there is a considerable variation in the coupon rates of existing stocks. They vary from 2½ per cent. to 15½ per cent. When the interest rate underlying the market for a particular term is greater than the coupon rate the capital value in the market would stand below its par value. The converse is true if the interest rate is above that offered in the market: the Government stock will then tend to stand above par. Currently (October 1990) some of the high coupon stocks issued in the mid-1970s are standing well above par. An investor purchasing today receives an interest cashflow return well above current long term interest rates in return for a par value below its market price with a consequential reduction in capital at redemption.

6–13   Stocks of a low coupon rate could be of interest to investors seeking capital returns, possibly for tax reasons. Gilt edged stocks are normally free of capital gains tax on sale or redemption. So an individual higher rate tax payer might obtain an attractive investment return by investing in low coupon gilt edged stocks producing a small income but high capital gains on maturity. Such stocks are not normally attractive to pension schemes because the total return (before tax) is usually lower than an equivalent term high coupon stock. Gilt edged stocks which are attractive to pension schemes tend to be the high coupon stocks of a medium to long term. With its tax-free status the pension scheme is not taxed on the high income received and need not be so concerned about any reduction in capital value over the period. This is compensated for by the higher income. The pension scheme is looking for total return, whether by way of income or capital.

6–14   Other forms of fixed interest security may offer higher yields. This is because of the higher risk attaching to them compared with government stock. However, there is an additional reason for the yield differential between gilt edged stocks and other securities. The gilt edged market is very large and amounts are easily bought and sold. Gilt edged stocks are therefore highly marketable. In practice there is also immediate settlement, and a relatively small difference (spread) between buying and selling prices on any given day.

6–15   Because of this high marketability some gilt edged investors attempt to add to their investment returns by exploiting anomalies in the market. Occasionally, yields on particular stocks for roughly the same coupon rate or term may get out of line. Investors can make a profit by switching from one stock to another. In practice, it is very difficult to exploit anomalies since the market is very efficient. Investors may also gain an increased yield from gilt edged securities by taking a view on the next change in interest rates. If they expect interest rates to fall they will invest long, if they expect interest rates to rise they will invest in shorter term securities.

The size of recent United Kingdom Budget surpluses has resulted in the **6–16** Government reducing the size of the gilt edged market. Many stocks have been repurchased early or consolidated or converted into other issues. Few new stocks are being issued. This factor has also tended to reduce their yields especially at the long end compared with other forms of investment. In the late 1970s and early 1980s, it was quite common for a pension fund to be invested 30 per cent., 40 per cent. or even more in gilt edged stocks. With the rise in the equity values over the bull markets of the 1980s, there has been a steady fall in the percentage of pension schemes' funds invested in gilt edged stock. A quite common percentage for a typical pension fund would now (1990) be of the order of 10 per cent.

Debentures and other commercial prior charges

These investments are similar to gilt edged securities. They are fixed **6–17** money stock secured against a volume of assets both as regards capital and income. Debentures are commercial prior charges which can be redeemable or irredeemable. However they differ from gilt edged securities in one major respect—they have only the backing of the resources of a single company or group of companies behind them, rather than the Central or Local Government. As a result the investment return to be expected from such investments is higher than that from gilt edged securities. Another reason for this is that they are considerably less marketable than gilt edged securities.

The yield very much depends on the financial soundness of the particular **6–18** company offering the stock. The best commercial prior charges or debentures usually give a yield of $\frac{1}{2}$ per cent. or more above that available on gilt edged stocks of a similar coupon and term. However, the margin can vary considerably depending on the incidence of speculative and other market influences. They are normally bought and held for a considerable period.

The best commercial prior charges/debentures are mortgage debentures, **6–19** being secured on a particular property or other real assets. The last 20 years or so however, have seen a considerable number of corporate borrowers issuing unsecured loan stock. As their name suggest these securities do not enjoy a charge on a particular asset. They do nevertheless have a priority above shareholders on a liquidation. There have been times when the differential between yields on unsecured and secured loan debentures has been very small. The unsecured loan stock may then be offering the investor or lender too small a premium for the extra risk involved.

Continental European countries have a substantially larger market in **6–20** commercial debentures than the United Kingdom has. Companies often use the facility to borrow through the debenture market instead of approaching banks for direct loans. In the United Kingdom a far greater proportion of corporate borrowing has been done by means of overdrafts. The Government hopes that with the reduction in the size of the gilt edged market an active market in United Kingdom corporate debentures will develop. This would enable British industry to borrow longer at lower rates of interest than the banks offer and hence possibly improve its competitive position against industry elsewhere.

Mortgages

6–21 Mortgages against interest in real property are prior charges, like the prior charges of a commercial company. Generally, too, they have been granted on a basis sufficiently conservative to make their security for all practical purposes absolute and in such circumstances the risk of loss is remote. In addition, it is customary for the rate of interest upon a well-secured mortgage to be at least one per cent. above that on Government securities. One is here speaking of commercial and industrial property mortgages since it is very unusual for pension funds to invest in mortgages on domestic property.

6–22   Such mortgages, therefore, combine to a very high degree the properties of security of capital and attractive interest yield. On the other hand their supervision is more troublesome than that of stock exchange investments, the capital involved is less mobile, all fixed interest investments give no protection against higher than expected inflation and in many cases they give a one-way option; if interest rates fall the borrower can usually repay (even if often subject to payment of a penalty), whereas if interest rates rise the lender frequently cannot increase the rate charged, although this is becoming more widely permitted under the terms upon which new mortgages are granted.

Indexed linked Government securities

6–23 These were first issued in 1981. They combine the traditional security of a Government stock with interest payments and redemption monies linked to the retail prices index. There is however a timing delay in the linking. Increases in the income, and on the capital when repaid, are made having regard to the retail prices index eight months prior to the event. Conceptually such stocks should be attractive to pension funds. However throughout the early 1980s there was in general a bull market in equities. Index linked stocks initially offered a real rate of return above retail prices index inflation of around two per cent. per annum. Their availability was restricted to tax approved pension funds and the tax free business of insurance companies, but since 1982 they have been available to all investors. With booming equity markets in most of the 1980s the real yield required by investors has risen and typically that available on index linked stocks recently (October 1990) has been around $4\frac{1}{2}$ per cent. Thus the investment performance of the stocks issued has not been spectacular. Many professional investment managers believe that real yields obtainable on index linked stocks can easily be bettered through traditional investment channels.

Equities

The essential difference between equities, which comprise the ordinary **6–24** stocks and shares of industrial and commercial companies, and their prior charges is that, instead of being entitled to a fixed interest return and to a fixed capital value at redemption, they are entitled ultimately to the whole residue of the company, both of income and capital. Moreover, if the income is not paid to them immediately as dividends it is usually put to reserve and may appear ultimately as additional capital.

It is not surprising therefore that, even with the application of a dividend equalisation policy such as many companies adopt, the dividends fluctuate. Accompanying fluctuations of dividend there are always fluctuations of market value, and for this reason equities have tended in the past to be unpopular with conservatively minded investors, particularly family trustees and others who require a reasonably stable income. Although equities suffer in bad times they benefit in good times and, unlike the prior charges, they progress gradually with the steady expansion of a business and the yearly allocations which it is customary for industry to make to reserves. There are many examples to illustrate how, from a small beginning, a company can expand into one of the leading companies of the country with resources amounting to millions of pounds.

There is one major factor which makes equities a suitable investment for **6–25** most pension schemes. Pensions provide income throughout retirement. In times of inflation pensioners would like to receive an income which increases and which offers protection in real terms. A final salary scheme offers inflation protection for non-leaver's at least up to the point of retirement and pension fund trustees must be looking for investments whose income and capital grows in line with prices and the growth of earnings. Although not offering a direct one-to-one link a good package of equities spread across several sectors and geographical locations can offer such protection. As the economy grows and economic output grows companies should prosper. Companies also trade in real terms and their profits ultimately grow with inflation. Companies also hold real assets with property and industrial machinery whose value also normally increases with inflation. Since the mid-1950's an increasing proportion of pension fund monies have been invested in equities.

The traditional way of reducing the risk involved in equity investments is **6–26** to spread the investment across several sectors and geographical areas. It is customary to subdivide equities (and, for that matter, prior charges, too) into many classes according to industries, commodities, geographical location, and the like. Such a classification is quite reasonable since the hazards within each group tend to be similar. It is therefore reasonable and expedient to judge an investment, first, by the general influences affecting the group to which it belongs and, secondly, by the special financial characteristics of the individual within the broader group.

A factor from which equities can gain is gearing. When a company has **6–27** substantial bank borrowings or has issued a fair amount of corporate debentures, then the amount of equity capital in the company compared with the total capital may be small. If trading and profitability grows it is the shareholders in the company who will ultimately gain considerably from that growth. All the other charges against trading profits are fixed in nominal terms or only fluctuate with short term interest rates. For example to take an extreme case, if out of £100,000 of total trading profits, £90,000 is taken in interest upon prior charges, then a reduction in profits for the next year by 10 per cent. will wipe out the amount of income available for equity shareholders. On the other hand if profits grow by 10 per cent. then the amount available for distribution to equity holders will increase from £10,000 to £20,000. So one factor to examine before investing in the equity of a company is how geared the company is. Highly geared shares tend to have more variable dividends than the shares of lower geared companies.

6–28   Before making a purchase of equities, information should be sought on the stability of the business and the reputation of the company's management. There are statistics available to help the investor in his stock selection. Three particular ones are the dividend cover, dividend yield and the price earnings ratio.

6–29   The profit earned, after all prior charges and corporation tax, measured as a percentage of equity share capital should be well above the net rate of dividend declared. The number of times the net rate of dividend declared divides into this net profit after prior charges and corporation tax is the dividend cover. This statistic gives the investor some guide to the degree profits could reduce before the current rate of dividend would not be covered or its continued payment would have to be out of reserves.

6–30   The gross dividend yield is the gross dividend paid last year divided by the current market price of the share. It gives the investor an indication of the income yield currently payable. However it may not be a sufficient guide. When the market is expecting an increased dividend, the gross dividend yield based on the last dividend will be lower than otherwise. However in practice if the dividend increases as expected that stock could be a good purchase. If the market is expecting future profits and hence dividends to increase, the dividend yield on stock will generally be lower than the rest of the market. If the market expects the company to go into decline, with either a steady dividend declaration or reducing dividends from reduced profits, then the gross dividend yield will be high. For smaller growing companies financing themselves from retained profits, not much of the profits will be distributed as income. However the prospects in the long term for growing dividends from such companies could be excellent. Such companies might offer a very low dividend yield compared with the market but be good investment prospects in the long term. Thus gross dividend yield can never be considered in isolation: it must be considered along with the future prospects for growth in the company's profits and hence dividend distributions. The graph opposite shows how the average dividend yield on the constituents of the F.T. Actuaries All Share Index has changed since 1962.

6–31   Another way of examining the same concept is by means of the price earnings ratio. This is the market price of the share expressed as a multiple of the earnings per share in the last financial year. The earnings per share

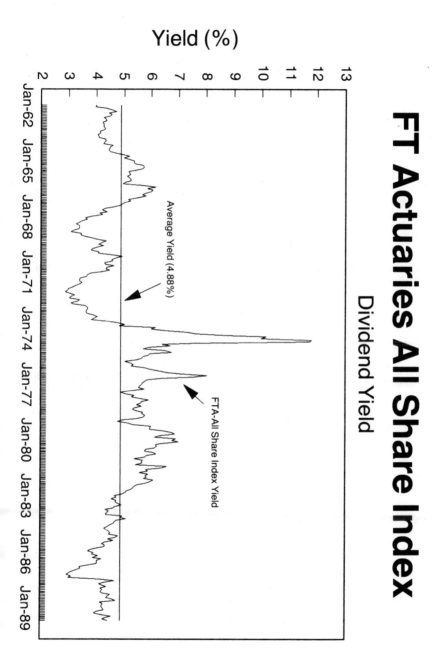

Figure 8

are measured after depreciation and corporation tax. For example if earnings per share are 25p and the current market price is £2.50 then the price earnings ratio is 10.

6–32   The concept of the price earnings ratio has however become more complex since the introduction of the system of imputation of corporation tax in April 1965. Under this system dividends free of basic rate tax can be paid out of a company's profits net of corporation tax. Before 1965 gross dividends (*i.e.* subject to income tax) were payable out of net profits. Individuals whose incomes are too low to pay tax and tax free institutions such as pension funds can claim a refund from the Inland Revenue of the hypothetical basic rate tax charged, in addition to receiving the net dividend from the company. As the Inland Revenue do not wish to be in the position of refunding tax before actually receiving it and corporation tax is not payable until sometime after the end of the financial year, the Inland Revenue insist that every time a net dividend is paid an additional payment known as advance corporation tax (ACT) is payable equivalent to tax at the basic rate. For example, when the basic rate of tax is 25 per cent., a net dividend of £75 also requires an ACT payment of £25 to be made at the same time to the Inland Revenue. This payment of £25 can eventually be offset against the company's total United Kingdom corporation tax liability. However, some companies may not generate sufficiently large trading profits to be able to offset the payment of ACT against mainstream corporation tax. This normally arises when companies are receiving large tax allowances or where most of the profits are derived from overseas profits which have already been taxed. In these instances the payment of ACT is effectively an extra tax payment.

6–33   It can be seen from the above that the total corporation tax payment of a company can vary according to the amount of dividends paid out. Earnings per share and hence the price earnings ratio may also vary depending on the distribution policy. Most (but not all) financial analysts use what is known as the net distribution price-earnings ratio which uses the actual tax paid. There are two main alternatives to this: namely, the nil distribution price earnings ratio, which presumes no dividends and hence no ACT, and the maximum distribution price earnings ratio which assumes all earnings are paid out as dividends.

6–34   Views vary between whether the price earnings ratio or the dividend yield is the best judge of a company. In practice both should be looked at as well as other financial ratios. A dividend yield might be more factual as it reflects actual income received or paid. However a company can have substantial retained earnings. The price earnings ratio reflects the totality of a company's profits but is dependent very much on the accounting practices used for that profit declaration.

Investment trusts and unit trusts

6–35 It may be uneconomic to have small holdings in a large number of companies. As well as the stockbroker's dealing charges being proportionately higher, there is also the problem of keeping a record of the increased number of transactions, collecting dividends, reclaiming tax, etc. One way of obtaining a reasonable underlying spread for the smaller fund is to invest in unit trusts or investment trusts.

The main differences are that an investment trust is a company quoted on the stock exchange and is a closed-end fund.

There are some fundamental differences between the two types of investment. A unit trust has no gearing; that is, it does not borrow from other sources. The price and performance of the unit trust is therefore directly related to the underlying assets held by its managers or trustees.

An investment trust can borrow from other sources and most do. If the **6–36** return on the extra assets held is greater than the cost of borrowing, the holders of the main investment trust shares gain from this gearing. Investment trusts have separately quoted prices which bear some relationship to the value of assets held but they often stand at a discount to the value of their underlying investment. The size of this discount varies from time to time. Unit trusts normally have set loadings for expenses, a bid and offer spread and an annual charge. With an investment trust the actual cost of the management of the investments is the cost incurred and charged to the trust itself. However sometimes within an investment management group notional charges can be made. They are therefore reasonable holdings, normally a less expensive investment route than unit trusts.

Both units trusts and investment trusts are normally exempt from capital gains on their internally realised investment profits.

Even for large schemes, investment in unit or investment trusts may **6–37** have a particular attraction. Many unit trusts and investment trusts specialise in narrow areas of the market. If a large scheme wishes to invest in one of these particular areas, say a particular overseas stock market, by going down the unit trust or investment trust route it might incur slightly more expense (compared with investing in direct holdings) but a greater spread will be achieved with ultimately less risk.

Property investment

As an investment asset, property has very distinctive features. By property **6–38** we mean land and buildings. First of all property is a real asset, that is its real worth should increase with inflation and increased economic activity. There is a limited amount of land available in any location and therefore to some extent a limited amount of property available. So, like equities, investment in property can provide both rising income and rising capital returns. However there are differences compared with equity investment. A ready market exists for quoted equities. Property is marketable but the period necessary to arrange the deal is considerably longer. To liquidate a portfolio of properties may typically take up to 12 months or longer. Also a considerable amount of professional advice is necessary in looking after a property portfolio. Reports of surveyors and estate agents on the underlying value of the property should be obtained and lawyers have involvement in the properties purchased and in any sub-leasing or renting arrangements.

6–39   Due to the time period in completing and arranging property deals, and the lack of liquidity of the property market, the actual market values are less volatile than those of equities. For some investors this makes property attractive. However, as with any other equity type investment, the value of property reacts to market pressures. Another factor in property investment is the actual size and value of one particular investment. This means that if the investor is to obtain a good spread of risk by holding several different properties, a considerable amount in total has to be invested.

6–40   Property can be divided into several types: freehold and leasehold, offices, shops, industrial property and residential. Each of these types has its own characteristics, but with all of them, factors affecting value include the location, the quality of the property, the age and condition of the property, the frequency of any rent reviews, the quality of the tenant and of any companies giving a guarantee regarding the future payment of rent. Each of the particular types of property has in addition its own characteristics.

6–41   Prime office property tends to have substantial value with each unit of investment itself being substantial. It is easier to obtain a spread of location by investing in several shops at different locations. However shop rents are directly related to the turnover expected in a particular location as well as the prosperity of the retail sector in general. Office and shop property tend to have a longer working lifetime than industrial units. As the demands of industry change a particular industrial unit can become obsolescent in design.

Residential property has typically less value attached to a particular unit but far greater administration is involved due to the greater number of units for a particular sized portfolio. Until recently in the United Kingdom residential tenants have had a substantial degree of protection both on the level of rents and security of tenancy. These two factors have made residential property unattractive for pension schemes.

6–42   As previously mentioned, the value of individual properties can be quite large and a small to medium sized pension fund may not be able to obtain a proper spread even if it intends investing a substantial proportion of its assets in property. If it intends to limit this proportion to 10 per cent. or 15 per cent., which has typically been the sort of proportion of a large pension funds' long term property holdings, then this problem of sufficient spread is greatly increased.

6–43   In the late 1960's and early 1970's several specialist pension fund property unit trusts were established with the intention of providing a vehicle by which a spread of property investments could be obtained by approved pension schemes. To cover the lack of marketability of property these unit trusts retain the right to delay the redemption of units. In the early 1980's the outlook for property investments compared with equities was poor. So many of the holders of units in property unit trusts decided to transfer their investment to general equities. There was therefore a substantial redemption of units from the property unit trust sector. As the underlying properties had to be realised the redemption of units was delayed in many instances. The underlying property investments were realised so in some instances it was in effect a forced sale. The end result was that many of the property unit trusts were wound-up.

There have been other attempts to allow institutional investors to share **6–44** in the value of particular properties. One way of doing this without the redemption problem is to try to create a secondary market in the units or in the particular investment vehicle. One such proposal is the creation of property investment income units in say one particular office block with these units being separately quoted on the stock exchange. As yet these ideas have not received substantial support.

Self investment

Self investment by scheme trustees is the investment of money back in the **6–45** employer's business. Self investment can take several forms: it can be the ownership of property occupied by the employer, it can be the provision of a short term or long term loan to the employer, the purchase of debenture stocks issued by the employer or the provision of equity capital via equity share ownership. One of the principle purposes of separately funding a pension scheme is to give security to pension rights outside the employer's business. Self investment conflicts with this concept.

Trustees of an occupational pension scheme are required to act in the **6–46** best interest of members. In the case of investment this entails obtaining the best investment return consistent with the required the level of security. In the case of *Cowan* v. *Scargill* concerning the Mineworkers' pension scheme it was decided that acting in the best interests of members of a pension scheme would normally mean acting in their best financial interests. Ulterior motives should not be involved. Accordingly the return obtained by the trustees should be at least that available on similar types of investment elsewhere. If this is so there must be other investors just as interested in making the investment as the trustees of the scheme. So the employer should be able to obtain the necessary finance elsewhere and the pension scheme money can be invested providing the proper security required (that is, without self investment).

There are other problems with self investment. The insider dealing pro- **6–47** visions of recent Government legislation can make it difficult for trustees who are also directors or senior managers of the business to trade legally at times when it might be thought necessary for the pension scheme to sell or buy holdings in the company. Some employers have used self investment partly as a means of providing greater protection against hostile takeover.

An occupational pension scheme, if its members are contracted-out of **6–48** the earnings-related part of the State pension scheme, has to report self investment to the Occupational Pensions Board in its annual return. If more than 10 per cent. of the assets of such a scheme consists of investments or loans to the employing company the Occupational Pensions Board require evidence that the scheme will still be able to meet in the opinion of the actuary, its liabilities with regard to contracting-out. This means that the actuary could still be able to give his actuarial certificate if the excess self invested assets were excluded for the purpose of this test.

6–49   Historically there has been one type of pension scheme where self investment is suitable. We are referring of course to small directly invested
schemes (less than 12 members) or schemes for controlling directors. In
these schemes there is normally a direct relationship between the members, the trustees and directors and senior managers of the business. They
are normally, apart from the separate pensioneer trustee required, the
same.

6–50   The small directly invested scheme provides a vehicle by which the
owners can provide for their retirement while at the same time providing
working capital for the business. The Inland Revenue require that no more
than 50 per cent. of the scheme's assets are loaned back to the employer
but there is no percentage ban on investment in property used within the
business. In practice the Inland Revenue will require evidence that there
are sufficiently liquid alternative assets to deal with the pension scheme's
cashflow and benefit provision. These schemes have to buy out pensions
via annuities within five years of retirement. So if a substantial number of
the scheme's members are nearing their retirement ages the scope for self
investment or loanback to the employer will be limited. The Inland
Revenue intend (October 1990) limiting loanbacks to 25 per cent. of the
scheme's funds, at least for schemes established after a date to be
announced.

6–51   The Social Security Act 1990 gives the Government regulation making
powers for restricting the amount of self investment to be permitted in a
pension scheme. In the case of small directly invested schemes, the existing
restrictions on self investment (including the Inland Revenue's loan restrictions mentioned above) are not expected to be made more restrictive
where all the members are trustees and investment decisions must be carried unanimously. In all other cases, the general intention has been stated
to be the achievment of a five per cent. maximum. However, the exact
amount of the maximum, what it should include and by when it should be
achieved has yet (October 1990) to be decided.

Chapter 27

INVESTMENT PRINCIPLES FOR PRIVATELY INVESTED SCHEMES

The essence of any funded pension scheme is the accumulation of monies **6–52** to support the later payment of the promised benefits. The investment return obtained is a critical factor in the total accumulation. A small increase in the investment return obtained over the long term can permit either a reduction in the employer contributions to the scheme or allows increased benefits to be provided. The rate of interest or investment return which matters is not that assumed by the actuary in his calculations but that actually obtained on the funds over the long term.

Broad investment policy is often decided by the trustees; possibly **6–53** influenced by the company, the advice received from stock brokers, any other day to day investment adviser and the actuary. It is unusual for broad investment policy to be delegated completely to an outside investment manager. By broad investment policy we mean the decisions concerning the percentage of monies to be invested in each sector; that is, in equities, gilt edged stock, property, overseas equities and other markets. For some funds day to day investment decisions (which particular stocks to buy and sell) have quite often been made by the trustees meeting half yearly, quarterly or monthly.

Nowadays routine investment decisions are generally delegated to one or more external managers or exceptionally, in the case of the very largest funds, to an internal investment department. Even the very large pension funds have moved towards delegation to external managers rather than running their own internal investment departments.

Two factors have resulted in this almost universal delegation. The first is **6–54** the volatility of world stock markets. It is not uncommon now for, say, the F.T. 30 Share or the F.T. 100 Share Index to move 20 to 30 points in a day. The timing of stock purchases has become more critical. As a result it is wise to delegate their selection and purchase to a full-time investment manager. He is more able to take advantage of temporary fluctuations or rapid changes in the market.

The second factor is the Financial Services Act. Under the Act any person involved in managing the assets of an occupational pension scheme is treated as carrying on investment business, and accordingly requires authorisation. However there is an exemption contained in the Act to the effect that pension trustees who delegate all day to day investment decisions to an authorised person need not themselves be authorised.

Although we discuss insured pension schemes in the next chapter there is **6–55** a point worth making about them here. In the past it has been argued that there are substantial risks in a directly invested scheme holding equities or other real assets, at least for smallish schemes who are better advised to use insurance contracts. However, the risk in a final salary scheme has to be measured against its liabilities, which are inflation related, and the ideal investments are those which offer some prospect of growth above inflation.

6–56 The ultimate return offered by an insurance policy must still depend on the return obtained on the underlying assets held. Short term capital guarantees will be of little value: long term capital guarantees of any significance will be obtained at a cost in lower investment returns. And it must be borne in mind that no private sector investment vehicle can guarantee a positive return above inflation. There can be as much if not more risk involved in investing in insurance policies as directly in equities, unit trusts and investment trusts. Over the long term few insurance companies will pay out more than they obtain on their own investments reduced by charges for their costs and profits.

Investment return

6–57 An essential feature of any investment is the return which it is anticipated will be received over the time it is held. Pension funds are normally long term investors. They are of course free to buy and sell existing holdings with the aim of maximising the medium to long term return on the monies held. By return we mean the interest or income received plus any capital profits and less any capital losses. The scope for increase in the future income from the security, as well as the extent to which any change in income will affect the underlying capital value, needs to be considered. These items have to be considered in the context of the economy as a whole and how they may be affected by fundamental changes in the economy.

Diversification

6–58 The risk of capital loss can be best minimised by spreading the investment holdings across different securities and different sectors. However spreading and diversification can be taken too far. Every extra holding gives rise to further work both in the recording and the collecting of income from that holding. In addition extra companies or sectors add to the companies or types of security whose performance should be regularly followed. A constant eye has to be kept on the existing holdings of a portfolio. A balance has therefore to be maintained between too much and too little diversification. A reasonable spread of risk can be obtained with as few as 15 to 20 stocks. The maximum number of stocks one can probably keep a reasonable eye on is somewhere between 30 to 50.

6–59 Diversification however can never be a substitute for sound judgment and care in the initial selection of securities. Even with sound judgment and great care an occasional loss is inevitable but if the portfolio is diversified the extent of loss due to one security is unlikely to be important. Such a loss should not be significant compared with the return obtained over the whole diversified portfolio. Diversification is therefore one of the cardinal principles to which all financial institutions normally subscribe.

Along with diversification, continued vigilance is also necessary; a mixed **6–60** bag of doubtful shares will still represent a hazardous investment. This is especially so if the risk of loss in each case is considerable. A mixed portfolio of sound investments provides greater security than each one of its components because the risk of loss in each case is small. Nevertheless, the need to keep a constant watch on a portfolio is one of the reasons why funds are well advised to place money in the hands of an outside manager (unless the fund is of such a substantial size that an internal full-time department, authorised under the Financial Services Act, could be considered viable).

The principle of diversification should be applied to all types of invest- **6–61** ment, to industries and to individual firms within industries. If this is done then losses which may occur within types of investment, peculiar to a particular industry or to a particular firm, will be minimised. For example if investment in the chemical industry were spread around the leading firms, then the losses would be minimised if one company showed poor results because of unsuccessful research. However if too high a proportion of the fund's assets had been placed in the chemical industry and the whole industry slumps then the fund suffers disproportionately.

Diversification can be extended to investments in different countries, **6–62** economies and stock markets. Such a course may nearly always imply the acceptance of a currency risk and possibly also a political risk in some instances. These risks vary enormously from country to country. The currency of some countries is so strong that investment income can be regarded as a hedge rather than a risk. Following the relaxation of foreign exchange controls and the removal of the investment currency premium, much United Kingdom pension fund money has been invested abroad. However it should always be remembered that for most United Kingdom pension funds liabilities are expressed and realisable in sterling. Cases do exist where part of the pension fund liabilities are in a foreign currency and in these cases it is definitely desirable to hold some investment in that foreign currency.

With the increasing sophistication of world stock markets and different **6–63** economies it has become common for most United Kingdom pension funds to invest up to 20 per cent. to 30 per cent. of their assets abroad. This trend started in 1970 when the outlook for United Kingdom equity shares was moderately gloomy. The proportion of overseas investment increased significantly after October 1979 when the Bank of England restrictions on overseas investment were lifted. From 1980 to 1982 United Kingdom institutions invested about 20 per cent. of new money each year overseas. Initially the most common stock markets invested in were those of the United States and Japan. Recently there has been investment in the stock markets of the European community and in other countries in the Far East as well as in Japan. Today there are few world stock markets where United Kingdom pension funds are not represented.

A problem with a large amount of investment abroad is that the number **6–64** of stock markets which have to be watched is larger. One way of obtaining a stake in overseas economies without directly investing overseas is to buy shares in a United Kingdom company which has substantial interests abroad. If this route is followed attention should be paid to the extent to which the company holds real assets (*i.e.* property and goodwill) outside the United Kingdom. A further factor to consider is the extent to which the United Kingdom company's overseas interests are diversified between different economies or concentrated in one foreign country. In extreme cases a United Kingdom company's overseas interests may be so substantial and so widely spread that it is immune from the effects of United Kingdom general economic activity whilst its overseas interests will hardly be affected by adverse developments in one particular country.

Choice of investments

6–65 In the light of the principle of diversification it remains to be decided how much of a particular fund should be invested in each type of investment. This decision can be divided into the split required between sectors (*i.e.* equities, fixed interest, property, overseas equities, index linked gilts and cash) and the split required between particular currencies and industries.

6–66 Pension funds are not static and quite clearly no simple fixed answer will suffice for all pension funds, for all circumstances, for all time. It is a cardinal principle of any investment policy that it must always be live and varying. It is rare for a completely passive attitude to investment policy to be adopted. It might be right to hold or sell some current investments but it is always important to consider and determine the reasons for the decision in the light of current circumstances.

6–67 There are two basic methods for deciding the split of the investments between different sectors and type of investments. The first is to decide the split by reference to the outlook for the particular investment sectors. The second is to decide the split by reference to the nature of the scheme liabilities. In practice a combination of these two methods should be used. We start by considering the first method, where investment matters are the only thing taken into account. To do this the characteristics of the different types of investments described in the previous chapter need to be considered.

6–68 For gilt edged stocks what particularly matters is the outlook for interest rates, the current shape of the yield curve as it changes for gilts at different terms, the coupon rate and redemption date of the particular gilt edged stock. Large capital profits can be made by holding long term, gilt edged stocks for a short time when interest rates fall substantially. The reverse is true and large losses can be made if one is holding that type of particular stock at a period of rapidly rising interest rates. Figure 9 opposite shows the yield curve for gilts of differing coupon and term.

6–69 With equities and commercial property it is the prospects for the economy, the particular industry concerned, and after that the particular company or site that matter. However the levels of the equity and property markets may not be totally unrelated to the levels of interest rates. When interest rates are low and borrowing is cheap there may be a greater level

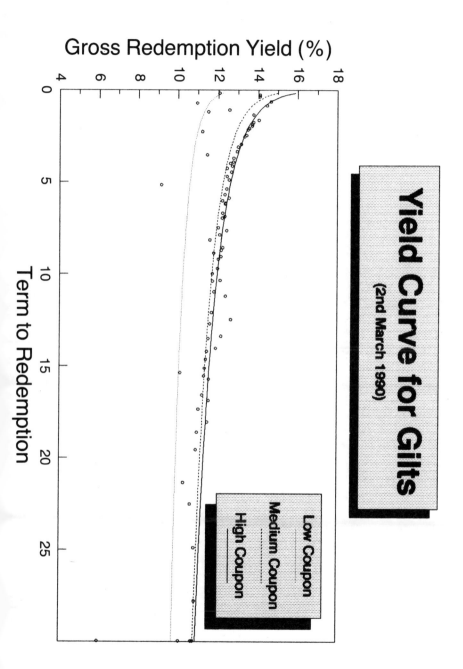

Figure 9

of speculative activity in the market. Investors may borrow to buy shares thus increasing market price levels. The other factor to consider for equity type investment is the likely rise in future income. For equities and properties the current yield of the investment, compared with the rates historically available, might give some indication of whether a particular investment is currently cheap or dear. However in making this decision the prospects for future rises or cuts in dividends or rents need to be considered. In addition the future capital requirements of the given company would need to be considered and how those capital requirements are likely to be financed. They could be financed by a future issue of equity, possibly depressing the current price; or by borrowing in the short term money markets; or by long term borrowing through the issue of debenture stock or some other financial instrument.

6–70　　There can be other pressures on market levels. The flow of new money into insurance companies and pension funds will affect the future demand for securities. The future capital needs of industry and the likelihood of future rights issues will affect the supply. If there is a large amount of takeover and merger activity where companies are using their own cash for the purpose then this makes more money available to the institutions for reinvestment.

6–71　　In the late 1960s and early 1970s the problem with the British economy was inflation with high interest rates and low growth in company profits culminating in a collapse in the stock market in 1973 and 1974. In the early and late 1980s we have seen in general steadily rising bull markets. This was due to a reduction in the rate of inflation and a tight monetary policy which enabled the economy to grow, producing in turn steady growth in company profits. The stock market collapse of October 1987 is looked upon at the current time (mid 1990) as a removal of an over-speculative froth in the market. Equity dividend yields prior to "the Crash" had been driven to an historic low of around three per cent. per annum. In recent years it has been more typical for equity dividend yields to vary around four per cent. to five per cent.

6–72　　Those directing investment policy must form their own opinions and make their own decisions in relation to the above topics. Fund managers must always be aware of future changes that could happen and give thought to the possibility of taking anticipatory action. Timing is of the essence in a good investment policy. Acting too early if one expects interest rates to fall in the long term can be as expensive as acting too late. An investment policy must not be pressed to the extremes. The great tests of a good investment policy are, first, that it does not leave the fund unduly susceptible to loss if movements are adverse and, secondly, that it does leave it receptive to profit if movements are favourable. The balance of moderation between the two extremes is delicate.

Matching assets and liabilities

6–73 The mix and nature of liabilities of a particular pension fund can differ from fund to fund. However all continuing funded schemes receive contributions which are to be invested to pay benefits possibly many years later. A fund gradually assumes liabilities in respect of its members which in general do not become payable for a long time. Just how long will depend on the ages of the members, the turnover of membership within the scheme, and the demographic experience of the membership. These factors will vary but it is possible to estimate the period over which the benefits will become payable. The benefit payments can also be of different types. By different type is meant whether they are fixed, whether they increase, and if so how increases are decided. Pensions can be fixed, increased on a discretionary basis, increased by guaranteed amounts each year or in line with the rise in the Retail Prices Index. It is possible to look at the likely benefit outgo of a scheme and estimate it by likely year of payment and nature of payment. This estimation could relate just to service accrued to date or to total service.

Having estimated the outgo of the scheme a similar exercise may be **6–74** possible for the investments. We may wish to choose the investments so that the timing and type of income they produce matches roughly the outgo. Under this technique the nature of the investments is decided by the nature of the liabilities.

To match a fixed pension an investment needs to produce a stream of **6–75** fixed income. As pensioners die over a period of years the income required will fall off. Accordingly the best match of investments that can be secured for such a set of liabilities is a package of Government gilt edged stock. These produce a fixed income for a fixed term with a return of capital at the end of that term. There are irredeemable gilts where the income continues indefinitely or until the Government decides to repurchase them. So by purchasing a package of gilt edged securities it may be possible to match the outgo for a set of fixed pensions.

Where pensions increase by fixed amounts it is just a question of appro- **6–76** priately altering the package of gilts purchased to take into account the increasing outgo required. To achieve this a larger amount of the income will probably need to come from capital redemptions. If the pensioners' retirement income is to increase by reference to increases in the RPI then appropriate gilt edged stocks (still) exist. Rather than purchasing ordinary gilt edged stocks, index linked gilts would be favoured.

Pre-retirement, the liability for deferred pensioners is either fixed or increasing in line with the RPI, in the private sector normally with a limit of five per cent. Again the appropriate investments for matching will be a mixed package of gilts, fixed and index linked.

Let us now consider the appropriate investments for matching the liab- **6–77** ilities in relation to members while they are in service. In a final salary scheme, the scheme's benefits rise in line with salary increases. Unfortunately no government or private sector company offers a financial security which supplies income and capital rising in line with earnings inflation. However earnings normally rise in line with economic activity in the country and changes in prices. This assumes that the distribution of wealth between workers and investors remains unaltered. So in general in the long term it is expected that equity dividends and property rents will rise in line with or bear some relation to the rise in earnings. Accordingly for active members equity type investments (*i.e.* equity stocks and real property) may be the appropriate investments.

6–78 One must of course consider just what liabilities are to be matched. With a continuing scheme open to new entrants it would be unusual to match precisely against the winding-up liabilities of the scheme. This would only tend to be done if the scheme was very poorly funded and there was a distinct possibility of wind-up. Such matching would be seeking to protect the basic benefits of the scheme. The winding-up liabilities do not normally cover all promised benefits. For members still in service the only pre-retirement revaluation included in the private sector would tend to be that under the provisions of the Social Security Act 1985.

6–79 Figure 10 opposite shows different distributions of assets produced by the above techniques for three differing age structures of scheme membership.

The new scheme has fewer pensioners than average whilst the mature scheme has reached stability with the ratio of pensioners to active members tending to remain constant.

6–80 The next stage of matching is to match against the liabilities taken on by the scheme if it is contracted-out on a GMP basis under the Social Security Pension Act 1975. The trustees of such a scheme (no doubt subject to agreement with the employer) have a continuing option at any time to contract back in. This could involve buying back into the State scheme or purchasing relevant benefits from an insurance company. The State buy-back terms include premiums to rid the scheme of any contracting-out liability not yet in payment called "accrued rights premiums" and premiums to cover guaranteed minimum pensions in payment, known as "pensioners' rights premiums." The first set of premiums are designed to move in sympathy with a portfolio of investments. This portfolio of investments for accrued rights premiums is notionally invested 35 per cent. in long dated United Kingdom Government stocks and 65 per cent. in United Kingdom equities. For current pensioners, the pensioners' rights premiums are notionally invested wholly in medium dated United Kingdom Government stocks. As regards securing GMPs in payment from an insurance company it should be noted that basic life office annuity rates normally move roughly in line with medium dated United Kingdom Government Stocks.

6–81 So, to protect the position of the contracting-out liabilities the actuary would consider what proportion of the scheme would have to be invested in gilts and equities in order to obtain the necessary match against the liabilities. He would look at the total accrued rights premiums that would have to be paid and the total pensioners' rights premiums. In theory, the scheme should as a minimum be holding equities equal in value to 65 per cent. of the accrued rights premiums and gilts to the value of the whole of the pensioners' rights premiums, plus 35 per cent. of the accrued rights premiums.

6–82 The fund is normally well in excess of the value of the bare minimum contracting-out liabilities and there is little risk of such liabilities being uncovered. However sometimes the funding level may be low or other liabilities may have greater priority in the scheme's winding-up rule than the payment of State scheme premiums. A particular item might be pensions in

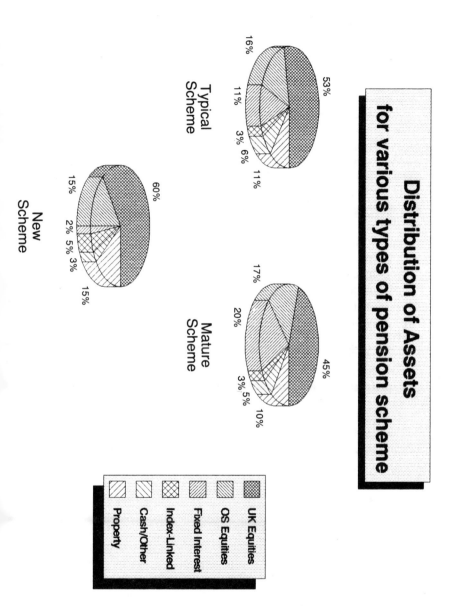

Figure 10

payment. In these circumstances the actuary will consider whether the scheme should hold extra gilt edged stock to match the current pension liabilities.

6–83   For a well funded scheme however whose projected liabilities for all accrued benefits, including future salary inflation, are covered by the existing fund, little restraint is normally placed on the investment policy by the contracted-out liabilities. There are some schemes where this may not be so, where the proportion of pensions in payment is substantial or the scheme is closed to new members and has relatively few members in service. In these instances the need to ensure that the contracted-out liabilities are adequately covered at all times might place a substantial restraint on investment policy. The scheme would need to hold a substantial proportion of its assets in gilt edged stock.

6–84   Matching against contracted-out and winding-up liabilities is essential in the case of a closed fund receiving little by way of contributions and paying out a substantial total in pensions. In this instance there may be a need to realise a significant number of investments over the years. If the term of the assets held is not closely related to the term of the liabilities a forced realisation of assets may become necessary at a time when market values are low. For this reason it may be necessary for the scheme to hold a substantial proportion of its assets in short dated securities, including fixed interest gilts. However if the scheme is substantially in surplus the existence of "free assets" gives it a greater freedom in its investment policy.

6–85   The sponsoring employer has always had an interest in the investment policy of his final salary balance of cost scheme. There is an increasing number of rules, both in the United States and the United Kingdom, on accounting for pensions. These dictate how surpluses and pension scheme deficits are to be accounted for and their emergence through the company's profit and loss account. The interest of companies in the investment policy of their funds has increased as a result and no doubt will continue to do so.

Asset Liability Modelling

6–86 Variations in a company's pension cost can have a substantial effect on declared profits. For this reason more sophisticated asset and liability management techniques are being investigated as a means of trying to control the emergence of surplus or to produce greater stability in the company's pension costs. These asset liability modelling techniques are very much in their infancy and can be expected to develop further in the next few years.

They work as follows. The asset liability modeller or actuary looks back at the past and makes assumptions for the future about the variability in statistical terms of the demographic experience of the scheme and of the economic elements (*i.e.* the investment return, earnings inflation and price inflation). These assumptions include the rate and age of new entrants into the scheme. He also considers how the investment return varies between different types of security and the variability of those returns. A substantial number of projections using these statistical assumptions is then made about the future trend of the pension fund experience. Different projection runs are done for different mixes of type of investment. From these projections a particular mix of investments which should produce a more stable investment cost for the future can often be determined. In doing the projections the extent to which surpluses and deficiencies emerge in the future is taken into account in the estimates of future pension costs.

The results of asset liability modelling depend very much on the assumptions made and the precise mathematical techniques involved. There are some pension scheme experts who are sceptical about the worth of these projections. The timescale involved is quite often substantially beyond the interest of most finance directors. The assets and liabilities of the scheme are being investigated over periods of 20 to 30 years in the future. Most companies in practice have a far shorter outlook. However as greater knowledge and experience is gained in the techniques involved there may come a time when they can contribute significantly to the running of a scheme. For a scheme with non-typical liabilities (for example, a particularly high proportion of pensioners or deferred pensioners) these techniques may already throw some light on what a sensible investment policy should be. **6–87**

Active investment policy

From time to time there will be market irregularities when a particular stock gets out of line with similar stocks. By out of line we mean that its price looks particularly cheap or expensive bearing in mind its prospects for the future compared with companies of a similar nature. An investment policy based upon the habitual exploitation of such difference is referred to as an active investment policy. If pursued successfully it can add a worthwhile investment return to the total. Such a policy can only be followed with stocks which are readily marketable and it does have a cost. Every time stock is bought or sold there are dealing expenses. These costs have to be paid for by the higher return achieved. **6–88**

Disposal of stocks

So far in this chapter we have talked in the main about the purchase and initial selection of investments. However there comes a time when stocks have to be sold or it is considered that a better investment return will be achieved by selling them. The original purchase price is never relevant to the decision to sell or hold a particular stock. In the long term, if a policy is followed of only selling stocks when they stand at a substantial profit to the price paid the investor finds he ends up hoarding a portfolio of poor investments. Any good investment has been sold off as soon as a realisable profit has been achieved without consideration for its future prospects. The portfolio the investor holds deteriorates as the proportion of underperforming stocks held for a considerable time grows. One of the first things an investor must learn is when to cut his loss and invest the monies obtained elsewhere. **6–89**

The reasons for selling an investment are the converse of the reasons for **6–90** buying one. Investments should therefore be sold when the investor concludes that the price is high or reasonable in relation to the prospects of income and capital growth, and better prospects are available elsewhere. It will be seen that the purchase price paid is not relevant to this decision.

Trustee Investments Act 1961

6–91 The Trustee Investments Act 1961 contains investment powers which are applicable to a trust unless the trust itself contains other wider powers. The investment powers contained within the Act are too restrictive for pension schemes which should adopt substantially wider powers, as discussed below.

Wider investment powers

6–92 All new schemes generally contain very wide investment powers. If wide powers are given, opportunities for profitable secure investment are not lost when they offer themselves, whereas they might be with a narrower investment power. We set out below a typical wide investment power, some aspects of which will have to be reconsidered in the context of any self investment restrictions imposed under the Social Security Act 1990.

Investment of Funds

1. Acquisition and disposal of investments

6–93 (1) The Trustees may retain any investments or property or any interest therein from time to time held by the Trustees and forming part of the Fund or sell or realise or otherwise deal with the same in such manner as they shall in their absolute discretion determine and may invest or apply in manner hereinafter provided any money forming part of the Fund and not immediately required for the payment of benefits and shall have power to sell or realise any investments or property or interest therein whether for providing money required for the payment of such benefits or for reinvestment or otherwise.

2. Permitted investments

6–94 (1) The Trustees may invest or otherwise deal with any money or other assets forming part of the Fund in such manner as they shall in their absolute discretion determine and in particular without prejudice to the generality of the Trustees' powers under this Rule:

(a) The Trustees may invest or apply any monies forming part of the Fund in or upon the security of any stocks, shares, debentures, debenture stocks, units in unit trusts or mutual or managed funds, bearer securities, any interest in land and any annuity policies and policies of assurance (being annuity policies or policies of assurance issued by any United Kingdom office or branch of any insurance company which is authorised to carry on ordinary long term insurance business under section 3 or 4 of the Insurance Companies Act 1982) or other investments or property whatsoever and wheresoever situate, whether or not involving liability, whether or not producing income and whether or not authorised by law for the investment of trust monies as the Trustees in their absolute discretion think fit.

(b) The Trustees shall have power to underwrite, sub-underwrite or **6–95** guarantee the subscription of any funds, securities, bonds debentures, debenture stocks and stocks and shares of any kind.

(c) The Trustees may place or retain any monies: **6–96**

    (i) on deposit or current account at such rate of interest (if any) and upon such terms as they shall think fit with any bank, investment company, building society, local authority, finance company or any United Kingdom office or branch of any insurance company as aforesaid, and

    (ii) on deposit upon such terms as they shall think fit with any company or undertaking other than a Participating Employer,

    (iii) on deposit upon such terms as they shall think fit with any Participating Employer or any other company or undertaking.

The Trustees shall not be chargeable in respect of any interest in excess of the interest (if any) actually paid or credited on any monies dealt with in accordance with this Rule or otherwise in respect thereof.

(d) The Trustees may enter into any transaction in connection with **6–97** financial futures, the lawful currency of any country and the purchase or sale of any assets or property for receipt or delivery at a future date and may grant or acquire call or put options over any assets or property.

3. Additional powers; land and buildings

(1) The Trustees shall, in relation to any real property or any interest **6–98** therein forming part of the Fund have the following additional powers:

    (a) power to keep any buildings insured against such risks and for such amounts as they think fit;

    (b) powers, in addition to the powers of management conferred by law upon trustees holding land upon trust for sale, to sell, exchange, convey, lease, charge, agree to let or otherwise conduct the management of any such property as if the Trustees were absolutely entitled to such property beneficially but so that, in exercising this power, the Trustees shall obtain and act upon such advice as they consider necessary (including advice from an independent valuer or independent valuers) in order to determine and agree the terms and conditions appropriate to each such sale, exchange, conveyance, lease, charge and agreement to let;

(c) power to apply any money for the time being forming part of the Fund in improving or developing any such property or in enlarging, improving, demolishing or rebuilding any building comprised in such property.

4. Additional powers; personal property

6–99 (1) The Trustees shall, in relation to any personal property, have the power to take such steps as they may think proper for the insurance, repair, protection, removal, custody, carriage and general maintenance of such property or any part thereof.

5. Participation in common investment fund

6–100 (1) The Trustees shall have power to enter into any arrangement with the trustees of any common investment fund authorised for the purposes of this Rule by the Principal Employer and approved by the Board of Inland Revenue (such common investment fund being an arrangement for the pooling of investments held for the purposes of retirement benefits schemes approved under the Income and Corporation Taxes Act 1988) on the basis that, in exchange for entitlement to share in any such common investment fund in accordance with its terms, any monies comprising the Fund or a part thereof or any investments or property representing the same, or as the case may be, any contributions payable to the Trustees under the Rules shall be paid or transferred to the trustees of such common investment fund to be invested or otherwise dealt with under such arrangement by the trustees of such common investment fund pursuant to the terms and conditions thereof. Upon and to the extent that any such payment or transfer is made the responsibility of the Trustees as to safekeeping and investment shall thereupon cease and the Trustees shall not be liable for any loss arising directly or indirectly in consequence of any such arrangement or in respect of any such payment or transfer.

6. Indemnity by trustees in connection with investments

6–101 (1) The Trustees shall have power to give any indemnity in connection with the exercise of their powers under this Rule and may bind the Fund to give effect thereto.

7. Nominee to hold investments

6–102 (1) The Trustees may appoint any corporate body to act as their nominee for the purposes of this Rule with power for the Trustees at any time or times in like manner to revoke or vary such appointment and any investments of the Fund may be made in the name of or transferred to the corporate body so appointed on the terms that the latter shall hold them as nominee for and on behalf of the Trustees and the Trustees may for this purpose enter into any agreement with such corporate body and may bind the Fund in respect of any indemnity to give effect thereto.

8. Power to raise or borrow money

(1) After obtaining the consent of the Principal Employer, the Trustees **6–103** may whenever they think it desirable so to do raise or borrow any sum or sums of money and may secure the repayment of such monies in such manner and upon such terms and conditions in all respects as they think it and in particular by charging or mortgaging all or any part of the Fund.

It will be seen that very little is excluded from the trustees' investment **6–104** powers. Investment in all types of equity stocks, unit trusts and managed funds is permitted. Trustees can underwrite offers of new shares. A wide power to invest in land and buildings is included and in addition the trustees can participate in a common investment fund if they wish. Common investment funds are described below.

Included within the above investment power is the ability to invest in **6–105** annuities or deferred annuities. One of the causes of a possibly heavy liability on a fund is if an unexpectedly high proportion of pensioners survive to advanced ages. In a fund with a large membership this is a very unlikely event. However if a scheme's membership is small the unexpected longevity of even two or three pensioners can have an embarrassing effect on the financing of the scheme. One method of reducing this risk is to buy annuities or deferred annuities from an insurance company for pensioners as they retire. This purchase might only be done for those pensioners who are considered to be in above average good health.

One of the effects of the accounting for pension cost standard in the **6–106** United States is that it has become quite common for smaller and medium (and even some large) pension funds of subsidiaries of United States companies to purchase annuities at retirement. If the pension costs are "settled" in this way FAS 87 and FAS 88 allow any "saving" (*i.e.* excess of reserve over annuity cost) to be used to reduce the accounting cost in the year of purchase. This applies even to deferred annuities for active members and some pension funds of U.S. subsidiaries have gone that far (that is, they have purchased the accrued rights of all members who have a fixed known liability, namely early leavers and any members who have opted out of the scheme). Trustees should of course be satisfied that the purchase of annuities is an appropriate investment decision.

Investment expenses

Even when the employer has agreed to meet all the expenses of administer- **6–107** ing the fund, it is usual for the fund itself to bear the expenses directly attributable to the buying and selling of investments and the management of those investments.

Common investment fund

6–108 In order to keep the liabilities separate it is not uncommon for a large holding company to have several pension schemes which each relate to a separate subsidiary. This might be the correct route to follow if the holding company wishes to limit any cross-subsidy of pension costs between the subsidiaries. However the smaller amount of monies resulting in each pension fund may limit investment opportunities. This can be avoided by having each of the pension funds of the subsidiaries participating in a common investment fund. This would be similar to investing in an internal unit trust. The investment policy can be tailored to the requirements of the participating funds' trustees. With proper accounting each scheme's share in the common investment fund is established and recognisable. However the larger fund available enables a wider spread of securities to be held and possibly new markets invested in.

Measurement of investment performance

6–109 From the late 1950s through to the end of the 1970s there was a steady increase in the United Kingdom in the number of pension schemes directly invested in stock exchange and other securities. As we have seen the long term cost of a final salary pension scheme is very dependent on the investment return achieved. It is not surprising therefore that both employers and trustees should show an interest in how their investment managers are performing. This is not a question of merely looking at a portfolio on a given date and at an investment income account covering a year or two. The measurement of investment performance has become an expertise in its own right. The practitioners include subsidiaries of consulting actuaries, pension consultants and stock brokers.

6–110 There are various ways of measuring performance. The investment return can be calculated with weightings according to timing of income and according to the amounts of money invested in particular stocks. Under either method the analyst concentrates on the total rate of investment return, *i.e.* the rate obtained by combining both income and changes in capital values. Most analysts compare the results of the individual fund with an array of other funds measured over the same period. This tends to produce a league table concentrating on short term performance. This is open to criticism. An investment manager needs several years to establish a record of how he deals with the markets in different situations. Pension fund money is generally invested for the long term and the manager needs to be measured over the long term.

6–111 As well as providing results for total rates of return investment performance analysts split the return obtained between and measure the performance in the different sectors and types of investment. An experienced analyst will go beyond analysing the return obtained and will provide sufficient information for the trustees to gain a valuable insight into what has happened and the reasons for why it has occurred. For example, a reasonable investment return obtained by the investment manager may be shown to have been the result of excellent sector selection combined with below average stock selection: average performance in both might have produced a better total result.

CHAPTER 28

INSURED PENSION SCHEMES

6–112 In one sense there is nothing special about an insurance policy. Like any other pension scheme investment it is just a way of accumulating money so that the benefits due can be paid. However insurance is about the sharing of risk. The pension scheme trustee needs to consider whether the risks the policy offers insurance against are significant and whether insurance offers sufficient protection in the case of his particular pension scheme. Here it must be remembered that salary inflation is a risk against which no scheme can insure.

6–113 Some types of insurance contract offer protection against mortality risk. For a small scheme this protection may be worthwhile but most pension schemes are large enough to bear their own risk regarding the accumulation of money pre-retirement. Some small schemes purchase annuities post retirement to protect against excessive longevity. Small and medium sized schemes (and some large ones) may reinsure lump sum death benefit risks separately.

6–114 Pre-retirement, some types of insurance policy offer protection against investment risks; that is the policy guarantees that the proceeds will not be dependent on market levels at the point of claim. Again, most pension schemes have a positive cash flow and forced realisations of investments are unusual. If forced realisations are likely then the scheme can still invest directly in stock exchange securities, holding investments of the appropriate amount and term. However this might not be possible for the very smallest of pension schemes and here insurance may have some role with regard to investments.

6–115 Historically insured schemes have covered all costs within one premium. It has not been easy for the trustees to see exactly how much of the total was being paid towards investment, administration, actuarial or legal costs. This lead through the 1950s to the late 1970s to a steady downward trend in the size of schemes moving from an insured towards a directly invested basis, where these items can be chosen and priced separately in a competitive environment.

Types of insurance policy

6–116 The types of contract offered by life offices can be broadly divided into the following four categories.

1. Non-profit group deferred annuities policy.
2. With-profits group deferred annuities policy.
3. Deposit administration.

4. Unit linked/managed funds.

1. Non-profit group deferred annuities policy

This was the first type of insured pension arrangement and was at one time **6–117**
very common. Today it would be exceptional to find a continuing scheme
insured on this basis. Individually it involves the provision by the life office
for a known life of a defined age a fixed amount of pension per annum or
cash at retirement age. Such group policies were issued at a time when gilt
edged securities and other investment yields were low. The guaranteed
return has varied from three per cent. to seven or eight per cent. per
annum. Such a return is very unattractive compared with returns available
elsewhere. Non-profit deferred annuities are also a very inflexible form of
pension investment. The nature of the investment is equivalent to a gilt
edged stock but tends to offer slightly lower yields due to the guarantees
involved. The guarantees offer little attraction for a pension scheme.

2. With-profits group deferred annuities policy

These are a development of the non-profit concept. They offer a low guar- **6–118**
anteed return, which perhaps varies between two per cent. and six per
cent. depending on contract, but in addition the pension scheme participates in the profits of the life office. They therefore offer a possibility of
yielding far more than their non-profit counterparts. The life office actuary
however controls the emergence of the investment profit by means of the
life office's bonus declarations.

The bonuses declared can take different forms. In the past life offices **6–119**
made bonus declarations every three years but there has been a recent
movement towards annual bonus declarations. In most cases they are
expressed as a percentage of the guaranteed benefits or of the premiums
paid and once granted cannot be taken away.

As life offices invested more in equity type investments and as the price **6–120**
of such investments rose, it was found that reversionary bonuses were not a
completely appropriate way to distribute capital investment profits which
had not yet been realised. As a result life offices began to introduce terminal bonuses which applied to policies maturing or becoming claims in any
given year. Terminal bonuses can be expressed as a percentage of the original guaranteed benefit, as a percentage of the reversionary bonuses
declared or as a percentage of the guaranteed benefits plus reversionary
bonuses.

A reversionary bonus scale can be heavily dependent on the length of **6–121**
time the money has been invested. In recent years investment returns in
some of the world markets have been so large that some life offices have
granted one-off special reversionary bonuses. The normal intention is that
the annual reversionary bonus should be a fairly stable item and change
slowly, hence smoothing out investment returns. It is in order not to give
the wrong impression, and so as not to hold back too much of the achieved
investment return, that some life offices have declared these one-off special
reversionary bonuses in some years.

6–122   With-profit deferred annuity contracts can offer an attractive investment return if held to their maturity. The total with-profit yield from all sources and different types of bonuses can vary between about 10 per cent. to just over 20 per cent. per annum depending on contract, term and life office.

Originally with-profits pension contracts provided an annuity payable from retirement age, offering protection against fluctuating annuity rates. Following the Finance Act 1970 most retirement benefit schemes offered a commutation lump sum option at retirement. If the with-profits contract offered an annuity there would be an option to convert the money into cash. This option might have a guaranteed conversion rate, with the actual rate used depending on annuity rates at retirement if it produced a better rate. Alternatively some with-profit contracts provide cash at retirement which is then used if required to purchase pension at the annuity rates prevailing. Again there might be a low guaranteed annuity rate contained within the policy.

Open market options

6–123 Because the office providing the with-profit contract might not be the one offering the best annuity rates at the time of retirement, many policies include an open market option. This is the right to take the cash available at retirement to another life office offering better annuity rates at the time. This open market option can apply just as much under deposit administration and unit linked/managed fund contracts described below.

Deposit administration contracts

6–124 Under a with-profit contract the benefits that are guaranteed are those at retirement or maturity of the policy. Should an employee leave service and request a transfer value then if a with-profit policy is held a surrender value will be needed for the benefits already purchased. Surrender values usually involve an element of penalty and can be unattractive. To meet this objection some offices offer a contract which promises a return of the capital value plus investment return to date as long as the proceeds are being used to purchase or provide a benefit. If the whole pension scheme policy were being surrendered or transferred elsewhere then this capital value guarantee would not normally be provided and some form of surrender penalty might be involved.

6–125   Capital guarantees cannot be provided without cost. Initially most deposit administration contracts were invested in gilt edged stocks of varying terms in order to provide the life office with a stream of capital returns out of which the promised cash could be provided.

6–126   Quite often under a deposit administration contract the monies will not be individually allocated in the names of the members but allocated to the trustees as one cash pool. The life office will offer a low guaranteed return and each year declare a total rate of investment return either as an additional bonus or as the overall investment return for that year. Some life offices have invested a substantial proportion of the monies underlying their deposit administration contracts in equities. To do this the life office will require an appropriate amount of unallocated reserve to help ensure that the capital guarantees promised can be met. Some of these deposit administration contracts also offer a bonus when the money is used for a claim, the size of the bonus depending on how long the money has been in the pool. This is very much akin to a terminal bonus on a deferred annuity with-profit contract. These deposit administration contracts can offer returns comparable with those of a good with-profit contract (possibly slightly less due to the guarantees offered) whilst providing small additional capital guarantees.

Managed funds/unit linked contracts

These are a type of insurance contract most closely akin to a directly **6–127** invested fund. They operate on a basis very similar to a unit trust. No guarantees are offered apart possibly from some guaranteed annuity rate for the purchase of pensions at retirement. However pre-retirement the investment return obtained moves in line with that of the underlying investments held. Several different unit linked or managed funds may be offered specialising in different sectors of the investment market. Usually the title "managed fund" indicates that the units are invested in all sectors. In addition there might be separate funds with units invested solely in the United Kingdom equity market, in overseas equity markets, in general international investments, in gilt edged stock and in property. It would be for the trustees to decide how much of the pension scheme to invest in each particular type of unit, although this could be delegated to the insurance company, acting as investment manager. Delegating such decisions would be the norm, following the Financial Services Act (see Chapter 27).

As with any other type of insurance policy, before selecting a contract it **6–128** is necessary to investigate the past return achieved and the general investment capabilities of the office. In a managed fund the investment management charges will, typically, be met by an annual charge and a bid-offer spread; that is, different prices for buying and selling units. Even though it is a unit linked policy some life offices might impose penalties of around 10 per cent. or 15 per cent. if the policy is surrendered. Such a penalty may be necessary to claw back any commission paid or initial expenses involved in establishing the scheme or policy.

Discontinuance

When selecting an insurance policy, trustees should always investigate **6–129** what the discontinuance terms would be if they subsequently decide to stop paying premiums and, possibly, take the money invested elsewhere. They should investigate whether the discontinuance terms are guaranteed or left to the life office's discretion at the time of discontinuance. It could be argued that since the trustees do not intend to discontinue the policy, the discontinuance terms are irrelevant. However, very few pension schemes remain unaltered over a period of time and the wishes of the trustees and the company may change. The future cannot be foreseen and the trustees may find that the policy needs to be discontinued at a time which was never initially envisaged (for example, following a merger with another company).

6–130   Discontinuance of insurance policies tends to involve some form of penalty as the life office may have had initial expenses in establishing it, including the payment of commission. The intention would have been to recoup these expenses over a possibly extended period and the life office will still wish to recoup them should the policy be discontinued. The discontinuance terms may differ depending upon whether the monies are being transferred elsewhere outside the life office, or to another type of policy within the same life office. The enhancement in the latter case can be as high as 10 per cent. or 15 per cent.

Controlled funding

6–131 When insured schemes were first established, it was common for the premiums to be decided on a member by member basis. On that basis the actual premium paid for each individual is that required to provide the benefits for him over his lifetime. Quite often the benefits related to future salary increases, as they affected accrued service, would not be funded until the salary increases were actually granted. Under controlled funding the group pension policy is just treated as any other asset of the pension fund. The life office actuary makes calculations in a manner very similar to that adopted by an actuary for a directly invested scheme. The one difference is that for his investment return the life office actuary makes an assumption about the likely rate achievable under his company's particular insurance policy. The actuary makes an assessment of the single long term contribution rate necessary to buy the benefits for all members of the scheme rather than producing individual rates. This single rate is then applied in the particular year and the resulting premium is allocated under some system to particular members (if it is allocated at all). In many cases the benefits for the older individuals are purchased first.

PART 7

INDIVIDUALS AND SPECIAL GROUPS

INDIVIDUALS AND SPECIAL GROUPS

Most of the chapters in this book are devoted to retirement provision **7–01** through occupational pension schemes. Such schemes cover groups of employees which are often large and homogenous. The principles which apply to such groups also apply to small groups of employees except that the medium of investment is more likely to be an insurance policy or policies.

Occupational schemes are not however available to all people. The self **7–02** employed cannot participate in an occupational pension and their pension arrangements are set up under different legislation. They are able to contribute to self employed retirement annuities and personal pension schemes. Personal pension schemes are also open to employees.

There are two other groups that also merit special consideration. The **7–03** first is senior executives, who have quite often been granted augmented pension benefits to make maximum use of the tax reliefs available. The second group are controlling directors of family owned companies who have been able to make finance available for the business from monies paid into a small self administered scheme. The different options which apply to these groups are described in the next chapters.

CHAPTER 29

SELF EMPLOYED RETIREMENT ANNUITIES AND PERSONAL PENSIONS

7–04 Self employed retirement annuities were first introduced by the Finance Act 1956. In very broad terms the legislation allowed individuals, both self employed and those in employment but with no other pension provision, to enjoy full tax relief on premiums payable within certain limits under specially approved annuity contracts with a life assurance company or a friendly society.

7–05 Originally, the maximum allowable premiums were severely limited in monetary terms. This was changed by the Finance Act 1980 which abolished the monetary limits while retaining limits expressed as a percentage of earnings. The Act also introduced favourable facilities for paying tax relieved contributions on earnings from earlier years. Self employed retirement annuities, although open to use by employees who are not members of an occupational pension scheme, have never been able to accept contributions from the employer directly.

7–06 The second Finance Act of 1987 made a number of changes, with effect from July 1, 1988. Although previously approved self employed retirement annuities remained open to accept further premiums, the legislation was replaced by legislation on personal pensions. These were to be broadly similar to self employed retirement annuities but with many changes of detail.

7–07 The first major change was the ability to accept contributions from an employer. The second was brought about by the Social Security Act 1986 which permitted personal pension contracts to be a vehicle for contracting employees out of the State earnings related scheme (SERPS). These two changes did not directly affect the self employed but their retirement provision was brought under the same legislation.

7–08 The legislation on personal pensions is now contained within the Income and Corporation Taxes Act 1988, sections 630 to 655. This is a consolidating act which also contains the legislation for self employed retirement annuities, in sections 618 to 629. In this chapter we describe how personal pension schemes operate as regards eligibility of earnings, contributions, benefits and investment media. We explain where the legislation for self employed retirement annuities is different.

7–09 The substantial tax advantages that apply to approved occupational pension scheme provision also apply to self employed retirement annuities and personal pensions. In addition, in the late 1970s and early 1980s, many insurance companies developed self employed retirement contracts which included or had alongside a facility for loans to the individual. These two factors resulted in a substantial growth in premiums paid.

180

As mentioned above personal pensions and self employed annuity con- **7–10** tracts are not just available to the self employed. They are also available to employees who are in "non-pensionable employment." In addition the Social Security Act 1986 made occupational pension scheme membership voluntary. So employees who are eligible for an occupational scheme have a choice: whether to provide for their retirement by joining the company pension arrangement or by taking out a personal pension scheme contract.

A personal pension scheme can only be a money purchase scheme, the **7–11** contributions to it going to the exclusive credit of the member. The advantages and disadvantages of money purchase schemes compared with final pay schemes were described in Part 2—Scheme Design. There is an additional point which can be made about personal pension schemes. Most employers who offer membership of a company scheme to an employee, be it a money purchase scheme or a final pay scheme, do so on a "take it or leave it" basis. In most cases the employer does not contribute to any personal pension scheme the employee might choose to join instead of the company scheme.

A possible exception is if a new senior executive is caught by the cap on pension provision in a company scheme approved by the Inland Revenue. In some cases it may be possible to provide more pension through a personal pension scheme than through the Inland Revenue approved company scheme. This possibility is discussed in a little more detail in Part 11.

Eligibility and contributions

There is a technical difference in the way personal pension schemes and **7–12** self employed retirement annuities are constituted. With self employed retirement annuities there is just a contract between the individual and the insurance company or friendly society and anyone with relevant earnings (see below) may pay contributions to it under that contract. Incidentally, no new self employed retirement annuities could be taken out after July 1, 1988. For personal pensions, the financial institution offering them first establishes a personal pension scheme. Conditions are laid down on who may become members of such a scheme. One condition is that the individual joining should be below the age of 75. If the individual wishes to make contributions himself, or if his employer is to make contributions on his behalf, then as with a self employed annuity the individual needs to have relevant earnings (see below).

There are three categories of individuals who can become members of a **7–13** personal pension scheme even if they have no relevant earnings. The first comprises those individuals who intend becoming a member of the personal pension scheme solely so that it can receive a transfer payment from another personal pension scheme or an occupational pension scheme. The second category comprises employees who are members of occupational pension schemes but who wish to become members of the personal pension scheme so that it can receive, no more than, any minimum contributions payable by the Department of Social Security. The employee is using membership of the personal pension scheme to contract-out of SERPS whilst remaining a member of a contracted-in occupational scheme. Finally, an individual who is a member of an approved occupational pension scheme may also become a member of a personal pension scheme if the only benefits the occupational scheme provides in respect of him are a lump sum on death in service or pensions for any surviving spouse or dependant.

7–14   For any year of tax assessment relevant earnings includes

> (i) income arising from a non-pensionable employment chargeable under Schedule E except any income arising from the acquisition or disposal of shares, an interest in shares or a right to acquire shares or income from any golden handshake;
> (ii) income from property which is part of the emolument of an office or employment;
> (iii) income chargeable under Schedule D arising from a trade or profession whether as an individual or in partnership;
> (iv) income from pension rights treated as earned income.

7–15   For an employment to be non-pensionable, service in that employment should be one to which an occupational pension scheme does not relate. As mentioned above an exception is that an employee can be provided with a lump sum on death in service or a pension for any spouse or dependent after his death. The occupational pension scheme in this context would be an approved scheme. An individual can be a member of an unapproved occupational pension scheme and pay contributions to a personal pension scheme or self employed annuity.

Any income received from an investment company of which the individual is a controlling director does not count as relevant earnings.

7–16   It can be seen that the personal pensions route will be available to an employed person who has decided not to join his employer's approved occupational scheme, even though such a scheme was available. However, it should be noted that the criterion for relevant earnings does not depend on whether or not all the earnings from a particular employment are pensioned. If the occupational pension scheme covers only part of the individual's earnings (say earnings excluding commission or earnings less a deduction for the basic State pension) then the employment would be one in which the service relates to an occupational pension scheme. There would be no relevant earnings from that employment. Similarly if the occupational pension scheme provides benefits which are well below those permitted by the Inland Revenue the individual cannot pay personal pension scheme premiums to make up any part of the difference. He is however able to pay AVCs to his employer's occupational pension scheme or to a free-standing AVC scheme operated by one of the institutions.

7–17   The contribution limits for a personal pension relate to net relevant earnings. For a Schedule E individual net relevant earnings will usually be equal to his total taxable non-pensionable earnings. For a self employed person net relevant earnings are earnings from self employment net of any deductions relating to capital allowances, business losses and stock relief.

For a personal pension the aggregate maximum contribution payable by **7–18** the member and his employer is set out below. The limits are related to the member's age at the beginning of the particular tax year.

Age	Tax year 1988/1989. Percentage of net relevant earnings	Tax year 1989/1990 and subsequent tax years. Percentage of net relevant earnings capped at £60K + indexation increase.[1]
35 or less	$17\frac{1}{2}\%$	$17\frac{1}{2}\%$
36 to 45	$17\frac{1}{2}\%$	20%
46 to 50	$17\frac{1}{2}\%$	25%
51 to 55	20%	30%
56 to 60	$22\frac{1}{2}\%$	35%
61 and over	$27\frac{1}{2}\%$	35%

[1] The cap on net relevant earnings for the tax year 1990/91 is £64,800.

The contribution limits are in addition to any contracting-out rebate and contracting-out incentive payment if the personal pension scheme is "appropriate" and the employee has decided to contract-out by means of that scheme.

The 1988/89 limits remain in force for self employed contracts for sub- **7–19** sequent tax years and the £60k indexed cap (see Chapter 30) does not apply to net relevant earnings for the purpose of such contracts. It should also be remembered that an employer cannot contribute directly to a self employed contract.

If an individual is paying contributions to both a self employed contract **7–20** and a subsequent personal pension scheme then the limits for the personal pension scheme are reduced by any amount paid to the self employed contract. Quite often the effect of this is that at the older ages, if an individual has earnings well in excess of the £60k cap, the allowable contributions to a personal pension scheme contract will be zero if the maximum is paid to a self employed annuity contract.

For the tax year 1987/88 contribution limits for self employed retirement **7–21** annuity contracts were similar to those for 1988/89. For tax years before that date the basic contribution limit was $17\frac{1}{2}$ per cent. From the tax year 1982/83 varying scales dependent on year of birth applied for those born in 1933 or earlier.

Both for personal pensions and self employed retirement annuities, **7–22** within the overall limit in each case, five per cent. of net relevant earnings can be contributed and specifically applied to provide lump sums or dependants' pensions on death prior to retirement.

Contained within the legislation on self employed annuities since 1988, **7–23** and repeated within the legislation on personal pension schemes, are provisions to carry back for one year to the previous year any contribution paid and a carry forward provision (for up to six years) for unused relief.

The carry back provision allows a contribution paid in a particular tax year to be deemed to have been paid in the previous tax year (if within the limits) with tax relief obtained in respect of that earlier year. This is especially useful in the case of the self employed individual whose actual taxable earnings are not known at the end of the tax year but only when his accounts have been prepared and his tax assessment agreed with the Inland Revenue.

7–24   The carry forward provision allows unused relief to be carried forward for up to six years. In other words it is possible to pay a premium greater than that allowed for a particular tax year of assessment if the maximum allowable retirement annuity premium was not paid in any one or more of the previous six years. When a contribution is paid on this basis the excess over that allowable in the current year is offset first against the earliest of any of the six years with unused relief.

Benefits from self employed retirement annuities

7–25   The benefits under these arrangements can only be drawn between the ages of 60 and 75 or earlier death and cannot be surrendered prior to the minimum age. Not all the benefit needs to be drawn at once. An individual could for instance go into partial retirement at age 60 drawing on some but not all of his self employed policies and then draw the balance of his benefit at a later age, say 65 or 70. The Inland Revenue may agree to the benefits being drawn before the age of 60 on grounds of ill-health or for special types of occupation.

7–26   Up to approximately one-quarter of the monies accumulated can be taken (between the ages of 60 and 75) as a tax-free lump sum with the balance used to provide a pension (which is taxable as earned income). The rule on tax-free cash is that the sum must not exceed three times the maximum pension which can be purchased with the residual monies. To gain maximum advantage from this rule most self employed retirement annuity contracts provide that the initial pension is payable annually in arrear and without guarantee. This maximises the initial amount which in turn maximises the lump sum. The residual annuity can then be rearranged to be paid in the form which is required, possibly monthly with some guaranteed period and with some contingent annuity to a surviving dependent.

7–27   The pension must be payable for life but a minimum guaranteed period of up to 10 years can be included. The pension can increase by virtue of bonuses or built in contractual increments whilst in payment. Provision can also be made for the pension to continue to the spouse or other dependants, or both, should the individual die first.

7–28   On death before the benefits are otherwise taken, the accumulated funds can be paid to a nominated beneficiary. The arrangement can be set up in such a way that the payment will be free of inheritance tax. As mentioned earlier up to five per cent. of net relevant earnings can be applied to the purchase of a life assurance policy providing death benefits only, and the proceeds of this can be paid in addition to any fund otherwise accumulated for retirement benefits.

Most self employed retirement annuity contracts give the member an **7–29** open market option. If better annuity rates are available elsewhere under another contract the money held can be transferred to it. Any commutation lump sum has to be provided from the new contract.

Benefits from personal pension arrangements

Retirement benefits from a personal pension scheme can be drawn at any **7–30** time between the attainment of ages 50 and 75. An earlier pension date may be permitted in cases of incapacity or with the approval of the Superannuation Funds Office for certain special occupations. As with self employed retirement annuities there is no requirement that the member must actually have retired for benefits to start. Personal pension scheme rules may allow members to select different pension dates for different arrangements held under the scheme.

On retirement, the possibilities are similar to those for self employed **7–31** annuities, but with several differences. The personal pension scheme administrator must purchase an annuity from an insurance company, with the individual having the right to choose which insurance company. As with self employed annuities the annuity must be payable for life and may be guaranteed for a period not exceeding 10 years. Again the annuity can be a level annuity, variable or increasing annually by a fixed percentage. The annuity should be payable normally at least once a year and can be paid more frequently. It may be paid in advance or in arrear.

The rules on the tax free lump sum are different from those applicable to **7–32** self employed annuities. For personal pension arrangements taken out before July 27, 1989, the maximum lump sum was 25 per cent. of the total fund excluding any part of that fund which had been assigned for the payment of a widow's, widower's or dependant's pension. For personal pension arrangements set up after that date the maximum is one-quarter of the total fund excluding any portion of it that is protected rights (*i.e.* benefits derived from minimum contributions from the D.S.S. or a transfer in either of such rights or rights to a guaranteed minimum pension). No lump sum can be paid under any arrangement irrespective of the starting date from that part of the fund constituting protected rights.

As with self employed annuities a contingent spouse's or dependant's **7–33** pension can be provided on the member's death on or after pension date. The rules on the provision of spouses's or dependant's pensions on death before the pension starts are similar to those for self employed retirement annuities. If no widow's annuity is payable on the member's death before vesting then the contributions paid to secure retirement benefits can be returned with interest or bonuses as a lump sum. Again up to five per cent. of net relevant earnings can be used to provide life assurance cover giving lump sum or spouse's or dependant's benefits.

A personal pension scheme must provide for transfer payments to other **7–34** personal pension schemes or occupational pension schemes and must be able to accept transfer payments from those schemes.

Investment media—Self employed retirement annuity contracts

7–35 The rules are less restrictive for personal pension schemes than they are for self employed retirement annuity contracts. Only United Kingdom life assurance companies or registered friendly societies are allowed to provide self employed retirement annuity contracts. In addition certain trust schemes approved by the Inland Revenue and established for the benefit of individuals engaged in or connected with a particular occupation can provide retirement benefits under similar rules.

7–36 An individual policy combined with a life assurance policy has been the method adopted by the greater majority of individuals effecting self employed retirement annuity contracts. The two main types of policy available from life assurance companies are with-profit and unit linked. The characteristics of these arrangements are explained in Chapter 28 on insured pension schemes. The best choice will not necessarily lie between one or the other but for a given individual could be a particular combination of the two. The investment performance of different life assurance companies can vary substantially and it may also be sensible to have a spread of different types of policy across two or three different life offices.

7–37 Most life offices offer loan-back facilities up to the current value of the policy if some other security is provided. Commonly the gross interest paid on the loan, less a deduction for expenses, is credited to the individual's accumulating fund. Tighter controls exist for loan-backs under personal pension schemes. These are explained below.

7–38 There are two variants on self employed retirement annuity contracts worth mentioning. The first is where the scheme for self employed provision is operated and documented as a life assurance contract. In this case however the life assurance company establishes a separate unitised fund for the particular contract and appoints an investment manager after consultation with the individual paying the premiums. In other words the individual can use his own investment adviser leaving the life insurance company to handle implementation. This method provides the individual with a greater degree of control over the investment of his retirement annuity premiums and can be a useful vehicle in the financial planning of partnerships. However with this type of contract the level of expense charges needs to be considered and watched carefully.

7–39 The second variant, which is only available to individual partnerships, is for some or all the partners to set up their own friendly society. Such a friendly society must have at least seven members. Friendly societies like life assurance companies were able to issue approved retirement annuity contracts. They are now able to establish personal pension schemes. The individuals concerned would control the friendly society and hence be able to direct the investments of their retirement annuity premiums. The arrangements are therefore not dissimilar to that described in the preceding paragraph but, dependent on the size of premiums, the expenses involved might be lower. A further advantage is that direct investment in property is possible in some instances.

Investment media—Personal pensions

The Government's intention has been to extend the competitive environ-   **7–40** ment and allow other financial institutions as well as insurance companies and friendly societies to make approved retirement provision available for individuals. The initial legislation was set out in the Finance (No. 2) Act 1987 and consolidated into the Income and Corporation Taxes Act 1988. This legislation set down approved providers for personal pension schemes. A personal pension scheme has to be established by an insurance company, a unit trust group, a building society, a pension company within the meaning of the building societies legislation, or an authorised bank. All have to be authorised under their particular part of the Financial Services legislation or banking or building society legislation. As a concession an existing retirement annuity trust scheme approved under section 20 of the Income and Corporation Taxes Act 1988, formerly section 226(5) of the Income and Corporation Taxes Act 1970, could establish a personal pension scheme and remain open to new members.

The intention was that a far wider market would be established. To date   **7–41** few building societies and banks have entered the personal pension scheme market. Also the number of unit trust groups providing personal pensions is very limited. Despite the intended extension the vast majority of personal pension schemes are offered by insurance companies. They continue to offer a choice of investment vehicles—with-profits, unit linked, deposit administration or possibly all types under one contract.

In his 1989 Budget Speech the Chancellor of the Exchequer announced   **7–42** his intention of making relaxations in the personal pension legislation so that the member could choose the underlying investments held. As previous legislation and practice stood, this remained the choice of the personal pension scheme provider although the member, by choosing the type of contract, could choose the sectors the money was invested in. In October 1989 the necessary memorandum was issued by the Inland Revenue.

The rules on the choice of investment severely restrict the degree of self   **7–43** investment available within a personal pension scheme. The effect of the memorandum is that the only form of self investment permitted is for the individual to purchase a property he or his partners do not already own. One of the prime effects of the requirements is to ban any deals between the personal pension scheme and any person connected with the personal pension scheme member. This will ban any investment in shares of companies which the individual controls or owns. It will also in practice stop the loan-back arrangements whereby the investment return obtained in future in the personal pension contract depends on the rate of interest paid on the loan to the member. However under this facility the personal pension scheme member can direct his investment to be held in particular quoted equities or other types of investment as long as there is no connection with himself, his family or his partners.

Chapter 30

SENIOR EXECUTIVES

Introduction

7–44 For a number of reasons, the pension benefits of senior executives often merit separate consideration. Their tax position makes it advantageous to take the fullest advantage of approved pension provision. Effectively this translates taxable income before retirement into taxable income after retirement when the marginal rate of tax may be lower. Even where the marginal tax rate does not reduce, there is the attraction of the gross investment build-up provided by the tax approved pension provision. Although tax rates decreased in the late 1980s, this reasoning is still valid albeit less important. In addition the attraction remains that part of the benefits at retirement are available as a tax free lump sum. Furthermore senior executives are more likely to have income not needed for the necessities of life, are often more at home with the complexities of financial planning and are more willing to contribute towards generous pension arrangements.

7–45 A further reason comes from the employer. It is frequently the employer's policy to encourage senior executives to retire at an earlier age than general staff. In such cases it makes sense for the employer to provide additional pension benefits for senior executives to ensure they are provided with adequate retirement income from the earlier age. In addition it must be remembered that for the higher paid the State retirement benefits represent a lower proportion of pre-retirement income.

Benefits

7–46 The range of benefits which might be provided by a typical company pension scheme has been discussed in some detail in earlier chapters of this book, in particular in Part 2. In order to ensure that the employer is able to recruit and retain high calibre senior staff improvements that might be considered for senior executives are as follows.

7–47 1. A lower normal retirement age may be provided. If the main company scheme provides for normal retirement at the age of 65 for men it is not uncommon for senior executives to have a lower normal pension age, of say 60 or 62. The Inland Revenue will not normally allow a normal pension age to be set below the age of 60 for men and 55 for women.

7–48 2. An enhanced rate of pension accrual may be provided—a two-thirds pension for less than 40 years' service. The provision of a two-thirds pension for as little as 20 years' service is frequently found. Before

March 17, 1987 the minimum service period for a two-thirds Inland
Revenue approved pension was 10 years.

3. At one time it was quite common for staff employees to have their **7–49**
pension commutation restricted to a lump sum of 3/80ths of final
pensionable salary for each year of pensionable service (the Inland
Revenue's uplifted scale permits one and a half times final salary
after 20 years). If this restriction was in place it was quite common
for it to be removed for senior executives who would be allowed to
commute pension up to their Inland Revenue maximum. Following
the changes in Inland Revenue limits in 1987, an employee's pension has to be in excess of 1/60th of final pensionable salary for each
year of service before he can take a commutation lump sum in
excess of the 3/80ths rate. So the fact that the executive receives an
enhanced accrual rate will mean he will be able to take an enhanced
tax free lump sum.

4. The lump sum payable on death in service is quite often increased to **7–50**
the maximum permitted by the Inland Revenue; that is, to four
times salary plus a return of any contributions paid by the executive.
Invariably this benefit is paid by a discretionary trust, so that it falls
outside the executive's estate for inheritance tax purposes.

5. Some executive schemes provide a widow's pension based on a pen- **7–51**
sion fraction of two-thirds of the member's benefit rather than one
half. The widow's maximum approvable pension is 4/9ths of salary
where the member has prospective service of more than 20 years (10
years for pre March 17, 1987 scheme members).

6. Improvements may be made to the pension provided on ill-health **7–52**
retirement. For example if the ill-health pension is not based on
notional service to normal retirement age for general staff
employees it may be so based for executives.

7. A higher level of guaranteed increases on benefits in payment may **7–53**
be provided. For example the staff scheme may provide guaranteed
increases post retirement at the rate three per cent. per annum with
a five per cent. per annum guaranteed increase being provided for
members of the executive scheme. This particular distinction will be
removed by the Social Security Act 1990, unless insufficient
surpluses emerge over the future lifetime of the staff scheme.

It would be unusual for all the benefit enhancements mentioned above to **7–54**
be applicable in a particular case. However there are many cases where say
three or four of them are provided.

Methods of providing executive benefits

The extra benefits offered to senior executives can be provided in different **7–55**
ways. There are two basic choices. The first is to provide the extra benefits
by augmentation in the main company pension scheme. The second
involves setting up a separate senior executive scheme. An argu-

ment in favour of a separate scheme is that a degree of confidentiality can be obtained which might not be possible if the benefits are provided from the main company scheme.

7–56   The cost of the senior executives' accruing benefits in the separate scheme would have to be included in the company's SSAP-24 disclosure in the company's accounts. This could however be on an aggregate basis across all schemes of the employer. A situation where SSAP-24 might require separate disclosure is if the senior executive scheme had a current funding level deficiency; that is, there was not enough money in the scheme to cover accrued benefits calculated on the basis of current salary.

7–57   From a funding point of view there may be some advantage in providing all the benefits for staff and senior executive from one scheme. A funding surplus for one category may be used to offset a deficit elsewhere and the progression of the company's total pension cost may be smoother. If the monies are in separate schemes then the restrictions on over-funding introduced by the Finance Act 1986 will apply to each scheme separately.

7–58   Should a separate fund be used to provide the whole of the senior executives' benefits or should the senior executives continue as members of the main company scheme, with the supplementary fund just providing the top-up benefit? From an industrial relations point of view the second route may be preferable. However if the top up is small then a separate senior executive scheme may be less viable if it is just to provide the top up benefits.

7–59   So far in this chapter we have assumed that the company will bear the whole or a substantial part of the cost of the extra benefits. It may well be that over and above the contributions the company are prepared to pay on his behalf a senior executive will want to divert part of his remuneration towards extra approved retirement provision.

The executive could pay additional voluntary contributions. These are limited to 15 per cent. of remuneration, inclusive of any scale contributions required of scheme members. Following the changes in pensions legislation and Inland Revenue practice in 1988 there is now no need for a regular commitment to pay additional voluntary contributions. Prior to that time the individual had to be prepared to pay AVCs for at least five years at an unreduced rate or until normal pension age if sooner.

7–60   If the 15 per cent. limit on employee contributions is likely to be a problem then the executive might wish to consider a salary or bonus sacrifice. Under these arrangements the employee would give up part of his salary or bonus in a particular year and the company would pay the equivalent amount of money into the company pension arrangement.

7–61   A possible disadvantage with salary or bonus sacrifice is that it reduces the individual's remuneration for pension purposes, which has a knock on effect on the maximum benefits he can draw at retirement (this point need not apply if the salary sacrifice is reinstated a year or more before retirement; the position with bonuses is more complicated and expert advice should be sought on the point). A salary reduction may also, unless positive steps are taken to the contrary, reduce the scale benefits the individual is entitled to under the main company pension scheme.

For a salary or bonus sacrifice to be effective the sacrifice has to be made **7–62** before the executive is contractually entitled to the remuneration. There are other technical details regarding the sacrifice that need to be satisfied to ensure that the employee is not taxed on the remuneration. For instance, there should be no agreement, explicit or implicit, in correspondence or revised contracts of employment or any associated literature that the entitlement to a higher salary or bonus can be reinstated as a result of any action of the executive. If so an adequate sacrifice would not have been made. In addition, it should not be possible for the executive to obtain the use and enjoyment of the employer's contributions other than as a retirement benefit.

Where an executive is providing additional pension for himself by salary **7–63** sacrifice it may be appropriate to provide the extra benefits by means of a separate investment vehicle. This could be documented as a separate individual pension scheme using an insurance policy or simply as an investment of the existing executive or company pension scheme. In this way the proceeds of the salary sacrifice can be clearly identified with no risk of that cross-subsidy between the executive and other members of the scheme.

The cap on approved pensions

The Finance Act 1989 will result in fundamental changes to senior execu- **7–64** tive pension provision. The principal change was the introduction of a cap on earnings on which approved pension provision can be based. The earnings cap was initially set at £60,000 per annum, for the tax year 1989/90 and is linked to changes in the RPI (for the tax year 1990/91 it is £64,800 per annum). The cap took effect for new members of existing schemes joining after June 1, 1989 and for new schemes set up after March 14, 1989. There are transitional arrangements to smooth in this change. For personal pension schemes the cap took effect on contributions paid from and including the tax year 1989/90.

Following the introduction of the cap it is now possible to provide unapproved pension arrangements (having a different tax treatment) on top of approved ones. These are described in detail in Part 11.

These changes may need to be taken into account when recruiting a new **7–65** senior executive. If the executive has a substantial approved pension promise from his current employer and his earnings are significantly above the cap there could be a substantial increase in cost if the new employer wishes to match the existing pension promise. The increase in cost can be minimised by going down the non-funded route (see Chapter 45) and also possibly by making maximum use of the approved pension scheme as now restricted. On this last point, the choice has to be made between putting the executive in one or more occupational pension schemes (main and/or senior executive) or a personal pension arrangement. If the executive has available from his previous employment large retained benefits (i.e. deferred pension rights or the prospect of a large transfer value) then a personal pension may be the better option.

Each case needs to be looked at individually. Which is better for a par- **7–66** ticular executive depends on the size of his existing pension rights, his intended date of retirement and the size or likely size of his earnings at retirement in relation to the pension cap. If further pension provision is required then this would be on an unapproved basis, which is described in Part 11.

Non-executive directors

7–67 Pensions for non-executive directors can be provided under an occupational pension scheme or as a personal pension. Which of the two is better will depend on individual circumstances. The Finance Act 1989 changes can fundamentally affect the position. For a personal pension the £60,000 indexed cap applies across all employments and self employments of the individual director. However the maximum contribution rates permitted, expressed as a percentage of capped earning, are now quite high. If the non-executive director intended retiring late, say beyond 65, then in some instances far greater benefits might be provided under a personal pension scheme. However for an occupational pension scheme the £60,000 indexed cap applies to earnings from any given company and its associated companies. So a non-executive director holding a number of directorships with non connected companies producing total earnings in excess of the indexed £60,000 could be better off with occupational scheme provision.

7–68   In making a comparison between personal company pension schemes for non-executive directors the fundamental difference between a money purchase arrangement and a final salary scheme should be born in mind, unless of course the company scheme is itself on a money purchase basis.

CHAPTER 31

CONTROLLING DIRECTORS

Introduction

Until 1973 controlling directors could not be provided with approved occu- **7–69** pational pensions. Any approved retirement provision they wished to make had to use self employed retirement annuity contracts. The Finance Act 1973 allowed controlling directors to become members of company pension schemes. They could participate fully in the type of company pension arrangements discussed so far including the possible top up arrangements for senior executives discussed in the previous chapter. However one or two special rules and minor qualifications apply to controlling directors and we mention these in this chapter.

The definition of a controlling director has changed from time to time. A **7–70** current definition (October 1990) for approved pension scheme purposes is a person who has at any time after March 16, 1987 and within 10 years of retirement, been a director and either on his own or with one or more associates beneficially owned or been able to control directly or indirectly or through other companies 20 per cent. or more of the ordinary share capital of the company. Associates include relatives (spouse, forebears, issue and siblings) partners and the trustees of any settlement in which the director or any relative of his has settled money.

The restrictions are introduced because the controlling director has sub- **7–71** stantial control of the business he is involved in and therefore has substantial control over his own earnings. If there were no restrictions he would be able to manipulate his earnings to obtain greater pension tax advantages.

The main restriction on the pension that a company can provide for its **7–72** controlling directors is that final remuneration, when calculated for the purpose of Inland Revenue maximum benefits, has to be based on the average of the last three years' earnings. For a normal employee or non controlling director whose earnings are less than £100,000 a year final remuneration can be the last year's salary plus the average of any bonuses or fluctuating emoluments over the previous three years. Another restriction is that if the controlling director remains in employment after the age of 70 his Inland Revenue maximum pension is the maximum at the age of 70 plus any actuarial late retirement or Retail Prices increase. This restriction applies to controlling directors who were members of schemes prior to the 1989 Budget changes. Under the new 1989 practice, pensions must not start later than the 75th birthday but accrual of further 30ths beyond the age of 70 is possible if the two-thirds maximum has not been reached.

Controlling director or small self administered schemes

Following the Finance Act 1973 a specific market and type of scheme has **7–73** developed for the controlling directors of private companies. For controlling directors who own their companies there can be a very substantial advantage in setting up their own pension scheme just for themselves, on a directly invested basis. Because the only members of such a scheme are normally controlling directors they can use the assets of the scheme to help the company in a way which would be inappropriate for an employee's pension scheme. Large numbers of such schemes were established in the late 1970s and early 1980s.

7–74   These schemes normally operate as follows. They make no promises other than to provide benefits on a money purchase basis, but may include a target consisting of the maximum benefits permitted by the Inland Revenue. The pension scheme deed permits investment back in the company subject to Inland Revenue restrictions. At the time of writing (October 1990) the Inland Revenue restricts self investment in the form of loans or owning the company's shares to 50 per cent. of the scheme's assets. There is a proposal further to restrict this to 25 per cent. for schemes approved after a date yet (October 1990) to be decided. The scheme could also own property which is occupied by the business. The Inland Revenue criteria here is that such investment is permitted as long as the schemes financing is so arranged that there are sufficient free assets at the time benefits become due for them to be met without the property assets having to be realised.

7–75   Substantial contributions to the scheme are actuarially justifiable when the maximum benefits targeted are those allowed by the Inland Revenue. This along with the self investment described above enables the pension scheme substantially to help fund the expansion of the company. Such methods of finance are attractive when individual tax rates are high. They are also attractive if the company happens to be in that band of corporation tax whereby the smaller company's corporation tax concession is being clawed back and the marginal rate of corporation tax paid is above the usual rate.

7–76   As tax rates have fallen, and since the time the employer's National Insurance contributions have been imposed on all earnings, it has been more attractive for some owners of small companies to take their financial rewards as dividends rather than earnings. This restricts the ability to use the pension scheme as a company finance vehicle because earnings are needed to be pensioned and dividends cannot be pensioned. The introduction of the £60,000 indexed cap on pensionable earnings in the Finance Act 1989, which affects new members and new schemes, also reduced the benefits that can be provided by these schemes and correspondingly their ability to be used as a company finance vehicle.

7–77   There was a time when these schemes were allegedly invested in unusual assets, that is, in such things as company yachts, villas in France, racehorses and holiday homes. In practice controlling director schemes were not generally invested in such investments. The tax advantages were too valuable to run the risk of prejudicing Inland Revenue approval.

7–78   Not all schemes take advantage of the facility to make loans back to the company. Many do however invest directly in property. In practice many of the schemes hold conventional pension scheme investments—equities, gilts and cash deposits. Subject to certain conditions the management of the investments is outside the scope of the Financial Services Act. However, if the controlling director does not have the time or inclination to manage an active portfolio then the scheme may well invest in unit trusts.

Special Inland Revenue rules

Because of the tax benefits and to stop abuse the Inland Revenue have 7–79 imposed some special rules on these schemes. For example, one of the trustees must be a person who is a pension specialist and approved by the Inland Revenue for this purpose. He is known as a pensioneer trustee. Initially the Inland Revenue stated that one of the principle reasons for having a pensioneer trustee was to stop the other trustees who are normally members of the scheme, just dividing the scheme assets up amongst themselves and disappearing with the assets having previously obtained substantial tax reliefs. The pensioneer trustee is required to be a party to any winding-up of the scheme and to report such an event to the Inland Revenue. Some pensioneer trustees are often also involved in the day to day running of the scheme, providing the necessary pensions expertise.

Another Inland Revenue rule relates to the investments of the scheme: 7–80 there is a total ban on loans to members and their families. Generally, these schemes are not large enough to bear all their own mortality risk. For this reason the Superannuation Funds Office require that within five years of retirement the given pension is provided by means of an annuity purchased from a life office. The Inland Revenue also require that any life cover promised to the member above the assets held be insured.

Restrictions on self investment introduced by the Social Security Act 1990

The Social Security Act 1990 introduced restrictions for normal occupa- 7–81 tional pension schemes regarding self investment. For the ordinary occupational scheme any self investment is to be limited to 5 per cent. of the total scheme assets. The requirement will be brought into effect by regulations but they have not yet (October 1990) been published. Controlling director schemes are exempt from these requirements as long as (i) all the members of the scheme are trustees, (ii) each member is a 20 per cent. director as defined for Inland Revenue purposes and (iii) the self investment decision must be with the agreement of all the trustees.

Directly invested or insured

Many insurance companies offer what they call "self administered 7–82 schemes for controlling directors." These are hybrid affairs containing many of the advantages outlined in this chapter, but not all. In particular, a typical insurance arrangement is likely to restrict the opportunities for direct investment in property. If the contributions exceed £10,000 or £15,000 a year these schemes may cost more than a privately invested scheme, due to the level of expenses charged. They tend to give the directors less control and less flexibility, particularly as regards the investments. The insurers may insist that any money not used for self investment is invested in insurance policies with the insurance company. The surrender penalties involved might result in a substantial proportion of the scheme's investments being locked into the insurance company for the duration of the scheme.

PART 8

OVERSEAS PENSION ARRANGEMENTS

OVERSEAS PENSION ARRANGEMENTS

Here we consider briefly the ways in which United Kingdom multi-national **8–01** companies may deal with their corporate pension arrangements abroad and we give a thumbnail sketch of social security and occupational pension systems outside the United Kingdom.

CHAPTER 32

MULTI-NATIONAL COMPANIES

8–02 For an international company based in the United Kingdom the pension arrangements set up in this country will be only a part of an overall strategy for making adequate retirement provision for its employees throughout the world. The considerations are numerous and depend on a number of factors and we do little more than broach the subject in this book. Expert advice is available and should be sought by anyone concerned with benefits on an international basis.

8–03 The problems can be different for different types of employee:

(a) those who work permanently in their own country
(b) those working permanently in a country other than their country of origin and possible retirement
(c) those who move frequently from one country to another.

8–04 Those individuals who are working in a country different from their country of origin and different from the country in which their employer is based are often referred to as "third country nationals."

8–05 A single scheme set up in the United Kingdom can, in theory, be a powerful weapon for pension provision if all the employees are paid by (or at least controlled from) that home base. The pension aspect of the transfer of employees between countries is more easily dealt with by such an arrangement, the overall strategy can be achieved more efficiently and there is scope for economies of scale in administration. Nevertheless, the taxation position on the contributions paid by the members and the employer (that is whether or not relief is available) may be inhibiting. Furthermore, it must be borne in mind that it is inappropriate, indeed undesirable, to have a common benefit structure because of the variation in social security arrangements and taxation systems which operate in different countries. There are after all some countries, such as Italy, where the generous pensions paid by the state mean that any further provision is superfluous. In other countries, such as France, membership of an industry-wide scheme may be obligatory with much the same result. There are other instances where the tax on personal incomes is such that a lump sum paid at retirement may be more advantageous to the member than a pension.

8–06 In practice a single scheme including overseas employees may prove to be feasible only when the employees outside the United Kingdom are on temporary assignments. Normally if the period of secondment is up to three years the Inland Revenue will allow the employee to remain in the United Kingdom scheme irrespective of whether he is employed by the subsidiary abroad or the United Kingdom employer.

There is one particular country with which the single scheme idea has **8–07** been practicable. This is the Republic of Ireland. Special provisions exist for a scheme established in either country to be approved for taxation purposes by the Revenue authorities in the other country. This means that employees in both countries can participate in the scheme with no taxation disadvantage. The practices of the two Revenue authorities are not identical nor are the two social security systems. Until the late 1980s it was quite common for both Republic of Ireland employees and United Kingdom employees to be in the same scheme. Recently however the two social security systems have diverged significantly. In addition some United Kingdom Revenue legislation which overrides on scheme rules takes no account of different Republic of Ireland practice. The value of the currencies of the two countries has also diverged. As a result the establishment of a common scheme for United Kingdom and Republic of Ireland employees has become less common. Indeed some employers with such schemes have split them into separate schemes for the employees of each in the two countries.

In general there are three practical ways of providing benefits for over- **8–08** seas employees. They are

(1) a single offshore scheme
(2) a series of local schemes or
(3) a United Kingdom scheme for employees not resident in the United Kingdom. These schemes were previously known as section 218 schemes (218 being a reference to the clause in the previous consolidated Income and Corporation Taxes Act of 1970). They now fall under section 615(6) of the Income and Corporation Taxes Act 1988.

We consider each of these types of scheme in turn.

(1) A single offshore scheme

It is not essential for the single scheme to be set up in the United King- **8–09** dom. It is possible to use an offshore tax haven for this purpose. The particular countries available in this connection change from time to time as do the advantages each can offer. Several are in the vicinity of the United Kingdom (at least at the time of writing) particularly the Channel Islands, while others are far-flung specks in the ocean. An ideal offshore scheme (and, as in most situations, the ideal will not be found) will give freedom from tax on the build-up of the reserves, no tax deducted at source from benefit payments, ample investment opportunities (not necessarily only in the tax haven), the facilities for the easy transfer of monies and the minimum of government supervision of the scheme. The position for a particular tax haven varies from time to time and is so fluid that any comments made now will become dated. This is an area where expert advice is needed and should be sought. A single offshore scheme established in a tax haven may be the vehicle most suitable for providing benefits for individuals who frequently move country and whose ultimate country of retirement is unclear.

(2) *A series of local schemes*

8–10   Local schemes have the merit of simplicity. There are rarely problems in the areas of tax relief, exchange control, scale and type of benefits and integration with social security systems. Such schemes will usually be most suitable for employees working permanently in their own country. On the other hand, the labour involved in the establishment of a series of schemes is considerable as is the running of the administrative systems. The method of build up of appropriate reserves (whether insured, privately invested or by book reserves) will depend on the legislation and practice of a particular country. The proportion of contributions absorbed by expenses may be considerably higher than with a unified scheme. This is especially so if there are only a few employees in each country.

8–11   Even when a system of local schemes is set up it does not follow that a given local scheme would be the most appropriate pensions vehicle for all employees working in the particular country. Employees working temporarily in their host country are probably best excluded from membership and provided for by means of an offshore scheme or a United Kingdom scheme for overseas employees.

8–12   One possibility with a network of local schemes is to introduce multinational pooling. Here the pension schemes set up in the various countries do not exist in complete isolation from each other. Each scheme would be insured with a different branch of an international insurance company. Alternatively, each scheme might be insured with the appropriate insurance company in a network of insurance companies co-operating so as to provide international pension coverage.

8–13   The advantages of such a link up are as follows.

(a) Due to the "pooling" of a larger number of lives the expense charges (when expressed as a percentage of premiums) made by the insurance company or companies in the network are smaller then they otherwise would be.

(b) The terms on which death and disability benefits can be provided are more generous than would otherwise be the case. In particular, the amount of the insurance on any one life which can be accepted without evidence of health is larger.

(c) There are facilities for transferring the accrued pension rights of an employee when he moves from one country to another country covered by a scheme in the network.

(d) The insurance company network can make available knowledge on the pension practice and social security arrangements applying in the different countries.

8–14   As an alternative, independent and privately invested local funds could be set up in countries where large numbers are employed and linked together possibly with a pooled investment fund to achieve the economies of scale similar to those available under an insurance network.

(3) *Schemes which fit the definition in section 615(6) of the Income and Corporation Taxes Act 1988*

In those overseas countries where pensions legislation may not be so far **8–15** advanced, particularly developing countries, it is sometimes convenient to provide pensions for employees sent out from the United Kingdom through a trust established in the United Kingdom. This may be the case even where the employees concerned are employed by the overseas company.

If it is established that the beneficiaries of such a trust are not resident in **8–16** the United Kingdom, tax relief on the interest income of certain types of United Kingdom investment is available under the Income and Corporation Taxes Act 1988. Section 47 gives relief on interest from certain British Government securities. Section 48 and section 65(4) give relief on interest and dividends from overseas securities.

Section 614(5) allows the reliefs referred to in the previous paragraph on **8–17** all forms of investment income and capital gains provided the pension fund comes within the definition contained in section 615(6). This is one which

(a) is bona fide established under irrevocable trust in connection with some trade or undertaking carried on wholly or partly outside the United Kingdom;

(b) has for its sole purpose the provision of superannuation benefits in respect of persons' employment in the trade or undertaking wholly outside the United Kingdom; and

(c) is recognised by the employer and employed persons in the trade or undertaking.

The sub-section goes on to say that duties performed in the United King- **8–18** dom which are only incidental to other duties outside the United Kingdom should be treated as performed outside the United Kingdom. Income tax is not deducted because of sub-section 615(3).

Note that even one member whose employment is wholly in the United **8–19** Kingdom would put the total fund outside the above definition. It would, however be permissible to grant paid-up benefits to a member returning to employment in the United Kingdom.

As far as benefits are concerned the expression "for its sole purpose the **8–20** provision of superannuation benefits" is broadly interpreted. The provision of a return of contributions on withdrawal, the payment of a lump sum on death, the provision of a spouse's pension or a lump sum on retirement will not put the scheme outside the section.

A transfer of assets in respect of an employee joining from a convention- **8–21** ally approved United Kingdom scheme to a section 615 fund will not normally be permitted. However transfers in the opposite direction are allowed.

There is no question of approval under section 615(6). A scheme either comes within the definition or does not.

Approval in the Channel Islands or the Isle of Man

8–22 If a company has employees in Jersey, Guernsey or the Isle of Man, it will be necessary for the scheme to be approved by the tax authorities in the Islands concerned. In the Isle of Man the rules are very similar to those in the United Kingdom. Their legislation tends to follow two or three years later.

8–23 Approval arrangements in the Channel Islands again are also similar to those of the United Kingdom but there are some differences. For example, neither Guernsey nor Jersey have any legislation requiring preserved benefit rights to early leavers. In Jersey the maximum widow's pension is one-half of the member's pension after commutation (Guernsey 2/3rds before commutation).

Transfers of employees to other countries

8–24 Reciprocal arrangements made by the Superannuation Funds Office (SFO) of the Inland Revenue now facilitate the making of transfer payments by a United Kingdom approved scheme to schemes approved in Ireland, Jersey, Guernsey and the Isle of Man. There are special arrangements regarding transfer payments to the pension scheme established for the staff of the European Community.

8–25 The SFO is willing to consider approving a transfer payment to overseas schemes. Provided the United Kingdom scheme has the power to make such a transfer, and the overseas scheme is willing to accept it, full particulars including copies of the documentation governing the overseas scheme should be submitted to the Joint Office of the SFO and the Occupational Pensions Board (OPB). The SFO's principle concern is that the overseas arrangement is a genuine pension arrangement and not just an ordinary savings vehicle.

CHAPTER 33

OTHER COUNTRIES WITH PARTICULAR REFERENCE TO THE EEC

EEC

Government sponsored social security schemes covering all employed **8–26** persons and including retirement and dependants' pensions are universal. The extent and type of additional occupational pension scheme coverage is summarised in the following table.

Country	Type	Method of Financing
Belgium	Employer funded arrangements. Both defined contribution and defined benefit.	Small employers generally– insured arrangements.
		Medium employers–Deposit administration contracts.
		Large employers–Private directly invested schemes called A.B.S.L.s.
Denmark	Employer arrangements, primarily defined contributions.	Most employers small so most plans insured.
France	Based on a points system approximates to career average revalued benefit.	Industry wide schemes financed on a pay as you go basis.
West Germany	Defined benefit arrangements.	Book reserve on employer's balance sheet with compulsory insolvency insurance.
		Some direct insurance arrangements with insurance companies.
Greece	Senior employees defined benefits.	Deposit administration contracts.
	For other employees high social security benefits adequate, little occupa- tional scheme coverage. In some industries there may be industry-wide union plans.	

Ireland	Funded employer arrangements.	Similar to United Kingdom
	Many defined benefit.	Directly invested schemes and insured arrangements.
Italy	Very high social security benefits–few occupational schemes– only for senior executives.	Where schemes exist–group insurance.
Luxembourg	Very high social security benefits–few occupational schemes.	Where schemes exist–group insurance or book reserves.
Netherlands	Law requires any pension promise to be funded.	Directly invested schemes and insured arrangements.
	Individual employer and industry wide schemes common.	
Portugal	Defined benefit schemes.	Schemes existing prior to 1986 pay as you go common.
		New schemes post 1986 required to be funded.
		Group insurance policies common.
Spain	Defined benefit schemes supplement social security system.	To be tax qualified, a scheme must be funded. Pay as you go with or without book reserves is still common.
		Directly invested schemes.
		Deposit administration contracts.
		Since 1987, book reserves and deposit administration scheme classed as non-qualified schemes.

Outside the EEC

8–27 Occupational pension schemes are rare outside the developed world, *i.e.* EEC, United States, the old British Commonwealth and Japan. Within the developed world, apart from a few exceptions, occupational pension scheme liabilities are funded in advance. Historically the United Kingdom, Australia, Canada, New Zealand, South Africa and the United States had similar systems. However, in the late 1980s most of these countries have had major tax reforms and the tax treatment of their pension schemes has diverged. The United States position is similar in many respects to that in the United Kingdom, the larger employers having defined benefit schemes. Smaller employers have recently tended to establish defined contribution schemes. In the United States there exist individual retirement accounts which are similar to the United Kingdom's personal pensions. There is a cap on earnings for pension scheme tax approval purposes in both countries.

New Zealand reversed the tax treatment of occupational pensions. It **8–28** was similar to the United Kingdom's with non-assessment on employees of the employer's contributions, gross roll-up on investments and taxation of pensions. From 1989 there is a tax on employer contributions, employee contributions are no longer tax deductible, investment income is taxed and benefits are no longer taxed. Australia has moved, but not completely, in the same direction, with a 15 per cent. tax on employer contributions, a 15 per cent. tax on investment income and reduced taxes on benefits.

In the Third World there are a number of government sponsored social **8–29** security arrangements of one kind or another. Where they exist they are usually based on a pay as you go system. In some countries promises have been given as to retirement provision whose fulfilment, as the proportion of pensioners in the population rises, will require contribution rates which the grandchildren of today's contributors will probably not countenance. This has already become a matter of concern in some developed countries.

PART 9

LEGISLATION

LEGISLATION

The legal framework within which pension schemes in the United Kingdom **9–01** must operate is to be found mainly in the following Acts of Parliament:

— The Income and Corporation Taxes Act 1988, which consolidates earlier legislation, and provides for various tax reliefs to be available to suitably approved schemes.

— The Social Security Act 1973 which lays down the rules on preservation of pension rights when employees change jobs.

— The Social Security Pensions Act 1975. In its original form, effective from April 6, 1978, this Act ensures that all employees qualify for an additional earnings related pension on top of the basic flat rate State pension, both being protected against inflation. It allows for members of occupational schemes to be contracted-out of the additional pension part of the State scheme (but *not* out of the basic pension) if their scheme is, generally speaking, as good as the additional pension part of the State scheme. It also contains provisions for men and women to have "equal access"—that is the same right of entry—to occupational pension schemes.

— The Health and Social Security Act 1984. This guarantees that early leavers get the benefit of increases in their guaranteed minimum pensions under contracted-out schemes from cessation of contracted-out service up to state pension age—the so-called "anti-franking" requirements.

— The Social Security Act 1985, which introduced an option for early leavers to transfer the "cash equivalent" of their accrued rights to a buy-out policy or to another pension scheme. The Act also required preserved pensions accrued since January 1, 1985 to be increased up to normal pension age by reference to the Index of Retail Prices, subject to a maximum increase of five per cent. per annum compound.

— The Social Security Act 1986. This introduced contracted-out personal pensions; outlawed compulsory membership of occupational schemes and specific personal pension schemes; required occupational schemes to provide an additional voluntary contribution facility; introduced a money purchase test as an alternative for contracting-out.

The Social Security Act 1989, which introduced the principle of equal treatment of men and women intended to take effect from January 1, 1993. This requirement was subject to important exceptions, particularly relating to pension ages and survivors' benefits.

Its requirements have however been made redundant in as much as they are overridden by the more comprehensive equality require-ments of the *Barber* judgment (see Chapter 42).

— The Finance Act 1989, which imposed a limit of £60,000 RPI indexed on pensionable remuneration under an approved occupa-tional scheme, and on remuneration by reference to which contribu-tions can be paid to a personal pension scheme. The limit does not apply to employees who joined the given occupational scheme before June 1, 1989, where the scheme was established before March 14, 1989. It applies to all personal pension schemes from the 1989/1990 tax year.

— The Social Security Act 1990, which will require pensions under final salary schemes to qualify for increases whilst in payment in line with increases in the Retail Prices Index, with a maximum of five per cent. This change will apply in respect of pensions accruing after a date to be appointed, but expected to be January 1, 1992. It is also expected that from the same date surplus above a prescribed level will have to be applied to provide similar increases to other pensions under final salary schemes. The Act also requires employers to make good any deficiency arising on the winding-up of a final salary scheme.

"Preservation," "contracting-out," and "equal access" are monitored by the Occupational Pensions Board (OPB) while the tax aspects are super-vised by the Inland Revenue Superannuation Funds Office (SFO).

The other area of legislation which affects pension provision is of course the State pension scheme generally which operates within the social secur-ity system in this country, and the Treaty of Rome in relation to non-discrimination on grounds of sex.

These various matters are dealt with in the following chapters in this Part and in Part 10.

CHAPTER 34

TAXATION ✓

Historical

The position can best be appreciated in its broad background in the light of **9–02** some historical facts. In the early part of the century, before the 1914–1918 War, there was no legislation directed expressly to the taxation of pension schemes. Under those conditions, no question of relief in respect of employee's contributions arose and the interest income of the fund bore tax in the normal way. The decision as to whether or not an employer's contribution was an expense of management depended on the facts of the case viewed in the light of the general principles governing income tax assessments of all kinds. The rates of tax were low enough to make the question relatively unimportant.

There were provisions governing the allowances to be granted in respect **9–03** of premiums paid upon life assurance and similar policies and these provisions applied to individual policies effected by members of a pension scheme.

Even in 1920, however, there was no legislation explicitly governing a privately invested pension fund and the immediate post-War years found these funds very seriously affected by income tax at rates much higher than before the War. The net rate of interest which could be earned on invested assets in the face of such high rates of tax was being seriously reduced and it was becoming more and more important that, if employers were to be encouraged to inaugurate and maintain funds, the contributions made by them should enjoy relief from tax. As a result the Finance Act 1921 provided, broadly, that contributions from both the employer and the employee to funds approved by the Inland Revenue ranked for full tax relief, and that the investment income of the fund was not taxable. Pension payments were taxable in the hands of the recipient as earned income.

The problems of insured schemes in the early days were not so great as **9–04** those of privately invested funds, because of the reliefs available on the premiums paid under the life assurance contracts bought by the employees' contributions; until 1947 the majority of companies running such schemes were content to ensure that employer's contributions were treated as an expense of management rather than to seek specific approval of the scheme from the Inland Revenue. Such privately invested schemes as existed, however, sought approval under the Finance Act 1921.

The Finance Act 1947 however, provided that unless a scheme was speci- **9–05** fically approved by the Inland Revenue then not only would the various tax reliefs available not apply, but the employee would have to pay income tax on the employer's contributions just as if that contribution had been income of the employee. The consequences of not obtaining approval were, therefore, severe and these same penalties still apply today. As a result, virtually all schemes applied for approval in one form or another and from 1947 up to 1970 a variety of different forms of approval grew up.

9–06   By 1970, the whole question of approval of retirement benefits schemes by the Inland Revenue had become exceedingly complex and the position was rationalised by the passing of the Finance Act 1970. This introduced in Chapter II, Part II a single Code of Approval for all schemes—at the time it was known as the "New Code of Approval"—and all schemes then in existence were given until 1980 in which to switch to approval under this New code.

The legislation is now comprised in the Income and Corporation Taxes Act 1988, which consolidated earlier legislation. Fundamental changes were made by the Finance Act 1989, which restricted the scope of approved schemes to earnings of £60,000 per annum, and removed the previous restrictions affecting concurrent unapproved arrangements. The changes affect schemes established after March 1989, and new entrants to existing schemes with effect from June 1, 1989.

The current position—approved schemes

9–07 The Income and Corporation Taxes Act 1988 provides for schemes to be both "approved" and "exempt approved." An "exempt approved" scheme is simply an approved scheme which has been set up under an irrevocable trust and since the full tax reliefs are available only to "exempt approved" schemes, in practice virtually all funded approved schemes are set up in this way.

The tax reliefs available to an exempt approved scheme are as follows:

— to the employer on his contribution to the scheme;
— to the employee on the employer's contributions (without this relief the employer's contributions would be taxable as part of the employee's income);
— to the employee on his own contributions to the scheme;
— to the employee on his lump sum at retirement and (provided that the destination of the benefit is governed by a suitable discretionary trust) to the recipients of a lump sum payable on death; and
— to the pension fund on the income from its investments whether by way of dividends, interest or capital appreciation.

These reliefs are of course extremely valuable, increasing the ultimate value of the benefits for which members qualify and reducing the amounts that have to be paid into the scheme in the meantime.

It should be remembered though that when a member's or widow's pension actually becomes payable under an approved scheme it is taxed under PAYE.

The Inland Revenue

9–08 The approval of pension schemes is looked after by a separate branch of the Inland Revenue known as the Superannuation Funds Office (SFO).

They are responsible for approving a scheme initially and they will then notify the local inspector of taxes for the district in which the scheme is administered. He will then deal with any tax payments or refunds and he will also deal with the PAYE tax on the pensions.

The SFO have a continuing involvement with the scheme once it is started and their initial approval given. The trustees have a responsibility to inform the SFO of certain events such as changes in the benefits and contributions or other alterations to the trust deed and rules, the admission of other employers to the scheme, and the payment of special contributions by the employer.

Conditions for approval under the Income and Corporation Taxes Act 1988

The basis for approval of occupational pension schemes under the legis- **9–09** lation is contained in Sections 590–596.

It is possible for schemes to seek approval under section 590 of the Act and approval must be given by the Inland Revenue if a scheme satisfies certain prescribed conditions. However, the prescribed conditions are so restrictive that this section is hardly ever used.

Instead approval is nearly always sought under section 591 of the Act but the difference here is that section 591 allows the Revenue complete discretion to impose such conditions on approval as it thinks fit. The Revenue's use of their discretion under section 591 extends into almost every possible provision of the scheme. Their practice is set out in a booklet of some 100 pages which can be obtained free of charge from the Superannuation Funds Office. It is referred to as "SFO Practice Notes (IR12)."

If the principles set out in these practice notes are not observed then it is most unlikely that a scheme will be approved. If, however, the principles are observed then normally it should be possible to obtain approval after a period in which the fine details are hammered out with the Revenue.

This means that a scheme can be explained to employees and put into **9–10** operation before formal approval is obtained—indeed it usually is—and it is not unknown for several years to elapse between establishment of the scheme and final approval.

The main principles are as follows.

— The scheme must be set up under irrevocable trusts.
— The benefits must conform with certain limits (detailed later in this chapter).
— The contributions must conform with certain limits (also detailed later in this chapter).
— Every member and every employee who has a right to be a member must be given written particulars of all essential features of the scheme which concern him.

The procedure for setting up a new scheme would typically be as follows. **9–11**

(a) A legal trust is established by the execution of an interim deed. This deed is usually fairly straightforward; among other things it appoints trustees, declares the existence and intentions of the trust, and declares that within a given period of time a definitive trust deed and full set of rules will be prepared which will qualify for approval by both the SFO and the OPB. Although straightforward, careful consideration should be given to the content of the interim deed. It should include powers to delegate, and a power of amendment. It should also ensure that disputes are avoided in the unfortunate event of a receiver or liquidator being appointed before the definitive deed is executed. For example, the disposal of surplus should be covered.

(b) A written announcement to prospective members is distributed and copies of this and the interim deed are submitted to the SFO and OPB.

(c) At the same time formal application for approval is made to the SFO. A prescribed form must be used for this purpose. The information required includes:

   (i) an actuarial report in the case of a directly invested scheme;
   (ii) membership statistics;
   (iii) the tax district(s) dealing with members' personal taxation and with the taxation of the employer(s);
   (iv) the names of those directors of sponsoring companies who will be eligible for membership;
   (v) information regarding any other schemes which cover the same employees.

(d) Tax relief is granted when a correctly completed application has been lodged (though "provisionally" pending formal approval) on the employees' contributions. Other reliefs will be granted only when formal approval has been allowed (*i.e.* when the final rules have been agreed) but will then be backdated to commencement.

9–12   Note that as far as the Inland Revenue is concerned any employee can join a scheme, including a director. However, there are some restrictions on the usual definition of final remuneration (used for the purposes of calculating maximum approvable benefits) in the case of any director (whether "controlling" or not) who has a substantial interest, broadly speaking 20 per cent. of the equity, in the company.

Note also that a single scheme can embrace a number of different benefit and contribution structures; in theory it is possible to have a different formula for every member.

Benefit limits

9–13 Inland Revenue limits vary depending on the date upon which an employee joins a scheme, subject to certain transitional arrangements, *e.g.* on the merger of schemes of the same employer.

A brief outline of the current limits for new entrants after June 1, 1989, where no transitional arrangements apply, is as follows.

Normal Pension Age	60–70 men; 55–70 women. (The Income and Corporation Taxes Act 1988 still discriminates against men in this context).
Maximum approvable pension at normal pension age	1/30th of final remuneration for each year of service, maximum 20/30ths. Overall initial maximum pension £40,000.* Final remuneration must be averaged over three years as far as fluctuating emoluments are concerned.
Maximum approval lump sum at normal pension age	2.25 times initial pension (before commutation or allocation). Maximum lump sum £90,000.* A lump sum cannot be paid in addition to the maximum pension–the maximum pension must be reduced by the pension equivalent of the lump sum.
Early Retirement	1/30th of final remuneration for each year of service, maximum 20/30ths or, if less, two-thirds of final remuneration less retained benefits from previous employments. Initial pension must not exceed £40,000.*
Leaving before retirement	There are restrictions on the maximum deferred benefits which can be granted to a member who leaves without becoming entitled to an immediate pension and for convenience these are explained in Chapter 35 on Preservation.
Late retirement	On retirement after normal pension age certain increases can be made to the maximum approvable pension and lump sum.
Surviving spouse's pension	On the death of a member the maximum approvable spouse's pension is two-thirds of the maximum approvable retirement pension for the member. If death occurs in service, the years between death and normal retirement date can be included in the calculation of the maximum approvable retirement pension.

Other pensions	Pensions can be paid to another dependant rather than to a spouse. Further, if there are two or more dependants (irrespective of whether one of them is a spouse) the limit is increased so as to equal the maximum approvable retirement pension for the member.
Lump sums for spouses and dependants	Except on conditions which are seldom attractive, lump sum payments are not allowed on the death of a pensioner (but pensions can be guaranteed for up to five years and any balance due on death paid as a lump sum). On death in service (before retirement age) a lump sum of four times salary (up to $4 \times £60,000^*$), can be paid in addition to a return of the members' contributions with interest (and also in addition to any spouse's or dependant's pension).
Cost of living increases	Automatic increases can be promised in line with increases in the cost of living as measured by the Retail Prices Index (RPI) published by the Department of Employment. The increases can be applied to the maximum pension, so a pension smaller than the maximum can be increased at a faster rate than the maximum.

Contribution limits

9–14 Members of a scheme may contribute directly in any year up to 15 per cent. of their earnings, on which full tax relief is granted, with earnings in this context restricted to a maximum of £60,000. (The £60,000* and the figures dependent upon it are increased annually in line with the RPI with some rounding up. For retirements and deaths in the tax year 1990/91 the figures above marked with an asterisk can be multiplied by 1.08).

There are no specific upper limits on contributions by the employer although at the other extreme and unlike the case of the employee, some contribution by the employer, and not merely a token one, is mandatory.

However, the only employer's contributions which attract tax relief without any doubt whatsoever are "ordinary annual contributions," *i.e.* those which the employer (with technical advice) expects will be required of him over a long period in order to finance the scheme. Usually "special contributions" can be made in addition, attracting immediate relief if they are not greater than the ordinary contributions in the same year or if they are made solely for the purpose of financing cost of living increases for existing pensioners. If larger special contributions are made, tax relief may be spread forward.

The liability of the scheme to tax

There are three areas in which those responsible for running an approved **9–15** pension scheme are likely to find themselves liable to tax. These are as follows.

(1) *Pensions*

All pensions payable from an exempt approved pension scheme are liable to tax as earned income and the person or body who pays the pension (whether this be the trustees, the employer, or the scheme's administrator) is responsible for applying PAYE and accounting for tax to the Inland Revenue.

(2) *Refunds of contributions*

When a member's contributions to an exempt approved scheme are refunded on leaving before retirement then tax is payable at the rate of 20 per cent. on the amount of refund due including any interest element. The tax has to be paid by the scheme administrator who may if the scheme rules permit make a corresponding deduction from the actual refund paid to the member.

(3) *Lump sum payments*

It is possible for schemes to commute pensions and pay out lump sums to members of amounts greater than those referred to earlier in this chapter if either

(a) the amount of the pension commuted is regarded by the SFO as "trivial" which at present (October 1990) means a pension of £2 (this is expected shortly to be increased to £5) a week or less; or

(b) the member's pension has been commuted in full on the grounds of exceptional circumstances of serious ill-health (which means that the member's expectation of life is unquestionably very short by comparison with the average for the same age and sex). At the time of writing (October 1990) this ill-health pension commutation facility is in doubt, especially for new entrants.

Broadly speaking, the amount of the lump sum which would otherwise have been paid if there had not been special circumstances is regarded as tax-free and the balance is chargeable to tax at the rate of 20 per cent. Again this has to be paid by the administrator of the scheme who may if the scheme rules permit make a corresponding deduction from the payment to the member.

Unapproved schemes

9–16 Employers may now provide benefits under schemes which are not approved by the Inland Revenue and (accordingly are not subject to the limitations and restrictions associated with approval including those referred to above) without prejudicing the tax exempt status of an approved scheme covering some of the same employees.

Such schemes could be useful, in particular to provide benefits where remuneration exceeds the indexed £60,000 per annum. The tax consequences of such schemes vary depending on whether the scheme is funded, or unfunded.

Unapproved funded schemes

9–17 Contributions made by employers for the provision of benefits in respect of an employee will be chargeable to tax in the hands of the employee in the year in which the contributions are paid. These employer contributions will qualify for relief against corporation tax.

No relief is allowed on employee contributions and it is anticipated that funded unapproved schemes will be non-contributory.

Benefits can be paid as a lump sum free of tax. However, any pensions paid will be taxed under Schedule E.

Investment income and indexed capital gains will be liable to income and capital gains taxes (at the standard rate if the scheme is appropriately set up).

9–18 Where the employer pays an identifiable amount towards the cost of instituting or administering an unapproved funded scheme, it will be a sponsored superannuation scheme for inheritance tax purposes. The effect of this is that the settlement charging provisions normally associated with trusts will not apply, and any lump sum death benefits payable at the discretion of the trustees will escape inheritance tax on the same basis as applies under approved schemes.

Unapproved Non-funded schemes

9–19 Benefits paid under unapproved non-funded schemes are taxable in the hands of the recipient under Schedule E. This includes pensions and lump sums payable on retirement or on death.

VAT

9–20 The application of VAT to funded pension schemes is as set out in the March 1983 H.M. Customs and Excise leaflet—700/17/53 Funded Pension Schemes. However, regard must be had to subsequent changes in the law.

The leaflet applies in cases where the contributions paid to the pension scheme are vested by trust in independent trustees who may be individuals or a corporate body (including the employer) in respect of supplies received on or after April 1, 1982.

This means that the employer, irrespective of whether the trustees are individuals or a corporate body, can claim input tax on the following items:

— Services in connection with the organisation and setting up of the scheme.
— Administration of the scheme (*e.g.* collection of contributions and payment of pensions).
— Advice on a review of the scheme.
— Implementing changes in the trust deed including drafting deeds and other legal instruments.
— Advice on the management of the scheme.
— Accounting and auditing services.
— Periodic actuarial valuations.
— Appraisal of investment performance.
— Other actuarial advice in connection with the scheme's administration.

In order to claim input tax on the above items, the employer must hold **9–21** the tax invoices in his own name from the supplier of the service. Thus, if the trustees pay for the supplies on the employer's behalf, the invoices must still be made out in the employer's name.

Any VAT on investment advice, brokerage charges and all other services relating to the acquisition, exploitation or disposal of assets, trustees' services (*i.e.* services of a professional trustee in managing the assets of the scheme) and any other services rendered to the trustees for their business as trustee to the scheme, cannot be treated as the employer's input tax even if those expenses are paid by the employer.

CHAPTER 35

PRESERVATION ✓

9–22 Under the Social Security Act 1973, occupational pension schemes are required to provide preserved pensions for employees leaving service. The Social Security Act 1990, extends these provisions to cover all circumstances in which pensionable service terminates. Thus, ceasing to be eligible on promotion and electing to opt-out of the employer's scheme will be included.

When first introduced in 1975, preservation applied to employees who had completed five years' pensionable service, and attained the age of 26. It now applies to employees on completion of two years' pensionable service.

9–23 Entitlement to a preserved pension means entitlement to a pension payable from the scheme's normal pension age, calculated on the same basis as applies to an employee who remains in service but related, in a final salary scheme, to earnings at the date pensionable service ends and pensionable service is completed. In a money purchase scheme the leaver with a preserved benefit is entitled to receive bonuses or investment returns on his accumulated account in the same way as a continuing member.

9–24 Various alternatives to "short service benefit," as the preserved benefits are called, are permitted. These include a reduced pension starting before normal pension age, an increased pension starting later, and a transfer to another scheme. It should be noted however that the alternatives are optional and accordingly depend on whether or not the occupational scheme contains the relevant provisions. Refunds of contributions are not permitted as an alternative, and accordingly this benefit can only be offered to employees with less than two years' pensionable service. However, under transitional arrangements made when the requirements were first introduced in 1975, employees who paid contributions before that date retain the right to take a refund of such contributions on leaving service. Again, it should be noted that provision for refunds is optional, and accordingly depends on whether the scheme rules permit it.

9–25 The benefits which must be preserved are the personal pension for the employee or accumulated account in a money purchase scheme, and any benefits payable, for example to a surviving spouse or dependant, on death after normal pension age. Where an employee is entitled to receive full benefits on a date earlier than normal pension age, otherwise than under special provisions for early retirement, his preserved benefits must be payable from the earlier date, but not earlier than the age of 60.

Where benefits, for example for past service, are improved, there are special provisions under which entitlement to the improvement for subsequent leavers can be calculated by reference to the proportion which their period of pensionable service completed after the improvement, bears to the period which would have been completed had they stayed until normal pension age.

Under the requirements, a member who leaves a scheme with preserved **9–26** benefits, and who rejoins the scheme, becomes entitled immediately to preserved benefits in respect of his subsequent period of service and does not have to satisfy the two years' qualifying period again. Under provisions dealing with short breaks in pensionable service, any break of less than one month is ignored, and where the break is a period of maternity leave, schemes must aggregate the period before the break with any period after the employee returns to work. This will determine whether the two years' qualifying period has been completed, if the employee subsequently leaves.

In order to ensure that the early leaver is not prejudiced, schemes must not contain any provision which results or could result in a member being treated less favourably in respect of his preserved benefits, than he would have been treated if he had remained in pensionable service.

In certain circumstances, scheme rules may provide for employees to **9–27** cease to be entitled to preserved benefits. For example, the rules may provide for an employer to be compensated in respect of any loss caused to him by any criminal, negligent, or fraudulent act or omission of the employee. An "employer's lien" rule is not however permitted to prejudice entitlement to guaranteed minimum pensions, or protected rights benefits for contracting-out purposes, and any benefits transferred in from another employer's scheme must still be preserved.

The preservation requirements were the first attempt to protect rights **9–28** under occupational schemes in respect of members who leave service. The provisions have been modified substantially since their introduction in 1975. The provisions are complicated and this chapter gives a simple outline of the main provisions. The rights of the early leaver have been considerably reinforced since 1975, with the introduction of mandatory increases in preserved benefits, and the right to a transfer to another occupational scheme, or to a personal pension scheme.

CHAPTER 36

SOCIAL SECURITY

Background

9–29 The current system of Social Security has developed somewhat piecemeal during the present century. The first old age pension was introduced in 1908; various other benefits followed and in 1925 we saw for the first time universal pensions payable without a means test (subject, however, to a contribution record).

A new scheme was born under the National Insurance Act 1946, as a result of the Beveridge Report of 1942, although some of the major principles of the Report were overturned in the Act. This scheme was wide-ranging in its application and it rationalised various existing arrangements but its main feature as far as this book is concerned was the retirement pension. This again was universal, subject to a contribution record, and the pension was 26s. a week for a single person and 42s. a week for a married couple. This was financed (along with some ancillary benefits) by a compulsory contribution (the National Insurance Stamp). The contribution was at the level of 9s. 1d. for employed persons, of which the employer paid 4s. 2d. and the employee 4s. 11d., and 6s. 2d. for the self-employed. The Exchequer boosted the contributions directly, from general taxation, to the tune of 18 per cent.

9–30 Although there was and still is a National Insurance Fund which receives most of the contributions and pays most of the benefit, there is not and never has been any "fund" in the normal sense. The Government Actuary's involvement is as a demographer rather than as an adviser on actuarial soundness or equity or insurance principles. Indeed the so-called "insurance principle" often referred to is now widely recognised as a myth. It has always been a myth, even in 1948, because benefits and contributions were never dependent on age or other relevant factors in any manner (apart from some arbitrary division as to sex). The "right to benefits" as a result of a contribution record has always been an ideology rather than a demonstrable fact. In truth the contributions at any time are determined largely by a consideration of what is required to cover the benefit outgo at that time.

9–31 The benefit outgo has increased substantially over the years, due largely to higher rates of benefit and a greater weight of pensions, from some £400 millions in 1950 to some £20,000 millions in 1982/83. In 1989/90 contributory benefits alone cost £30 billion. Until 1961 these increases were covered by corresponding increases in the flat National Insurance Stamps (and in the Exchequer's contributions) but it was then felt by the Government that the practical limits of this procedure were approaching. Accordingly an additional earnings related contribution was introduced in 1961. It was also felt that these additional contributions should carry a right to additional benefits (despite the fact that the contributions were going straight towards paying for the flat pension) and so the "Boyd-Carpenter Graduated Scheme" was born. The additional contributions levied were originally $8\frac{1}{2}$ per cent. of earnings between £9 and £15 a week, in respect of employed persons only, and they were shared equally between employer and employee, with each £15 (for men) or £18 (for women) of contribution securing an eventual pension of 6d. ($2\frac{1}{2}$p) per week. An employer could choose to "contract-out" of this Graduated Scheme and to pay a somewhat higher flat stamp.

The benefit outgo continued to soar, however, and further increases **9–32** were made over the years in both the flat and graduated elements, with all except the first of the increases in the Graduated Scheme being compulsory rather than optional. Thus, by 1975 the maximum total graduated contributions in respect of an employed person had risen from 51p per week to £5.82, while the maximum reduction in total contributions, by "contracting-out," was 60p per week.

In the early 1970's the Government felt once more, as benefits continued to rise, that changes were required and the Social Security Act 1973 brought about the cessation of the Graduated Scheme in April 1975. The Act provided for another scheme, the State Reserve Scheme, but after a change of Government in 1974, this part of the Act was repealed. It also introduced the "preservation" requirements for occupational schemes. These survive and are discussed in Chapter 35.

In addition, the Social Security Act 1973, with effect from April 1975, **9–33** took a step towards official recognition of the mythological character of the "insurance principle" and what is effectively a payroll tax was introduced, instead of the flat stamp, to finance the major part of the flat benefits (the rest continuing to come directly from the Exchequer). The total payroll tax was 14 per cent. of earnings up to £69 per week, of which $8\frac{1}{2}$ per cent. was paid by the employer and $5\frac{1}{2}$ per cent. by the employee, with the main benefit a retirement pension of £11.60 per week for a single person and £18.50 per week for a married couple (subject to an appropriate contribution record). At the same time a self-employed person became liable to pay an earnings related tax, equal to 8 per cent. of earnings between £1,600 and £3,600 per annum, in addition to a flat stamp of £2.41 per week. Increases in these figures have taken place since April 1975.

This system is still in force, but the new Government soon enacted **9–34** further large changes, in the Social Security Pensions Act 1975, providing for additional earnings-related benefits and contributions effective from April 6, 1978. This Act, along with remnants of earlier legislation consolidated in the Social Security Act 1975, forms the main state Social Security provision in this country as far as pensions are concerned.

The main features of this legislation as it affects pensions (and other benefits which are generally accepted as part of a pension arrangement) are described below. Persons are classified as Class 1, 2 or 3, the respective statuses being employed, self-employed, and non-employed. (There is also a

Class 4 contributor, who for all practical purposes is the same as a Class 2 contributor.)

The present position

9–35 Very broadly, there is a two-tier structure, the first tier compulsory and featuring a flat benefit financed by earnings-related contributions, and the second tier optional, being fully earnings related on both sides. However, the complex interaction between the two militates against separate treatment. Thus, it is unfortunately necessary to look at both tiers together before considering the option to "contract-out" of part of the benefits and contributions.

Contributions

9–36 The main feature of the contribution system is that it is earnings related. No contributions are required from those earning less than the lower earnings limit which is currently (April 1990) £46 per week and which in practice is altered by regulations every April. Contributions by the employer for those earning more than this figure range from five per cent. in respect of earnings from £46 to £79.99 a week to 10.45 per cent. in respect of earnings of £175 a week and higher. Employees' weekly contributions, for those earning more than £46 a week, are two per cent. of £46 plus nine per cent. of that part of weekly earnings which exceeds £46 but does not exceed £350 (the upper limit for employees).

As will be seen later, contracting-out reduces these contributions, on earnings between the lower and upper limits by two per cent. for employees, and 3.8 per cent. for employers.

Self-employed persons pay a flat weekly contribution of £4.55 under Class 2, plus 6.3 per cent. of any earnings between (presently) £5,450 and £18,200 a year, under Class 4.

Those not coming into any of the above categories, *e.g.* the unemployed, may if they wish pay (presently) £4.55 a week to fulfil the requirements regarding a contribution record in order to qualify for benefits.

Benefits—retirement pension

9–37 The main benefit from the scheme is a retirement pension. This is in two parts, the first being a flat pension (April 1990 to March 1991, £46.90 a week; from April 1991 to March 1992, £52 a week) which is roughly equal to the lower earnings limit. The second pension (applicable only to employed persons) is earnings related and for employees retiring up to the year 2000 is equal to $1\frac{1}{4}$ per cent. of the total pay between the lower and upper limits earned in the best 20 years prior to retirement (and after the start of the scheme in 1978). In other words, anyone contributing to the scheme for at least 20 years, will receive annually as his second pension one quarter of his average pay between the two limits during his best 20 years. For employees retiring after the year 2000, the pension will be progressively reduced over the succeeding 10 years to 1/5th of average pay.

There is however a system of "index linking" designed to compensate for the decline in the purchasing power of money. The first element in this system is that the pensions then in force—both the flat part and the earnings related part—are reviewed annually by the Secretary of State in relation to his estimate of the general movement of prices and, provided Parliament approves, a corresponding increase is made each year.

Secondly the earnings related pensions accrued, but not yet in force, are **9–38** reviewed similarly in relation to earnings.

This retirement pension is available, subject to certain contribution conditions, from the age of 65 (men) and 60 (women). Alternatively, the pension can be deferred until full retirement, though not beyond the age of 70 (men) or 65 (women), in which case it will be payable at an enhanced level.

The retirement pension is available to all who qualify according to their **9–39** contribution record. For a married couple the first component is increased so that their combined total is not less than a certain figure (from April 1990 to March 1991, £75.10 a week; from April 1991 to March 1992, £83.25 a week).

We now come to ancillary benefits, and only those normally considered part of a pension scheme are described.

Dependant's pension—death in retirement

On the death of a married male pensioner before the year 2000, the first **9–40** component of his state pension (without the increase for a married couple, referred to above) is payable to his widow for life, along with an amount equal to his second component pension.

However if the widow is receiving a State pension herself, based upon her own career, this will be reduced where necessary to ensure that (a) her total "first component" pension does not exceed the full rate of a single person's first component pension (currently £46.90 a week), and (b) her total second component pension similarly does not exceed the maximum possible single person's second component pension (*i.e.* that payable to an earner whose earnings have always been at the upper limit).

Similar provisions apply to a widower except that he must have been over age 65 (or an invalid) when his wife died.

Where death occurs after the year 2000 the additional pension payable to the widow or widower of a pensioner will be one-half of the calculated rate.

Dependant's pension—death in service

The benefits payable to a widow on the death of her husband before pen- **9–41** sionable age depend on her age at that time. Where the widow is under the age of 45 with no dependent child, she receives the lump sum widow's payment of £1,000. If the widow is over 45 but under 60, with no dependent child, she receives the widow's payment and a widow's pension. A widow under 60, with a dependent child receives the widow's payment, and a widowed mother's allowance.

Statutory sick pay schemes

9–42 A statutory sick pay scheme, which covers most employees, started on April 6, 1983. Briefly, statutory sick pay is now paid by an employer if an employee is absent through sickness for four or more consecutive days, and continues for up to 28 weeks of illness, not necessarily consecutive, in any one tax year. Employers are able to recover the gross amount of any statutory sick pay they pay by offsetting it against the payment of National Insurance contributions. Thus, in essence, the Government has put upon the employer the responsibility of administering the short term sickness provisions.

Chapter 37

CONTRACTING-OUT—THE LEGISLATION

In Chapter 36 we considered the State scheme in its totality. Not all of it is **9–43** compulsory, however, and in this chapter we consider that part from which it is possible to "contract-out." It should be noted that contracting-out is available only in respect of Class 1 contributors, *i.e.* employed persons.

Reduction in contributions

By contracting-out, the contributions payable to the State scheme by the **9–44** employee and employer are reduced by 2.0 per cent. and 3.8 per cent. (of earnings between £46 and £350 a week) respectively (figures applicable at September 1990).

It should be recognised that an employee's contributions to an approved occupational scheme qualify for tax relief whereas those to the State scheme do not.

The total rebate on contracting-out is intended to reduce in the future for technical and demographic reasons. It has already come down from 7 per cent. in 1978 to 5.8 per cent. with effect from 1988 and is likely to be just below 3.5 per cent. by the year 2027 when all contributors will have become subject to the Social Security Pensions Act 1975 from the youngest possible age (16).

Reduction in benefit

A person who participates in the State earnings related pension scheme is **9–45** entitled to the additional earnings related pension, including increases during payment in line with increases in the RPI.

A contracted-out person is similarly entitled, but the amount is reduced by his guaranteed minimum pension (see below). This includes increases in the guaranteed minimum pension during payment at a maximum of three per cent. per annum compound, in respect of any part of the guaranteed minimum pension accruing after April 5, 1988.

Similarly, a deduction equal to the widow's guaranteed minimum pension is deducted from the widow's additional pension under the State scheme. The amount so deducted includes increases in the widow's guaranteed minimum pension accrued since April 5, 1988, at the maximum rate of three per cent. per annum compound.

Since its inception in 1978, a number of changes have been made in the **9–46** conditions for contracting-out. Originally schemes had to provide the better of the guaranteed minimum pension and either a final salary benefit calculated as 1/80th of final pensionable pay for each year of contracted-out employment, or an average salary revalued benefit, similar to the guaranteed minimum pension. These alternative minimum requirements have been dropped, and schemes contracted-out on a defined benefit basis need only guarantee that benefits will not be less than the guaranteed minimum.

The conditions for contracting-out—Schemes providing "Guaranteed Minimum Pensions"

9–47 It is possible to contract-out of the State scheme's additional earnings related component if the employee is a member of an occupational scheme which provides pensions broadly speaking not less than those which would otherwise have been payable from the additional earnings related component of the State scheme. These are known as the "Guaranteed Minimum Pensions" or GMPs for short.

Early leavers

9–48 If a contracted-out member leaves an occupational pension scheme before retirement, then steps must be taken to secure the guaranteed minimum pension which the member has earned during his period of contracted-out service.

If the member is able to take a refund of his own contributions, then the GMP liability can be transferred back to the State by a payment to the State scheme of a sum equal to the total amount by which the contributions of the member and his employer have been reduced because the member was contracted-out. This sum is known as the "Contributions Equivalent Premium" or CEP for short. A CEP can also be paid where the member becomes entitled to a deferred pension provided the period of contracted-out service is less than two years and provided the preservation provisions of the Social Security Act 1973 do not operate.

If the member joins a new employer who also runs a contracted-out scheme then the GMP liability may be transferred to the new scheme by payment of a suitable transfer value.

9–49 If, however, the member becomes entitled on leaving a scheme to a deferred pension and a CEP is not paid then the GMP has to be preserved within the scheme. This GMP must be protected against inflation during the period up to State pension age and there are three options available.

   (i) To increase the pension fully in line with increases in earnings in accordance with orders made each year under Section 21 of the Social Security Pensions Act 1975.
   (ii) To pay a special premium to the State scheme known as a "Limited Revaluation Premium" which allows the scheme to limit its increases to five per cent. per annum.
   (iii) To elect for the GMP to be increased at a fixed rate of $7\frac{1}{2}$ per cent. per annum regardless of the level of inflation.

Buy back facility

It is possible for a contracted-out scheme to cease to be contracted-out pro- **9–50** vided that the appropriate consultation with any recognised trade unions is carried out. A scheme would also cease to be contracted-out if it had to be wound up. In either case there are special provisions for buying back the GMP liabilities into the State scheme and in particular there are two important safeguards. First, the revaluation of GMPs over the preceding five years can be limited to 12 per cent. per annum. Secondly, the premiums which have to be paid to the State scheme, in order to buy back in, vary according to market conditions, thus protecting schemes against sudden falls in the market value of their investments.

Schemes providing protected rights benefits

Since April 1988 schemes have been permitted to adopt an alternative **9–51** money purchase contracting-out test.

An amount equal to the reduction in National Insurance contributions must be applied on a money purchase basis to provide pensions known as "protected rights benefits" for the contracted-out employee and any surviving spouse.

Certain newly contracted-out employees included in a new scheme may qualify for a special incentive payment in respect of the period from April 1987 to April 1993, of two per cent. of earnings between the lower and upper earnings limit. This incentive payment is made by the Government to encourage contracting-out, and must also be used to provide protected rights benefits.

In the case of an employee entitled to protected rights benefits in respect **9–52** of any period of contracted-out employment, the deduction from his additional pension under the State Scheme for the same period will be equal to his guaranteed minimum pension. Depending on investment performance, and prevailing annuity rates when his pension is bought, his protected rights benefits for the period could be less than or more than his guaranteed minimum pension. The age of the employee is also a crucial factor, and contracting-out on a money purchase basis is not considered advantageous for older employees; that is for men over about the age of 45, and for women over about the age of 40.

The above is a bare outline of the contracting-out conditions. Fuller details are set out in the various OPB memoranda which are issued from time to time.

CHAPTER 38

CONTRACTING-OUT—THE DECISION

9–53 Employers sponsoring schemes in existence in 1978 had to consider whether their employees in the scheme should be contracted-out of the State earnings related pension scheme (SERPS) or not. Some 90 per cent. of occupational scheme members at the time were in fact contracted-out. The corresponding percentage of schemes themselves was something like 75 per cent. This reflected the fact that smaller schemes were less likely to have contracted-out their members initially. Most of the schemes which initially contracted-out have remained contracted-out where the scheme still exists.

9–54 Since 1978 there have been substantial changes and revisions in the contracting-out terms. In 1983 the contracting-out rebate was reviewed for the first time. The rebate is reviewed every five years. At the second review, in 1988, substantial changes were made to the terms of the market level indicators and also the facility to contract-out of SERPS on a protected rights/money purchase basis was introduced. It also became possible to contract-out of SERPS by means of a minimum-contribution-only personal pension scheme while at the same time remaining in an occupational pension scheme.

The Government also offered an extra incentive rebate for newly contracted-out occupational schemes which are defined as schemes contracting-out for the first time after January 1, 1986. The extra incentive rebate was to apply from April 6, 1988 to April 5, 1993. It was always vital that the contracted-out decision should be kept under review.

9–55 The above changes have made it necessary to reconsider the decision every five years. In addition newly established schemes have to make the decision for the first time. Due to the changes and new options introduced since 1978, the decision has become more complicated. Expert advice was needed in 1978 and the situation today is certainly no different as regards such need.

The basis on which the decision must be made includes the financial implication as regards cost and future risks. This latter item includes consideration of the financial terms for reinstatement back into SERPS should the scheme at a later stage cease to be contracted-out. Other matters to be included are the implications for administration and benefit design. In the rest of this chapter we discuss the above matters in the context of how they affect the actual decision to contract-out and the method chosen.

Financial considerations
GMP contracted-out schemes

9–56 GMP contracting-out is fundamentally an arrangement where the amount of the rebate in National Insurance contributions is invested in an occupational scheme. In return the employer promises to provide a certain level of benefit, the guaranteed minimum pension, to contracted-out members. The alternative is for the employer and employee to pay full National Insurance contributions with the amount of the rebate going to the State. Therefore the first financial effect to consider is how the amount of the rebate may best be invested. The decision can be viewed as a comparison between investing in the State and investing privately. The basic question is whether by investing the rebate an occupational pension scheme can securely provide the guaranteed minimum pensions it is promising.

When investing to provide guaranteed minimum pensions, the important factor regarding investment return is the real return available over earnings (not prices). Over a long period increases in earnings have fairly consistently outpaced increases in prices by about two per cent. per annum.

The table below shows some approximate figures for the yields obtained **9–57** by investing in cash on deposit, fixed interest United Kingdom Government stocks and equities, over periods ending with December 31, 1988.

Data Summary
Average return to 1988 over stated period

Period (years)	Gilts	UK Equity	Overseas Equity	Cash	Property	Earnings	Prices
1	9.4	11.6	30.6	10.1	30.2	7.9	6.8
2	12.8	9.8	9.0	10.0	23.7	8.2	5.2
3	12.4	15.4	18.6	10.4	16.9	7.8	4.7
4	12.1	16.7	17.0	11.0	14.4	7.6	5.0
5	11.2	19.5	19.8	10.9	13.0	7.4	4.9
10	14.5	21.3	16.3	12.5	13.8	9.8	7.9
15	14.3	19.0	13.9	11.9	11.2	11.6	10.4
25	8.8	14.3	n/a	10.1	n/a	10.7	8.7

Equities have been the best of these investments. The main reason has **9–58** been the underlying growth in equity dividends as company profits have increased. Depending on timing, investment in overseas equities and sometimes property have shown similar results as investment in United Kingdom equities. There have been periods when the erosion of the value of money has severely hit investments fixed in money terms, like cash or gilts. However in recent years a real rate of return has been available even on these investments. All in all it would seem most appropriate to take the view that at least a small positive real rate of return will be available in the long term.

The rebate percentage is applied to the band of earnings between the **9–59** upper and lower earnings limit. The rebate has been reduced at each of the quinquennial reviews. From April 1978 to April 1983 it was seven per cent., from April 1983 to April 1988 it was 6¼ per cent. and from April 1988 to April 1993 it is 5.8 per cent. The rebate from 1988 onwards takes into account the fact that the occupational pension scheme now has to provide index linking on post-1988 GMPs whilst in payment up to a limit of three per cent. per annum. This increase in cost was compensated for by the GMP accrual rate being cut back.

9–60 As an illustration of the effect of the real rate of return, we set out below what the raw rebate would be for an average scheme based on different real rates of return and different interest rates. These are the figures that would have been applicable from April 1988. The actual 5.8 per cent. rebate include a 0.4 per cent. margin above the Government Actuary's raw calculated figure.

Rebate required by average scheme

Real return	1%	$1\frac{1}{2}$%	2%
Interface rate			
7%	6.1	5.6	5.2
$8\frac{1}{2}$%	5.3	4.9	4.5
10%	4.6	4.2	3.9

As can be seen from the above the real rate of return above earnings assumed is crucial. A one per cent. difference in the real rate of return can make a difference of the order of one percentage point in the rebate required to meet the benefits. However with the extra 0.4 per cent. granted this time, apart from the most pessimistic combination of assumptions, the actual rebate is higher for each example shown than that required for the average scheme. This is before any further two per cent. incentive for a newly contracted-out scheme is taken into account.

9–61 Another factor that emerges from the table is that the absolute level of return is also important. This is because GMPs are not totally inflation-linked after retirement. Pre-1988 the occupational pension scheme did not have to increase any GMP in payment. Now any GMP accruing after April 5, 1988 has to be increased each year by the lesser of the rises in the RPI or three per cent. The effect of this is that the higher the rate of interest earned post retirement, the easier it is for a scheme to provide the GMP Naturally the converse is also true. The point is demonstrated by the cost of immediate annuities which is less at times of high interest rates and more at times of low long term yields.

9–62 As usual in actuarial calculations regarding pension schemes, the interest rate assumed means the expected total return for the future, *i.e.* both income and capital appreciation. At the time of writing (October 1990) one can buy fixed annuities on the basis of the yield from about 11 per cent. to $11\frac{1}{2}$ per cent. per annum. However if the rate of inflation were brought down then absolute rates of interest would fall, both short and long term. The cost of providing GMPs would then rise significantly even if the real rate of return remained undiminished.

9–63 Another vital factor in the decision is the actual age and earnings distribution of the scheme membership. This affects the actual level and value of

GMPs which the particular scheme is undertaking to provide. The rebate has been decided by considering this question in approximate terms over the whole population of both sexes in contracted-out schemes. Generally it is cheaper to provide a GMP for a younger member than an older one and also cheaper to provide the benefit for a man than for a woman. The reasons for these differences in cost derive primarily from the different rates of accrual of GMPs and the different State pension ages for men and women combined with the expected greater longevity of women.

As the distribution of members with regard to earnings, sex and age dif- **9–64** fers between different employers the effect or rebate required will vary. A difference which arises just from age alone can cause a significant difference in the underlying cost of providing the guaranteed minimum pension.

Originally the accrual of GMPs varies from 1/80th for those men born **9–65** before April 5, 1933 and women born before April 5, 1938 to 1/196ths for those men born after April 5, 1962. In 1988 GMP accrual rates were reduced by 20 per cent. so the maximum rate of accrual for post-1988 GMPs is now 1/100th. The variation with age in the cost of providing a GMP does in fact derive primarily from these different accrual rates and the different period over which a real rate of return is earned prior to retirement. This makes the age distribution of members of a scheme of vital importance. An individual conclusion needs to be drawn for each scheme.

To give further encouragement to employers to contract their employees **9–66** out of SERPS the Government decided to offer an extra incentive for a period of five years. The incentive is received by those occupational pension schemes contracted-out for the first time on or after January 1, 1986. The scheme receives the incentive for any employees who have not been previously contracted-out by another scheme of the employer. There are also further complicated rules which restrict the receipt of the incentive in certain cases. The purpose of these rules is to stop abuse of the incentive being claimed where it was not intended to be received. The incentive is an extra two per cent. of earnings between the upper and lower earnings limit. Accordingly there are very few new schemes with an age distribution which would currently on pure cost grounds justify the employees all remaining contracted-in.

We turn now to the longer term risks involved in contracting-out. Look- **9–67** ing ahead there could be changes to the State scheme and to the partnership between State and occupational pension schemes. In practice such changes did occur in 1988. SERPS pension accruals were cut back and there was a substantial change in the contracting-out terms. There was also a fundamental change in the way market level indicators for State scheme premiums were calculated.

Prior to 1988 market level indicators were decided by just looking at the **9–68** current yields on equities and long term gilts. Because market levels had risen dramatically through the mid-1980s the Government argued that occupational pension schemes had a substantial advantage by contracting-out. It decided to claw back some of this advantage if a scheme subsequently contracted back in. As a result the basis of the market level indicators was changed in 1988 so that in practice (if there had been a substantial improvement in market levels over the period the scheme had been contracted-out) some of this investment gain would be paid back in increased State scheme premiums on a scheme's ceasing to be contracted-out.

9–69   Existence of a buy-back facility through the use of the State scheme premiums was originally meant to be a safeguard against the fundamental risks involved in contracting-out. In a sense this safeguard is still there. Even in 1988 the Government had to give notice of the changes then made. There was a time when, if the employer was not happy with the new terms for contracting-out and the new buy back terms, he could have bought back into the State scheme before the change.

9–70   Another form of risk is the possibility of a substantial deterioration in financial conditions. This is more likely than a sudden change in the structure of contracting-out. This leads us to a second safeguard. The buy-back premiums are tied to market levels and this offers some protection. In addition there is a facility to limit the section 21 order to 12 per cent. for the last five years prior to ceasing to be contracted-out. This protects the scheme's contracted-out liabilities or buy back terms from a period of excessive high earnings inflation not matched by an increase in investment return.

9–71   For a particular scheme the underlying rebate necessary to provide the GMP could be calculated for a particular set of assumptions, *i.e.* investment returns, earnings inflation, turnover and mortality. All these factors could be projected and evaluated by the actuary in the same way as when he arrives at a funding rate for the occupational scheme. However there is a subtle difference between a funding rate and an estimation of the cost of providing guaranteed minimum pensions. The cost of being wrong in an occupational scheme does not normally affect the long term benefits paid out and could be corrected from valuation to valuation. However if the contracting-out decision is based on a false estimate the loss or gain is a true one which cannot be reversed. Although the scheme could pay State scheme premiums, thus giving the liability for guaranteed minimum pensions back to the State, the scheme will still have made a loss or gain compared with the position if the employees had never been contracted-out and participated in SERPS in the first place.

9–72   Another factor affecting the cost of contracting-out is the tax relief available on employees' contributions to approved occupational pension schemes. Tax relief is not available on National Insurance contributions to the State scheme.

It should be noted that GMP contracting-out involves the employer in financial loss or gain compared with his employees participating in SERPS. In the next few paragraphs we discuss money purchase contracting-out. Here any gain in contracting-out is passed to the employee by higher benefits being provided than those granted by the State. The converse is of course also true. If on an individual basis the employee's age is too old to justify contracting-out, then he will receive lower benefits than if he had remained in SERPS throughout.

Financial considerations—money purchase contracting-out/protected rights

The financial basis of protected rights contracting-out is completely differ- **9–73** ent from that attaching to GMP contracting-out. The Government felt that although many large to medium employers had contracted-out many small employers let their employees remain in SERPS. The Government wanted to encourage private pension provision and stated itself to be concerned about the emerging costs of SERPS early in the next century. The Government felt that the guarantees involved in G.M.P. contracting-out were a disincentive to the smaller employer. Under money purchase contracting-out the rebate and any two per cent. incentive due is notionally held separately as part of the member's fund on a money purchase basis (called protected rights).

There are rules as to how this accumulated money must be applied in different contingencies. At the age of 60 or later retirement the accumulated money must be used to provide a pension or purchase an annuity escalating at the lesser of three per cent. per annum or the rise in the RPI. A contingent widow's or widower's pension of one half the member's pension must attach to this pension on death after retirement. On death in service the protected rights fund has to be used to provide a pension for the widow or widower. If there is no spouse a dependant's pension can be provided or the protected rights fund can be paid out as a lump sum.

As can be seen there are no financial risks for the employer in money **9–74** purchase contracting-out: as mentioned earlier it is the member who accrues any financial gain or loss. The flat rate rebate for contracting-out remains the same regardless of age so a young member can have a substantial financial gain by contracting-out of SERPS on a money purchase basis. Members nearer pension age on the other hand would receive less benefit from contracting-out than if they remain in SERPS. The cross-over ages are round about 45 for men and 40 for women.

The charts on page 234 (figure 11) gives estimated ages at which it is **9–75** beneficial for the contracted-out employee to "rejoin" SERPS, or cease to be contracted-out. The estimates were calculated using the assumptions set out by the Life Assurance and Unit Trust Regulatory Organisation (LAUTRO) for controlling quotations on benefits from personal pension schemes. LAUTRO gave two sets of assumptions and we have used the more optimistic set. The principal elements of it are a 13 per cent. per annum investment return and a 10 per cent. rate of salary increase.

Before money purchase contracting-out was permitted all members in **9–76** any given category of employment in a scheme had to be contracted-out or not contracted-out, regardless of age or sex. From 1988 onwards an employer could in practice elect to contract-out those employees who opted at their own choice to join the contracted-out section of the scheme. This is a very useful facility in a protected rights scheme because above the cross-over ages it is increasingly in the member's interest to cease to be contracted-out and to participate in SERPS.

The Government has introduced some simple investment restrictions for **9–77** the money purchase contracted-out scheme, because the benefit the mem-

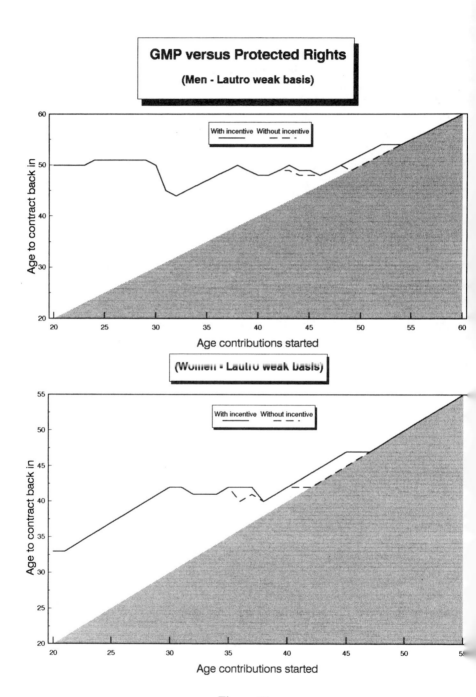

Figure 11

ber receives depends so much on the investment return and the benefit is a substitute for a State benefit. The restrictions are not onerous and can be easily complied with by a middle of the road investment policy. There are restrictions concerning concentration of investment in any particular security. Investment in the employer is limited to no more than 10 per cent. of the scheme's resources. This might be changed by the regulations under the Social Security Act 1990. These restrictions can only be viewed as reasonable, bearing in mind that the benefit is a substitute for a SERPS benefit and that, if the investments fail, the individual might fall back on the social security system.

Administration—G.M.P. contracted-out schemes

As indicated in Chapter 39, running a GMP contracted-out scheme **9–78** involves an increase in administration. This factor should be taken into account when considering the basic decision to contract-out or not. To enable the smooth operation of a GMP contracted-out scheme it is essential that second tier National Insurance contributions are recorded or alternatively the relevant earnings factor based on those contributions. This enables the administrator to calculate any guaranteed minimum pensions without recourse to the contracting-out group of the D.S.S. Also a great deal more form filling is required for any contracted-out scheme when a member leaves, transfers his rights elsewhere, dies in service or retires.

The small to medium sized scheme can consider the use of a computerised administration package to help solve these problems.

Administration—protected rights

In addition to the form filling for early leavers and retirements there is an **9–79** additional complication for schemes contracted-out on a money purchase basis. One of the requirements of money purchase contracting-out is that the employer pays the employer and employee share of the National Insurance contribution rebate (*i.e.* minimum contributions) to the trustees of the occupational pension scheme by the 19th day of the month following the one in which the contributions are due. If the employer has several pay sites he needs to impose a strict discipline to ensure that this condition is met. If the deadline were regularly missed, the Occupational Pensions Board could withdraw the contracting-out certificate.

Another problem in contracting-out on a money purchase basis is that it **9–80** is not possible to pay a contributions equivalent premium for leavers with less than two years' service. For these individuals protected rights must remain in the scheme, or can be transferred to another scheme, or used to buy a section 32 policy or personal pension. However unless the member agrees to the transfer, or requests a transfer in the first place, the trustees could end up administering quite small money purchase funds for a long period.

As with any money purchase scheme, the administration of a money purchase contracted-out scheme requires great discipline. In a final salary scheme the ultimate benefit does not depend on the prompt investment of monies. The prompt investment of monies just saves the employer cost in that the investment return is earned sooner. But in a money purchase scheme investment delays directly affect the member's ultimate pension.

Integration with the State scheme

9–81   One of the initial problems involved in the decision to contract-in or out is the complicated nature of the SERPS pensions. If a scheme wants to contract-in and cut back the benefit levels by exactly the amount of SERPS benefits, as much administration is involved in the operation as is involved in contracting-out. In addition the ultimate benefit formula would be so complicated few members would understand it. This factor tipped the balance towards many employers initially contracting-out in 1978. This factor is also involved in why many existing contracted-out schemes have remained contracted-out. For new final salary schemes it remains true to say that the easiest way to integrate one's pension provision with SERPS is to contract-out of it. A further factor is that in practice good real returns on investments have been achieved.

9–82   It is sometimes argued that the contracted-out scheme cannot be flexible enough when it comes to early retirement and pension commutation (the guaranteed minimum pension has to be paid in pension form and cannot be commuted). If a member retires early the pension in payment when State pension age is reached has to be at least the guaranteed minimum pension. This might restrict the age at which early retirement can be permitted or the cash sum that can be taken on early retirement. But if the scheme is not contracted-out then presumably the relevant pensions (and amount of pension commutation) would be cut back appropriately.

9–83   Early retirement is a greater problem in a scheme which has been contracted-out on a money purchase basis. The current rules require that protected rights cannot be taken earlier than the age of 60. However, pensions from SERPS cannot be taken earlier than State pension age.

9–84   With money purchase contracting-out available (and with the availability of contracting-out via a minimum contribution-only personal pension) an employer wishing to operate a contracted-in occupational pension scheme can do so without his employees losing the opportunity to contract-out via another vehicle. It makes sense for younger members of contracted-in occupational schemes to contract out using a minimum contribution-only personal pension.

Political considerations

9–85   Governments have promised generous State pensions with nothing more to back that promise than the expectation that future generations will pay for them. This may not be so. The security of a separate pool of assets has to be worth something. If the State later goes back on its promise, and this happened for future accrual in 1988, then those employees in a contracted-out scheme backed by a separate well funded pool of assets will have greater long term security.

Conclusion

Apart from the complications of administration (which in some instances **9–86** have turned out worse than originally expected) contracting-out seems generally to have been the right decision. We have had a good period of high rates of real return from investment. This alone has justified contracting-out for most schemes, except perhaps those with a very high average age of membership. The large real rates of return obtained have helped to pay some of the costs of administration. However for the small to medium sized employer (who has not the staff or is not willing to pay for specialist administration) money purchase contracting-out, perhaps by means of a personal pension scheme, should still be considered for or by the younger employees.

CHAPTER 39

CONTRACTING-OUT—THE ADMINISTRATION

9–87 The many aspects of running a pension scheme are covered in detail in Part 4 of this book. We deal here with a number of additional aspects which need to be born in mind when running a contracted-out pension scheme.

Termination of contracted-out employment

9–88 The bulk of the extra administration involved with a contracted-out scheme arises on the termination of a member's contracted-out employment. This most often happens when the employee changes jobs but it also embraces the member who opts out of the scheme while still in service, who retires, dies before retirement or whose scheme as a whole ceases to be contracted-out.

The various procedures are laid down in leaflet NP29 issued by the DSS. This leaflet runs to 77 pages and it is beyond the scope of this book to cover all the procedures in detail. In brief it can be said that when a member's contracted-out employment terminates then certain forms have to be completed for the DSS. In addition in some cases premiums have to be paid to the State scheme in order properly to preserve the member's guaranteed minimum pension entitlement. A summary of the various options for preserving the GMP entitlements of early leavers has been given in Chapter 36.

Notices and consultation

9–89 There are various notices which have to be issued and consultations which must be carried out with recognised trade unions in running a contracted-out scheme. These are described in detail in OPB Joint Office Memorandum No. 66 headed "Elections and related procedures." This memorandum describes the procedures that must be followed when the scheme first contracts-out. These procedures can also be relevant with a scheme after it has contracted-out. For instance, if a group running a contracted-out scheme acquires a new company and the employees of that company are to be offered membership of the scheme, then a contracting-out election has to be made for those employees with reference to the scheme. This will normally be done by making a formal election to add the new company to the contracting-out certificate held by the group holding company.

9–90 Before an election can be made the OPB require three months' notice to be given to the employees who are to be contracted-out. They will usually agree to a shorter period, of at least a month, if permission is requested in writing. If there are any recognised trade unions, consultation must be undertaken with them. In particular, any recognised trade union must consent to a shorter period of notice to the employees before the notice period starts. Specimen notices of the intention to contract-out are included within the OPB's memorandum. Notices must be issued to the employees, the trade unions and the trustees. The election procedures have to be gone through whenever a category of employment or a group of employees has its contracting-out status changed.

Supervision of scheme resources

The OPB have a responsibility to satisfy themselves that the assets of a **9–91** GMP contracted-out scheme are sufficient to provide the promised GMP liabilities. This means that they must satisfy themselves that the scheme's assets will be sufficient on a winding-up to cover the GMP liabilities and any other liabilities (such as current pensions) which rank on a par or ahead of the GMP liabilities. Full details of their requirements are set out in OPB Memorandum No. 76. In particular an actuarial certificate is required at least once every three and a half years stating that in the opinion of the actuary if the scheme is wound up at any time within the succeeding five years the resources of the scheme are likely in the normal course of events to be sufficient to meet the full GMP and other priority liabilities. Various other certificates from the life office are required in the case of insured schemes. Various annual statements are also required. In the case of a directly invested scheme, Form OP21 has to be submitted three months following the end of each scheme year. This relates to the audited accounts that have to be signed either by a trustee, the scheme administrator or the scheme's auditors. Form OP21 requires the following details to be given.

(a) Any self investment (investment in the business of the employer or that of an associated company) if this exceeds 10 per cent. of the scheme's total resources.

(b) Any concentration of investment (where an investment in one undertaking exceeds 10 per cent. of the scheme's resources).

(c) Confirmation that the actuary has been given the opportunity of considering any change which might affect the scheme's current actuarial certificate. For example, there might have been radical changes in the investments, large scale redundancies or a significant number of early retirements with enhanced benefits. If there are any such circumstances full details must be given to the actuary concerned.

(d) Confirmation that the employer has paid contributions in accordance with the actuary's certificate.

(e) Confirmation that the scheme's accounts have been audited and whether or not they were qualified.

9–92 The supervision of resources by the OPB is different for money purchase contracted-out schemes. Here no actuarial certificate is required as there are no guaranteed liabilities. Instead form OP21(MP) has to be completed each year. Here the trustees of the scheme have to certify that the employer has paid the minimum contribution within the required time limits; that is, by the 19th of each month following the month in which the corresponding National Insurance contributions were due. In addition, this form requires confirmation that the investment rules for money purchase contracted-out schemes have not been breached, the scheme's accounts have been audited (and whether qualified) and that the minimum contributions received have been promptly invested and allocated to members.

Conclusion

9–93 It can be seen that running a contracted-out scheme is more complicated than running one that is contracted-in. Extra form filling is required when members leave, die or retire. Notices and consultations are required when there are changes in the categories of employment eligible for membership of the scheme. The Occupational Pensions Board would have to be satisfied that either the GMP and other priority liabilities are being adequately funded or in the case of a protected rights scheme that the minimum contributions are being paid on time. For both types of schemes they have to be satisfied that the assets are being suitably invested. If a contracted-out scheme is being set up then expert advice is needed in order to comply with all these various requirements. When making the financial decision it is clearly essential that the cost of the extra administration involved is taken into account.

CHAPTER 40

DATA PROTECTION ACT 1984

General

The Data Protection Act 1984 regulates the holding and use of personal **9–94** data on computers. It does not affect records maintained manually. The Act makes it an offence to hold personal data or operate a computer bureau unless registered. It enables individuals to have access to personal data held in respect of them, and to claim compensation and other remedies for damage and distress arising from inaccuracy, loss or unauthorised disclosure. We refer below to the important "data protection principles," introduced by the Act which data users and others are required to observe. There are several exemptions from the requirements, including an exemption relating to payrolls and pensions. In this chapter we consider the advantages and disadvantages of registration on the one hand, and the alternative of relying on the exemptions.

Certain definitions are critical to the interpretation and scope of the Act, and some of the more important of these are set out below.

Occupational Pension Schemes

As far as pension schemes are concerned the main question facing **9–95** employers and others concerned with scheme administration is whether or not they will qualify for exemption from the provisions of the Act under Section 32 which relates to remuneration and pensions. Where the exemption applies there is no need for registration and the rights conferred on individuals under the legislation, *i.e.* access to the data and compensation for inaccuracy, loss, etc., do not apply. The exemption and the conditions which apply to it are tightly drawn and the general view is that registration is the preferred alternative.

The exemption for payrolls and pensions

The exemption applies to personal data held *only* for **9–96**

" . . . calculating amounts payable by way of remuneration or pensions in respect of service in any employment or office, or making payments of, or of sums deducted from, such remuneration or pensions."

"remuneration" includes benefits in kind and "pensions" includes gratuities and similar benefits.

However to qualify for the exemption the data must not be used for any other purpose, and may only be disclosed as follows.

(a) To any person other than the data user, by whom the remuneration or pensions in question are payable.
(b) For the purpose of obtaining actuarial advice.
(c) For the purpose of giving information about the persons in any employment or office for use in medical research into the health of, or injuries suffered by, persons engaged in particular occupations or working in particular places or areas.
(d) If the data subject (or a person acting on his behalf) has requested or consented to the disclosure of the information either generally or in the circumstances in which the disclosure in question is made.
(e) If the person making the disclosure has reasonable grounds for believing that the disclosure falls within paragraph (d) above.

The above sets out the persons to whom a disclosure may be made without losing the benefit of the exemption. There are also other circumstances in which data may be disclosed which would have the same effect, for example disclosure to the data subject himself or his agent, disclosure for obtaining legal advice, for the purposes of audit, or for the purpose only of giving information about the data user's financial affairs.

9–97   As stated above, it will be noted that the exemption and conditions which apply to it are tightly drawn and where for example data is disclosed otherwise than as permitted, the exemption ceases to apply. This would mean that an employer or trustees seeking to rely upon it would become unregistered data holders for the purposes of the legislation and accordingly be liable to a penalty. On conviction on indictment this carries an unlimited fine, and on summary conviction a maximum fine of £2,000.

Registration

9–98   Where data held by an employer or scheme trustees is to be used for purposes other than calculating remuneration and pensions, or where the conditions attaching to the use of the exemption are considered too restrictive, it will be necessary to register under the Act's provisions. As part of the registration procedure the following have to be described.

(a) the personal data to be held, and the purposes for which the data are held or used,
(b) the sources from which the data are to be obtained,
(c) the persons to whom the data may be disclosed,
(d) any countries outside the United Kingdom to which the data may be transferred.

9–99   It is then an offence under the legislation for data to be obtained from sources other than those described, to be disclosed to persons other than those described, and to be transferred to a territory outside the United Kingdom not specified in the registration. The terms of the registration will need careful consideration in order to ensure that all data, purposes, sources, recipients and potential destinations are covered.

Where data falls outside the exemption, the "data subject," *i.e.* the **9–100** scheme member or a member of his family, can claim compensation for actual damage incurred and any associated distress arising from inaccuracy in the data. It will therefore become easier to establish a claim for compensation where for example, due to an error in the data, the pension quoted to an employee near to retirement is higher than it should be. The rights conferred on data subjects under the legislation reinforce the importance of recording data correctly. A data subject cannot claim compensation for inaccuracy where he himself or a third party is the source of the incorrect data and the data identifies him or the third party as such. It is a defence for the data user to prove that he had taken reasonable care to ensure accuracy.

Data subjects can also claim compensation if a data user's poor security has resulted in loss or unauthorised disclosure of their personal data causing them actual damage and distress. Again, a defence of "reasonable care" is available.

It should be noted that a scheme member or other person in respect of **9–101** whom personal data is held is entitled to be supplied with a copy of all such data. The extraction of data in use when the request is made will in most cases be straightforward. The retrieval of historic data retained in respect of an individual may be much more difficult. Consideration should therefore be given to the routine erasure of data which need not be retained, and to ensuring that, as far as possible current records are comprehensive. This will help to minimise the circumstances in which archived material needs to be recovered in order to satisfy the subject access requirements.

The exact identity of the "data user" may be difficult to determine in **9–102** some cases: it may be the employer or the trustees or perhaps both. Data user is described as " . . . a person who holds data, and a person holds data if among other things that person (either alone or jointly or in common with other persons) controls the contents and use of the data comprised in the collection in which it is included." In some cases scheme trustees will have separate data and themselves be in control of it. However, in many cases the employer will have pensions data included in his collection, and will make this available to the trustees. It will then be necessary to consider who is the data user and it may be that an employer with a sophisticated system catering for his own needs, those of the trustees and a number of associated employers, will be a data user who also carries on a computer bureau within the definition in the legislation, and be required to register as such. In some cases joint registration may be appropriate.

The alternatives

The alternative courses of action, namely registration or relying on the **9–103** exemption, can be summarised as follows.

Use of the exemption

— No need to register.
— No risk of claims under the legislation for damage and distress.

— The data subject has no right of access to the data.
— Use of data for any other purpose or unauthorised disclosure will give rise to penalties. In an organisation of any size the risk of this happening must be considerable.

Registration

— The data may be used for any purpose, and disclosed to any person, described in the registration.
— The data subject has a right of access to his personal data.
— Risk of claims for damage and distress arising from errors, unauthorised disclosures, etc.

Employers and others concerned with scheme administration need to identify the areas in which data are held and to examine the purposes for which such data are used, or are likely to be used as systems develop. As stated above registration emerges as the preferred alternative in a case of any size or sophistication.

Definitions

9–104 Certain definitions in the Act are crucial to its interpretation. The most important of these are the following:

"Data" means information recorded in a form in which it can be processed by equipment operating automatically in response to instructions given for that purpose.

"Personal data" means data consisting of information which relates to a living individual who can be identified from that information (or from that and other information in the possession of the data user), including any expression of opinion about the individual but not any indication of the intentions of the data user in respect of that individual.

"Data subject" means an individual who is the subject of personal data.

"Data user" means a person who holds data, and a person "holds" data if

(a) the data forms part of a collection of data processed or intended to be processed by or on behalf of that person as mentioned above; and

(b) that person (either alone or jointly or in common with other persons) controls the contents and use of the data comprised in the collection; and

(c) the data are in the form in which they have been or are intended to be processed as mentioned in paragraph (a) above or (though not for the time being in that form) in a form which they have been converted after being so processed and with a view to being further so processed on a future occasion.

A person carries on a **"computer bureau"** if he provides other persons with services in respect of data, and a person provides such services if

(a) as agent for other persons he causes data held by them to be processed; or

(b) he allows other persons the use of equipment in his possession for the processing of data held by them.

"Processing," in relation to data, means amending, augmenting, deleting or re-arranging the data or extracting the information constituting the data and, in the case of personal data, means performing any of those operations by reference to the data subject.

"Disclosing," in relation to data, includes disclosing information extracted from the data; and where the identification of the individual who is the subject of personal data depends partly on the information constituting the data and partly on other information in the possession of the data user, the data shall not be regarded as disclosed or transferred unless the other information is also disclosed or transferred.

The Data Protection Principles

Data Users are under an obligation under the Act to comply with eight **9–105** Data Protection principles. The eighth principle also applies to computer bureau.

The eight principles are as follows.

1. The information to be contained in personal data shall be obtained and personal data shall be processed fairly and lawfully. Employees should be made aware of the purposes for which data are to be held, and given details of the organisation's data protection policies. A reference in the pension scheme booklet should be normal practice.

2. Personal data shall be held only for one or more specified and lawful purposes. This principle will be complied with if the data user processes data in accordance with the purposes he has registered.

    To simplify the registration process, the Registrar has devised Standard Purposes. Data held for pension scheme administration purposes will normally be registered under Standard Purpose P033—Pensions Administration.

3. Personal data held for any purpose or purposes shall not be used or disclosed in any manner incompatible with that purpose or those purposes. Again, this principle will be complied with if the data are used or disclosed in accordance with the registered details.

    Employees should be advised of likely disclosures when the data are first collected, and disclosures should be restricted to the minimum required. In particular, any request for information should not be complied with unless the pension scheme administrator is convinced of its validity, and that the disclosure complies with his registration.

4. Personal data held for any purpose shall be adequate relevant and not excessive in relation to that purpose or those purposes. Information should be restricted to the minimum necessary for adminis-

tration purposes, and any data which cannot be reasonably justified should not be held.

5. Personal data shall be accurate, and where necessary, kept up to date. Accurate and up to date data are fundamental to good pension scheme administration. Where appropriate, employees should be given the opportunity to check data held in respect of them, and to correct any errors. This is best achieved by the use of periodic benefit statements. Checks should be built in to software so as to limit the extent of possible errors.

6. Personal data held for any purpose or purposes shall not be kept for longer than necessary for that purpose or those purposes.

    Pensions data will often be held for long periods. Nevertheless, consideration should be given periodically to deleting data which is no longer required, particularly historic data in respect of individuals.

7. An individual shall be entitled without undue delay or expense, to be informed by any data user whether he holds personal data of which that individual is the subject, and to access any such data. Individuals should also be entitled to have incorrect data corrected or erased.

    All current and historic data must be disclosed in response to a request for subject access. Care must be taken to verify the identity of the individual applicant prior to disclosure. A fee may be charged for subject access, although many pension scheme administrators will allow access free of charge. Once the identity of an applicant has been established, the data user has 40 days to comply with his request. Any coded information must be explained, when the data is provided to the individual.

8. Appropriate security measures must be taken against unauthorised access to, or alteration, disclosure or destruction of, personal data, and against accidental loss or destruction of personal data.

    Attention should be paid to the security of the computer installation, and to the reliability of staff with access to the computer. An adequate degree of supervision should be maintained, so as to ensure that security is effective to maintain confidentiality.

CHAPTER 41

FINANCIAL SERVICES ACT

The Financial Services Act, which came into force on April 29, 1988, regu- **9–106** lates investment business activity in the United Kingdom. There are special provisions affecting pension scheme trustees, who need to consider whether authorisation is required under the Act. Authorisation is achieved by membership of one of the "Self Regulatory Organisations" established under the Act. For scheme trustees the relevant Organisation is The Investment Management Regulatory Organisation (IMRO).

One of the main functions of scheme trustees is the duty to invest. The Act confers a special status on any person involved in managing assets held for the purposes of an occupational pension scheme. Under Section 191, trustees involved in managing scheme assets are treated as carrying on an investment business, unless all decisions, or all day to day decisions, are taken by an authorised professional.

The activity of managing assets is not defined in the Act. Under the IMRO Rules it is described as "keeping under review how much of the fund should be for the time being invested and what those investments should be."

Similarly there is no guidance in the Act as to what constitutes a "day to day" decision. This could relate to either the frequency or the nature of the decision.

Where a portfolio is managed by a professional manager on a fully dis- **9–107** cretionary basis, *i.e.* the manager and not the trustees actually make the decisions, authorisation is not required. This leaves the trustees free to make strategic decisions, for example how much of the fund is to be invested in investments of a certain type or in a specified sector. However, where trustees wish to become involved in routine investment decisions, membership of IMRO is appropriate. A special category of membership has been created for this purpose, restricted to authorisation of scheme trustees for investment management purposes only.

Where the portfolio consists of stocks and shares and Government **9–108** securities, the position is straightforward. Greater care is required where the assets comprise insurance contracts and managed funds. In these cases, the investments held by the trustees under the Act are their rights under the contract, or the units held. Unless decisions in relation to these investments are properly delegated, the trustees run the risk of prosecution under the Act.

Interests under an occupational pension scheme are specifically excluded **9–109** from the definition of investments. There is therefore nothing to prevent trustees from giving advice to scheme members concerning their benefits under the scheme, and the option to transfer benefits from one scheme to another.

9–110   The giving of advice to members concerning specific alternative investments available on cessation of pensionable service, for example a buy-out contract with an insurance company, or a personal pension scheme, is covered by the legislation, where this activity is carried on as a business. It should be noted that the giving of advice by pension scheme trustees is not automatically treated as carrying on an investment business in the same way as involvement in managing assets. Nevertheless, in practice trustees should not get involved in giving advice in these areas in which the Act applies—this should be left to the authorised professional.

PART 10

SEX DISCRIMINATION

SEX DISCRIMINATION

In this part we look at the developing picture affecting employee benefit **10–01** schemes in the context of equal treatment for men and women.

In the United Kingdom, pension schemes have largely been excluded from sex discrimination law concerning employment matters, but this is changing as a result of Directives issued by the European Commission, and decisions of the European Court of Justice indicating that pensions are pay within Article 119 of the Treaty of Rome.

As a result of the Directives, the Social Security Act of 1989 was intended to require United Kingdom pension schemes not to discriminate on grounds of sex with effect from January 1, 1993. The intention was that pension ages and survivors' benefits would be excluded. However, the 1993 proposals have been made redundant by the judgment in the European Court case of *Barber* v. *Guardian Royal Exchange*. From May 17, 1990, the date of the judgment, United Kingdom pension schemes should not discriminate on grounds of sex, at least in respect of benefits accrued for service from that date. It is not yet clear (October 1990) to what extent the judgment applies to pension benefits accrued before that date.

CHAPTER 42

PENSION AND RETIREMENT AGES

10–02 In the United Kingdom, employment legislation requiring equal treatment for men and women originally excluded any provision for death or retirement.

In 1978, equal access requirements were introduced. Under these provisions men and women had to be offered membership of occupational pension schemes on the same terms as regards age and length of service and, until April 6, 1988, as to whether the scheme was voluntary or compulsory.

10–03 The current position is both confusing and unsatisfactory. It is obviously necessary to consider United Kingdom domestic employment and pensions law, but both of these need to be examined in the context of European law.

Until November 1987, the upper age limit for unfair dismissal was the age of 60 for women, 65 for men, unless an earlier normal retiring age could be established. This concept of normal retiring age related to the age at which employees in fact retired. Where employees in the relevant category of employment in practice retired at various ages, no "normal" retiring age could be established and the upper age limit became 60 or 65.

These discriminatory provisions were challenged by Health Authority employee Helen Marshall. She was dismissed at age 62 and claimed that, had she been male, she would have been allowed to work until age 65. Her claim succeeded before the European Court of Justice.

This resulted in the Sex Discrimination Act 1986, the relevant provisions of which became effective in November 1987. Under that Act men and women have the right not to be dismissed on the grounds of having reached a given age until the age of 65, unless an earlier normal retiring age, common to both sexes, has been established.

Women thus have the right to work until the same age as their male colleagues, which will often be the age of 65.

10–04 The equal access requirements affecting pension schemes continue unchanged. Under United Kingdom domestic law, one can still (October 1990) discriminate between men and women on pensions and contributions. In practice most schemes have not discriminated, except in relation to pension ages, and survivors' benefits and the use of different factors for men and women (for example in calculating an early retirement pension). It will not be possible for these exceptions to continue, (see below), following the European Court ruling in May 1990 on the case of *Barber* v. *Guardian Royal Exchange*.

10–05 The position under United Kingdom legislation was to change with effect from January 1, 1993. From that date the principle of equal treatment was to apply in "employment related benefit schemes," including occupational pension schemes. Schemes were then generally to provide for contributions and benefits to be calculated on the same basis for men and

250

women. But pension ages and survivors' benefits were specifically excluded under the legislation. Both Government and the European Directive on which the legislation was based clearly envisaged that discrimination in these important areas would be allowed to continue after 1993.

Barber v. Guardian Royal Exchange (G.R.E.)

United Kingdom legislation which permits discrimination has been chal- **10–06** lenged in a number of cases appearing before the European Court. In particular, the cases of *Barber* v. *G.R.E.*, and *Clarke* v. *Cray Precision Engineering*, must be noted. Both relate to whether pension benefits fall within the definition of "pay" under Article 119 of the Treaty of Rome. This requires Member States to ensure that men and women receive equal pay for equal work, and the definition of "pay" is widely drawn to include any consideration whether in cash or in kind which the worker receives.

In the *Barber* case, Mr. Barber was made redundant at the age of 52. **10–07** Under the arrangements for early retirement he was not eligible for an immediate early retirement pension. This was available for both men and women retiring within 10 years of normal pension age, which was 65 for men, and 60 for women.

Mr. Barber claimed that he should be entitled to an immediate pension under the arrangements, since he would be so entitled if he was a woman. The European Court decided in favour of Mr. Barber.

In the *Clarke* case, Mr. Clarke was made redundant at the age of 60. Under the pension scheme the pension age for men was 65, and for women 60. The early retirement pension payable to Mr. Clarke at age 60 was approximately one-third less than the pension which would have been payable to a woman retiring at the same age, with the same service and salary history. Mr. Clarke is expected to succeed in his claim.

In the case of *Barber* v. *Guardian Royal Exchange* the European Court decided that pensions are pay under Article 119. Consequently the proposed changes in United Kingdom pensions legislation intended to become effective in 1993 are redundant. Full equality will apply, enforceable through United Kingdom Industrial Tribunals.

The effect of the ruling in Barber v. G.R.E.

Following the ruling in this case it is clear that if it is necessary to know the **10–08** sex of a scheme member in order to determine the pension or death benefit payable to or in respect of that member then unlawful discrimination is involved. It is generally agreed that this applies in respect of all pension scheme benefits which accrue after May 17, 1990, the date of the Court ruling. It may also apply to benefits in respect of service prior to that date, but the position is far from clear at this time (October 1990) and may not be resolved without a further reference to the European Court.

Achieving equality—new money purchase schemes

The complications brought about by contracting-out are discussed at the **10–09** end of this chapter. We discuss here the achieving of equality with non-contracting-out benefits.

For men and women in the same job category, the employer's contribution rate must not vary. It follows that for identical service and pay the accumulated sum at retirement will be independent of the individual's sex. However, the ruling in *Barber* v. *G.R.E.* indicates that the pension provided by the accumulated cash must itself be independent of the individual's sex. And that is not possible unless the trustees use unisex annuity conversion rates.

Unisex annuity rates are not generally available in the market place at the moment, except in relation to protected rights under money purchase contracting-out. Except for substantial well-established money purchase schemes, it is probably unwise to try to compete with insurance companies in the running of a directly invested annuity fund for pensioners.

10–10 The following suggestion may be effective. Have one's scheme rules require the retiring member to instruct the trustees to purchase, with the accumulated money purchase account, an annuity from an insurance company of the individual's choice, at such an annuity rate as the individual has negotiated with that insurance company. The scheme rules might go on to require that if the trustees have received no instruction on the matter within, say, six months then they will pay a pension calculated from the individual's accumulated account by applying an annuity rate determined by the trustees after obtaining the advice of the scheme's actuary. He would no doubt advise a rate having regard to the annuity market current at the time, having regard to the need not to discriminate between men and women, and having regard to the need to protect the pension fund. This is achieved by recommending an uncompetitive rate obtained from the market for women retiring at the given age.

10–11 Of course, equality must also be achieved in the scheme in every other respect, and this should be easily achievable (but see contracting-out below). Thus, for example, the age range during which an accumulated cash sum must be converted to an annuity or pension must be the same for both sexes. As another example, the proportion of the account which can or must (in accordance with the scheme rules) be taken in retirement cash form must be the same for men and women.

Achieving equality—new final salary schemes

10–12 All pension ages must of course be the same for both sexes and clearly they should be the same as the normal retirement age. Early and late retirement reduction and increase factors should be independent of sex, perhaps determined by the actuary having regard to the proportion of men and women in the scheme.

The following alternative to having equal pension to retirement cash conversion factors is worth considering. This is to promise the same pension accrual rate for men and women (for example, 1/80th of final average pay for each year of scheme membership) plus a separate retirement cash accrual rate identical for men and women (for example, 3/80ths of final average pay for each year of scheme membership, as in the Civil Service Scheme).

Achieving equality—existing money purchase schemes

No additional factors are involved here other than those discussed above **10–13**
under the heading *Achieving equality—new money purchase schemes*.

Achieving equality—existing final pay schemes

If cost is no problem then equality is best achieved by equalising the pen- **10–14**
sion age of men downwards to that of women. Male members of the
scheme within, say, 10 years of their original pension age at the time of the
change might need to be given the right to retain their previous pension
age. If that is done then existing women in the same age group would need
to be given the same option.

The remarks made earlier about early, late and cash commutation factors in relation to new schemes apply equally of course to existing schemes.

Equalising pension ages at the existing higher age applicable to men is **10–15**
much more difficult, if not impossible, to achieve. It can, of course, be
done for new staff and contract law and the vast majority of pension
scheme rules should not prevent it being achieved in relation to the pension
accrued for service after the change is announced to existing staff (with,
possibly, appropriate notice). The rules of the scheme will probably prevent the pension age of women being increased in relation to the pension
accrued for service up to the date the change is to be made.

Under the ruling in the case of *Barber* v. *G.R.E.* it may not be necessary
to achieve equality in relation to pensions accrued for service up to May 17,
1990. Unfortunately, the ruling was ambiguous on the point and (October
1990) it is not known when the point will be settled.

Equality in contracted-out benefits

The contracting-out terms and conditions required, for example, that the **10–16**
protected rights of a woman contracted-out on a money purchase basis
must be available only from the age of 60 onwards, at the member's choice,
whereas for men the requirement applied from the age of 65. Equality
could not be achieved except at the employer's expense. A similar point
applies in respect of GMP contracting-out, except that the position is considerably more complicated.

As matters stand, the Government altered the requirements for money **10–17**
purchase contracting-out: following the Social Security Act 1990, protected
rights in occupational pension schemes must be available from the age of
60 onwards, regardless of sex. Consequently, achieving equality with
money purchase contracting-out presents no problems.

The Government has however taken no action to equalise the GMP
contracting-out requirements. They are unequal in three main respects.

(i) A woman's GMP must be available to her on retirement from any
age from 60 onwards. A man's GMP cannot be made available to
him before the age of 65.

    (ii) As a consequence of the differing pension ages for the GMP, the GMP accrual rate is different for men and women having the same salary. At any given age below 60, the woman's accrued GMP would be larger than that of a man of the same age and having the same salary history.

   (iii) A leaver's preserved GMP must be indexed appropriately (see Chapter 37) up to State pension age (65 for men, 60 for women) and this increase must be on top of the scheme's scale pension.

10–18   In the light of these inequalities, the only way to comply with the *Barber* judgment is to calculate the member's benefit (*e.g.* transfer value on leaving, pension at retirement) twice: as if the member is a man, taking account of the GMP requirements for men, and similarly as if the member is a woman. The results will always be different and the member should be granted the larger benefit.

    At this time (Autumn 1990) the Government seems reluctant to equalise the GMP contracting-out requirements ahead of equalising State pension ages (which is not yet required under European law). And it seems reluctant to consider equalising the State pension ages ahead of the next General Election.

    Existing GMP contracted-out schemes should seek expert advice. A new scheme, irrespective of whether it provides money purchase or final salary type pensions, should consider contracting-out of SERPS on a protected rights basis.

CHAPTER 43

INDIRECT DISCRIMINATION

In the United Kingdom, as in Europe as a whole, over 80 per cent. of part- **10–19**
time workers are women. Employers are under no specific duty not to discriminate against part-timers. If an employer's part-time workforce is
evenly divided between men and women, no claim for discriminatory treatment could arise if, for example, they are excluded from membership of
the pension scheme. However, where such an exclusion in practice affects
a significantly higher percentage of one sex, a claim of indirect sexual discrimination may be made. It would then be up to the employer to establish
that the exclusion from membership is justified on grounds other than sex.
Where no such justification exists, a claim based on European law is likely
to succeed.

In the case of *Bilka-Kaufhaus* v. *Weber von Hartz* [1986] CMLR 701, a **10–20**
German department store admitted employees to its pension scheme after
20 years' service, 15 of which had to be as a full-time employee. The claim-
ant had completed only 12 years' full service, and was thus excluded.

As is usual, the majority of part-time employees were women. Indirect
discrimination was established, but the employee's claim for compensation
failed when the employer was able to establish that the discrimination was
justified. The employer successfully claimed that it was the long established
policy of the store to discourage part-time workers generally, irrespective
of sex, and their employment policies were tailored accordingly.

In the United Kingdom, there are no specific provisions, affecting pen- **10–21**
sion schemes, which prohibit indirect discrimination either relating to eligibility or benefit provision. The changes referred to in Chapter 42, which
were due to become effective from January 1, 1993, would outlaw both
direct and indirect discrimination.

However, there is nothing to prevent a United Kingdom employee pur-
suing a claim based on European Law. The employee would claim that his
(or more likely her) treatment was contrary to Article 119, based on the
Bilka or *Barber* decision. In the absence of justification by the employer it
is our view that the claim would be successful, if the part-time employees
affected were predominantly of one sex.

Chapter 44

OTHER BENEFIT SCHEMES

10–22 The 1993 changes apply to "employment related benefit schemes." These include schemes providing benefits on termination of service, on retirement, old age or death, in sickness or invalidity, in the event of accident, injury or disease connected with the employment, and also schemes providing benefits during unemployment or expenses incurred in connection with children or other dependants.

As a general rule, the current law requires men and women to be treated equally in many of these schemes, and this has been the position since the Sex Discrimination Act 1975. This is because, as mentioned above, the exemption has applied only to provision for death or retirement.

10–23 Permanent Health insurance schemes (described in Chapter 9) are a case in point, particular now that men and women in the same job category must have equal normal retirement ages. For example, if men are to be covered for benefits from such a scheme while in service up to a normal retirement age of 65 then so must women (in the same job category) now, before 1993.

From January 1, 1993 the discrimination allowed on death benefits will no longer apply and if, for example, a lump sum is payable in respect of male employees on death in service before the age of 65 then the same must apply in respect of women in the same job category. Given the results of the *Barber* v. *G.R.E.* case, discrimination on death benefits should be avoided from May 17, 1990 onwards.

PART 11

UNAPPROVED PENSION SCHEMES

UNAPPROVED PENSION SCHEMES

The 1989 Finance Act made two fundamental changes to the tax treat- **11–01**
ment of pension provision. As explained earlier it placed a cap of £60,000
for the year 1989/90 on pensionable remuneration under an approved
scheme. As a transitional arrangement the limit does not apply to
employees who joined an approved scheme before June 1, 1989, provided it was established before March 14, 1989. The £60,000 cap is
increased each tax year in the line with rises in the RPI with some rounding up. For the tax year 1990/91 it is £64,800.

Until the Finance Act 1989, if an individual employee had some form **11–02**
of unapproved pension promise that unapproved benefit counted as a
retained benefit for the purpose of Inland Revenue limits. As a result an
individual could not have retirement benefits from an unapproved pension scheme so that the total exceeded Inland Revenue limits if he was at
the same time a member of an approved pension scheme. The 1989
Finance Act removed benefits provided by an unapproved arrangement
from inclusion in the Inland Revenue limits test for approved schemes. It
is now possible to have benefits in excess of those approvable by the
Inland Revenue as long as any excess is provided by an unapproved
scheme: simultaneous membership of an approved and unapproved
scheme is permitted.

The imposition of the cap on pensionable earnings in approved **11–03**
schemes causes a problem for employers wishing to recruit high paid
employees. In his existing position the employee's pensionable earnings
would not be restricted, assuming the transitional arrangement mentioned above applied, and by moving jobs he could experience a severe
reduction in his pension expectations (or rather on the amount of that
pension which could be provided from an Inland Revenue approved
scheme). However the employer is now free to promise additional, unapproved, pensions. There are two main forms of unapproved pension provision, the non-funded one and the funded one. We describe these in the
following chapters.

The same basic principle applies to the availability of corporation tax
relief for the employer and the tax treatments of the two types of benefits. Corporation tax relief is received at the point the employee is taxed
in respect of the unapproved arrangement. For a non-funded arrangement this is at the time payment of the benefit is made whether as a pension or lump sum. Death benefits are subject to inheritance tax. For a
funded scheme, the employee is taxed as soon as the employer makes
contributions with a view to the provision of a retirement benefit. So as
soon as the employer makes a contribution to a funded unapproved

scheme the employee is taxed at his marginal rate of income tax on the contribution, and the company receives corporation tax relief on it. If appropriately set up, death benefits from a funded unapproved scheme are not subject to inheritance tax.

CHAPTER 45

UNAPPROVED NON-FUNDED SCHEMES

General

The employer makes a contractual promise to pay given retirement bene- **11–04**
fits to the employee, and possibly death benefits too. In most cases the pension promise is of a final salary nature, usually making the approved
(defined benefit) scheme pension up to the level it would have been had the
£60,000 indexed cap not been introduced. There is no reason, however,
why the promised pensions should not be of a money purchase nature,
even though the arrangement is not being funded. The employee could, for
example, be provided with a lump sum at retirement derived from the
notional accumulation of a notional contribution by reference, say, to the
total rate of investment return obtained by the approved scheme.

The pension promise would have to be expensed under SSAP-24 and, on
the non-funded route, a provision for the liability would build up on the
company's balance sheet. No corporation tax relief would be received until
the benefit was actually paid and in theory a deferred tax credit would build
up for the corporation tax relief that could be expected when the benefit
was paid. However the various accountancy standards have caused problems with this approach and we described the practical effects towards the
end of Chapter 25.

Security

The problem with this approach for the employee (the senior executive one **11–05**
is trying to hire) is that the pension promise depends on the company having sufficient assets or other resources at the time payment is due. There is
no separate asset providing security for the pension promise. Some security
might be provided by placing a first charge on some existing asset of the
employer, such as a property or a particular piece of machinery. There is a
danger that if a new asset were specifically acquired for this purpose the
Inland Revenue might view the payment made to meet its cost as "a payment made with the view to the provision of the retirement benefit pursuant to a retirement benefit scheme." If this argument succeeded the
employee involved would be taxed on the value of the purchase price of the
asset.

If an existing asset were used to provide security for the pension promise
then some restraint is placed on the use of the asset in the employer's running of his business. Pension promises can cover a considerable period of
time and the asset might become redundant and have little value. So if this
charging route is followed it is suggested that the pension promise include
the establishment of a trust with independent trustees to police the operation of the arrangement. A further advantage of the trustee route is that

they would be able to represent the employees' interests and agree with the employer on the substitution of other worthwhile assets from time to time as a first charge against the promise. This would apply for example if the existing asset were no longer needed for the business and the employer wished to sell it.

11–06   It might be thought that requests for some sort of security back-up to a non-funded pension promise would only be thought necessary by the executive who is joining a medium to small company. However, even the largest of companies are subject to take-over and possible break-up for selling off as smaller components. And short of a takeover, there can be nothing in the pension contract to prevent a holding company selling off a subsidiary to a smaller organisation (or a similar disposal occurring in respect of part of the business).

Documentation

11–07 Managements will change from time to time even without the occurrence of a merger or takeover. Thus, sound business principles dictate that the individual being promised a non-funded pension should insist on a formal written contract (for possible vetting by his legal advisers).

The contractual promise can be in the form of a letter but that should not lead anyone to think that its drafting is a simple or straightforward affair.

Over the years, cases have arisen where company chairmen and senior personnel officers, anxious to recruit individuals they may know and respect, have written informally to the individual offering, for example, a pension of two-thirds of final pay. Only subsequently are questions raised about Inland Revenue approval, benefit limits, and retained benefits—questions which are all too familiar to the pensions professional.

11–08   Is the position any easier with an unapproved scheme? We suggest not. A simple letter seeking to put the executive in the same position as if no earnings cap applied to him under the executive approved scheme may have unintended consequences. The contractual promise itself, if not properly written, could be a benefit in kind for tax purposes. An election to transfer benefits under the approved scheme, when the executive subsequently leaves, may simply increase his entitlement under the unapproved promise (unless of course that promise has been correctly drawn up). It is also necessary to consider carefully the cashflow position of the company. No such consideration arises in the case of benefits which are provided under an approved funded scheme, since the cash will be available and any large unexpected payment, for example on death, may very well be insured.

11–09   It is clear that a detailed analysis of the approved executive arrangements is required before a form of words can be agreed upon for the unapproved arrangement. All the circumstances in which benefits become payable under the approved arrangements will be relevant in determining the form of the promise. There are some considerations which do not arise with the approved scheme which are relevant to an unapproved pension scheme contract. Clearly, this is no area for the inexperienced.

CHAPTER 46

UNAPPROVED FUNDED SCHEMES

Contributions

It is thought that cases will arise where a company is anxious to hire an **11–10**
executive whose approved pension expectations are constrained by the cap
and who insists that his unapproved pension be funded.

As previously mentioned, employer contributions to an unapproved **11–11**
pension scheme will be assessed on the executive for tax as if the contribution were additional pay. Yet the executive will not benefit from the contributions until he retires. Bear in mind, however, that having been taxed on
the contribution input the benefit outgo is not taxed provided it is paid in
lump sum form, as opposed to pensions which are taxed. So it is worth considering paying the individual an additional, non-pensionable salary, out of
which, after income tax, he can pay the tax on the contribution input. The
contribution input is smaller than it would otherwise be since paid, eventually, as a retirement lump sum it will be free of tax.

For every £1,000 the employer would have paid to an approved scheme, **11–12**
we suggest that he contributes to the unapproved arrangement the sums
shown below where we also show the employee's tax payments. The
figures are based on the assumptions that the employer's National Insurance contribution rate is 10.45 per cent. on salary payments made to the
employee; that the employee pays no National Insurance contributions on
his top slice of pay and that he has a marginal tax rate of 40 per cent.

**Suggested contribution to the funded unapproved pension scheme per
£1,000 otherwise payable to an approved scheme**

Payments by the employer Payments by employee

£		£
575.93 to scheme	Tax at 40% on the scheme contribution	230.37
	Tax at 40% on the pay	153.58
383.95 in non-pensionable pay		383.95
40.12 N.I. contribution		
(10.45% of 383.95)		
1,000.00		

These figures would of course change with changes in tax and National
Insurance contribution rates.

11–13   The £575.93 (per £1,000 otherwise paid into an approved scheme) is invested by the unapproved scheme, subject to tax as described below, and the proceeds are paid in lump sum form to the executive when he retires. The proceeds would be available for transfer to another unapproved scheme should the executive leave service before retirement (unless, perhaps, if the service were less than the two year period at which the preservation legislation first applies).

On the above figures are related to "£1,000 otherwise paid into an approved scheme," but what does that amount to? We should mention that our discussion here is based on the assumption that the employer is seeking to put the executive in a similar position, as nearly as possible, to that he would have been in had the £60,000 indexed cap not been introduced—without additional cost to the company or to the executive.

11–14   If the approved scheme is a money purchase scheme the straightforward approach is to restrict pensionable salary, on which contributions to the approved scheme are calculated, to the indexed £60,000 and to treat the balance of the executive's salary as pensionable in the unapproved arrangement described above. Thus if the executive is paid £10,000 per annum in excess of the indexed £60,000, and if the employer normally contributes 10 per cent. of pay into the approved money purchase scheme, we would have a gross contribution of £1,000 per annum to be treated as above. In this example, the employer might be able to pay more than 10 per cent. of the indexed £60,000 into the approved scheme and, short of extraordinarily good investment results, not exceed the approved benefit limits related to the idexed £60,000. Actuarial advice should be sought in respect of each new executive hired at a salary near to or above the indexed £60,000 per annum. In some individual cases a way to maximise approvable benefits might be by means of a personal pension scheme (which could be combined with an unapproved top-up promise where necessary).

11–15   Where the approved scheme is a final salary scheme, one way of calculating a rational contribution for the unapproved scheme is as follows. First calculate the maximum pension that can be provided for the individual in the company's approved scheme. This will be determined by the individual's total potential service with the company and by his pension benefits from his previous employments including the current one from which he is moving to join the company. The actual result would probably be expressed in final salary form as a proportion of the £60,000, RPI indexed, less the previous service pension provision. From this the final pay unapproved top up pension can be determined and from that the actuary can calculate the SSAP-24 cost to the company, on agreed assumptions, on the basis notionally that the extra pension will have been provided through the approved scheme.

What would go into the unapproved scheme is then 57.59 per cent. of that SSAP-24 cost, with 38.40 per cent. being paid to the employee as extra non-pensionable salary and 4.01 per cent. being retained for the employer's National Insurance contributions, in accordance with the split shown in the schedule above.

11–16   Note that the retirement lump sum produced is what the 57.59 per cent.

accumulates to after being invested by the unapproved scheme. The SSAP-24 cost, to which the 57.59 per cent. is applied in order to produce a contribution, could be reviewed from time to time, or it might be fixed at the outset (itself as a percentage of the executive's pay in excess of the indexed £60,000 per annum). The end result is a money purchase benefit, not the value of the difference between the executive's final pay pension with and the final pay pension without the £60,000 indexed cap applying. Moreover, the investment build-up in the approved scheme is taxed as indicated below—there is a straight loss in favour of the tax authorities compared with the gross build-up obtainable by an approved scheme.

Whether the company should feel obliged to make up that loss to the **11–17** executive it is trying to hire may well depend on how well advised he is and on how anxious the company is to hire him. Two points may be of relevance here. First, if the company is trading reasonably well, the cost to the company of an unapproved non-funded pension need not be any greater than if it could be provided through the approved scheme (see next chapter). So, the company might argue, why should they go to any additional expense merely because the individual wants a funded rather than a non-funded arrangement? Second, the simplest approach may be to maximise the provision in the approved scheme and pay the individual some, almost arbitrarily decided, additional pay by way of compensation for the £60,000 indexed cap restriction, and leave it at that. This "simplest" approach may give rise to problems of comparability between senior executives affected by the cap and those already in the company unaffected by it. The number in the first category will increase with time, since the £60,000 cap is indexed by the RPI rather than in line with earnings growth.

Taxation of investment build-up in the unapproved pension scheme

If the unapproved funded scheme is correctly set up, and as a trust, its **11–18** investment income is subject to the same taxation as any other trust which does not have the special privileges of an approved pension scheme trust. This means taxation on the investment income, and on realised capital gains above indexation, at the standard rate. If the scheme is not correctly set up, and is not set up as a trust, then the investment income and indexed capital gains are taxed at the individual's marginal tax rate. At current rates (1990) this means a difference of 15 percentage points for the executive member of the scheme.

It is this difference of the 15 percentage points that makes an unapproved funded scheme more attractive for the executive's retirement provision (above the cap) then paying the contribution to him for him to invest on his own account. It is relevant to note too that contributions to a pension scheme, whether approved or not, do not attract employer's National Insurance contributions whereas of course pay does.

Inheritance taxes

Approved pension schemes are exempted from the inheritance tax pro- **11–19** visions for trusts since they count as "sponsored superannuation schemes." An unapproved funded scheme can also count as a sponsored superannuation scheme if it is set up in the correct manner. Expert advice should be sought.

CHAPTER 47

COST COMPARISONS

An approved scheme compared
with an unapproved non-funded scheme

The essential difference in cost between these two types of scheme arises **11–20**
from the fact that the contributions to the approved scheme are invested
free of tax, whereas the "contributions" (SSAP-24 expense) to the balance
sheet in the case of the unfunded scheme are in effect invested in the company, which suffers corporation tax on its profits.

Consequently, if the company's profits at the margin (on new investment) net of corporation tax are sufficiently high, a non-funded pension
promise (non-contributory on the part of the member) need not cost any
more than if it were coming from an approved scheme. Note, however,
that any lump sum (and any pension) coming from an approved non-
funded scheme is subject to income tax in the recipient's hands. An
approved scheme of course can pay tax free retirement cash within the
Inland Revenue's approval limits (see Chapter 34).

The only direct way to compensate the executive one is trying to hire
(who is protected from the effects of the cap if he does not change jobs) for
any missing tax-free retirement cash is to pay him a grossed-up amount,
giving rise to a straight cost increase for the company.

The unapproved funded scheme

As indicated in the last chapter the essential point here is that the invest- **11–21**
ment build-up suffers tax, albeit at the standard rate, whereas the investments of an approved scheme do not. This produces a difference in cost.

With the approved scheme, the member is not taxed on the employer's
contribution input but then (tax free retirement cash apart) he is taxed on
the pension when he receives it. With the unapproved funded scheme the
employee is taxed on the contribution input but the whole of the retirement benefit can be paid as a tax-free lump sum. From a cost point of view,
and apart from the tax-free retirement cash available from an approved
scheme, there is no difference in cost between the two here. As indicated
in the last chapter, with the unapproved funded scheme one can pay part of
the contribution as salary to compensate the individual for the income tax,
and then invest the net contribution to provide a benefit which is tax-free in
the recipient's hands. There is the cost difference arising from the National
Insurance contributions which the employer has to pay on any part of what
would otherwise have been a contribution which is paid to the employee to
compensate him for tax, but the major difference in cost between an
approved and an unapproved scheme arises from the taxation on the
investments.

INDEX